PLANNING YOUR
FINANCIAL FUTURE

Planning Your Financial Future

TAX SHELTERS, ANNUITIES, IRAs, KEOGHs, STOCKS AND OTHER INVESTMENT OR RETIREMENT OPPORTUNITIES

Elliot Raphaelson
New School for Social Research

1807 1982

175 YEARS OF PUBLISHING

A Ronald Press Publication

JOHN WILEY & SONS

New York • Chichester • Brisbane • Toronto • Singapore

This publication is designed to provide accurate and
authoritative information in regard to the subject
matter covered. It is sold with the understanding that
the publisher is not engaged in rendering legal, accounting,
or other professional service. If legal advice or other
expert assistance is required, the services of a competent
professional person should be sought. *From a Declaration
of Principles jointly adopted by a Committee of the
American Bar Association and a Committee of Publishers.*

Library of Congress Cataloging in Publication Data

Raphaelson, Elliot.
  Planning your financial future.

  "A Ronald Press publication."
  Includes Index.
  1. Finance, Personal.   2. Retirement income.
3. Old age pensions.   I. Title.

HG179.R324   332.024'01   81-11629
                                    AACR2

ISBN 0-471-08134-5

Printed in the United States of America

10 9 8 7 6 5 4 3 2 1

Preface

The old expression about the certainty of death and taxes has been revised: The certainty of inflation must be added to the list. Although most people expect inflation to be with them for as long as they live, few people have made a conscious effort to analyze its impact on the retirement planning process.

The objective of this book is to analyze every major aspect of the retirement planning process with special focus on inflation and tax saving considerations. The book has been written primarily for those individuals who expect to work many more years and who want to retire in comfort without worrying whether inflation will erode the purchasing power of their retirement assets. Major considerations of private, employer, and Social Security pensions plans are examined, and tax aspects, inflation, and personal decision making are stressed. Several sections of the book are devoted to the advantages and disadvantages of traditional investments both before and after retirement. Real estate investment is discussed with major emphasis on owning condominiums both as a hedge against inflation and a tax shelter.

The book also includes a review of newer forms of investment that have become popular because of recent excellent investment growth. The advantages and potential pitfalls of investing in gold, silver, platinum, diamonds, and foreign securities are presented.

Many important contributions to this book are from my bright, inquisitive students at The New School for Social Research in New York City who have provided me with basic issues and questions of concern to them in a frustrating inflationary environment requiring sound solutions to difficult financial problems.

My students, you, and I are all faced with important planning and retirement decisions that are certainly made more difficult by inflation, unstable economic conditions, and the many complex investment options available to us. In this book I have tried to present every major factor involved in the retirement planning process: the issues and alternatives with all of their associated advantages and disadvantages. The final decisions are yours. I hope this book will make it easier for you to make the right ones.

ELLIOT RAPHAELSON

Englishtown, New Jersey
October 1981

Contents

1 Need for Retirement Planning

Most people will find that they have insufficient assets and income to maintain their standards of living when they retire. In fact, a significant percentage will find that their standards of living are *much* lower during retirement than during their working years—even with Social Security, private pension plans, and an independent savings and investment program.

The major causes of insufficient retirement income are inadequate planning; erosion of assets because of inflation; poor investments; lack of knowledge about pension and investment options; a poor life insurance program; inadequate estate planning; and failure to take advantage of available and legitimate tax shelters.

This book addresses these subjects so that individuals can do their own retirement planning—with the aid of competent professionals when required—in the fields of law, taxes, investments, and administration.

There are no simple solutions, and many of the issues and alternatives are complex. Moreover, general economic conditions, investment opportunities, and applicable federal and local laws will continue to change, as will your own situation. These factors make retirement planning a moving target, and, accordingly, plans must be revised on an ongoing basis. If it seems that the planning process is not worth the effort, remember that the number of years you will enjoy in retirement will probably approach 50% of the years you worked. Moreover, the decisions you make regarding retirement will have a dramatic impact on your closest dependents. You will find that the earlier you start the retirement planning process, the easier it will be to develop an effective plan that will enable you and your closest dependents to retire comfortably.

IMPACT OF INFLATION

One of the most severe handicaps for anyone contemplating retiring is inflation. It is unrealistic to ignore it, and it is difficult to predict what a realistic rate should be (see Exhibit 1-1). For planning purposes an inflation rate of 10% seems reasonable based on present government policies, labor union pressures, and the international environment. As economic conditions change you must change your assumptions to ensure that your total retirement plan is based on the latest information available.

A high inflation rate has an impact on many facets of your life that in turn affect your retirement planning. A continuing high rate of inflation means that when you retire you will need a much higher income than you would if you retired now. The further away retirement is for you, the more income you will need.

Inflation will have an impact on the adequacy of any pension benefits you expect to receive upon retirement. Currently your Social Security benefits are

Exhibit 1-1   Impact of Inflation

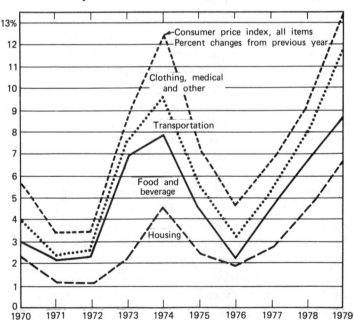

indexed to inflation. However, the Social Security system is not adequately funded. Congress is faced with a number of unattractive options. These include continuing to raise Social Security taxes, taxing Social Security income, reducing Social Security benefits, and reducing the frequency of indexing. It is not easy to predict changes Congress will make.

If Congress does decide to cut back on Social Security retirement benefits in any way, the impact will be felt by the segment of the population that is eligible for Social Security retirement income. Anyone who is planning retirement based primarily on Social Security income must certainly monitor carefully any proposed changes to these benefits. It would be to your benefit to let your congressman know your feelings about any changes in Social Security that are not in your best interests. The segment of the population that is or will be eligible for Social Security retirement benefits is too large for any congressman to ignore.

Most private pensions have no automatic protection from inflation. The formulas used to compute retirement income generally are based on years of service and levels of income during specified time periods. Some corporations have been more generous than others in raising pensions after retirement. For practically all private pensions the decision to raise benefits is a voluntary one, and in practically every case the rate of increase does not keep pace with inflation. Therefore, you should assume that any private pension you receive *will not* keep pace with inflation. You really cannot count on more than the benefits outlined in your employer's pension program in compliance with the Employee Retirement Income Security Act of 1974 (ERISA).

CHANGING INVESTMENT ENVIRONMENT

The inflation rate also should have an impact on your investing and savings programs. Assume that the rate of inflation averages 10% until you retire. Assume also that the average return on the money you have invested or saved over that time has been 6% after taxes. You have essentially lost 4% of your purchasing power *each year*. You would be breaking even if you earned 10%. You are ahead of inflation only if your rate of return exceeds the inflation rate.

There are a few ways to look at this problem. If you have a sufficient asset base to afford the loss in purchasing power, you can accept a rate of return that is less than the inflation rate. Your asset base would be shrinking with respect to inflation, but you would still be able to maintain an adequate standard of living because you had a large asset base to begin with. Accordingly, you could select safer investments even if you did not expect to "beat" INFLATION.

If your asset base is not large to begin with and you do not expect a large retirement income from other sources, your problem becomes more difficult. You may feel that you cannot afford any investment in which the expected rate of return is less than the inflation rate. In that case you will have to accept more risks in your investments to obtain possible higher returns.

In this book investments are subdivided into two categories: traditional investments and inflation investments. Traditional investments include common stocks, bonds, real estate, and mutual funds. Inflation investments include gold, silver, diamonds, platinum, and foreign stocks. In the 1970s in the aggregate and with the exception of real estate, investments in the inflation investment category have outperformed traditional investments. This is not to say that investment performance in the 1980s will be the same. The point is that investors who are concerned about inflation must be aware of changing economic and international conditions. There is no "perfect" investment all the time. An investor who wants to retire with an adequate income in the face of continuing inflation must be aware of investment trends and alternatives. Very few people are in the enviable position of having sufficient assets to stay with traditional investments over long periods of time, knowing that they will be provided with an adequate income in an era of high inflation.

IMPORTANCE OF TAX SHELTERS

One of the most serious problems facing practically all U.S. workers is higher taxes caused in large part by inflation. Congress passed a tax bill in 1981 that will index federal tax tables to changes in inflation. This adjustment does not become effective until 1985. Moreover, it is an admission by Congress that inflation cannot be effectively controlled. Until 1985 even if your pay increase is equal to the inflation rate, you have less "real" take home pay because you are in a higher federal tax bracket, and a higher percentage of your wages and other income goes to federal, state, and local governments in the form of increased taxes. Moreover, it will become even more difficult to save and invest for retirement.

In the face of this serious problem, you must take advantage of every legitimate tax shelter available to you that is consistent with your lifestyle and your investment and retirement objectives.

2 Estimating Your Retirement Needs

Most retired people are dissatisfied with their lifestyles because of inadequate assets/income. The major reasons for this situation are: (1) inadequate planning, (2) inflation, and (3) insufficient career income to establish adequate pensions and asset bases. In this book the emphasis is on effective planning in an inflationary environment. We cannot control inflation. We can, however, predict its impact when you do retire. When you establish your retirement objectives and plan, you must make certain assumptions concerning inflation in addition to the assumptions you make regarding your desired lifestyle in retirement.

YOUR LIFESTYLE IN RETIREMENT

Just as individuals have different lifestyles and standards of living during preretirement, the same situation will exist during retirement. Your objectives will be unique, and you must give them some thought during your preretirement years when you make the difficult decisions as to how much, if any, of your earnings you want to put aside for your retirement.

First you must determine your desired income in retirement. A simple approach is to use a percentage of your current income. That percentage can be more or less than 100%, depending on your objectives. Most people feel that they can live comfortably on 70–80% of the after-tax income they receive during their peak earning years in "constant dollars." Constant dollars are dollars that are adjusted for inflation.

Example

Assume that in 1980 Mr. Jones is earning $30,000 after taxes. He feels he can live comfortably in retirement on $25,000 in 1980 dollars. He would like to retire at age 65, in 1990.

Exhibit 2-1 shows the impact of inflation assuming a rate of 8%. For Mr. Jones to retire in 1990 and maintain a standard of living equivalent to $25,000 in 1980 dollars, he must make substantially more than $25,000 in 1990. As shown in Exhibit 2-1, at an 8% inflation rate $1 in 1980 will be equivalent to $2.15 in 1990. Thus in 1990 Mr. Jones will need an income of $53,750 if he wants the equivalent of $25,000 in 1980 dollars.

Unfortunately an 8% rate of inflation may be too conservative based on recent U.S. experience. A rate of 10% may be more realistic. It is not so important that your initial assumptions regarding the inflation rate be exactly accurate as long as you modify your assumption based on actual inflation rates and your changing retirement objectives.

Rather than take a simple percentage to determine your income requirements, you may prefer to prepare a detailed budget. It is unlikely that a budget prepared

Exhibit 2-1   Impact of Inflation[a]

Year	Monthly Income Required to Produce Equivalent of $1,000 Currently	Purchasing Power of $1,000 Per Month Fixed Income
1	$ 1,080	$926
2	1,166	857
3	1,260	794
4	1,360	735
5	1,469	681
10	2,158	463
15	3,172	315
20	4,660	214
25	6,848	146
30	10,062	99
35	14,785	67
40	21,724	46

Source: Trust Department, Chase Manhattan Financial Planning Report.
[a]Rate of inflation = 8%.

many years before your retirement would be realistic. However, it would still be worthwhile since it would force you to address expenditures you may not have now, and you may be pleasantly surprised to discover that many of the current expenses you do have—especially those related to employment—will not be required in retirement. A list of the major budget categories is contained in Exhibit 2-2.

One item that will continue to be significant for you in retirement is the cost of housing. Since this topic is so important and somewhat complex, a separate section is devoted to real estate in Chapter 12.

YOUR RETIREMENT OBJECTIVES

Like Mr. Jones, you should make some preliminary decisions regarding your retirement. Specifically, you should try to answer the following questions:

1 At what age would I like to retire?
2 How much income would I need to satisfy my retirement objectives in today's dollars?
3 How much income will I need when I take inflation into account? (Use Exhibit 2-1)

Exhibit 2-2 Budget Categories—Expenditures

Fixed	Discretionary
Housing	Leisure and vacation
Food	Entertainment
Clothing	Charitable
Taxes (income/Social Security)	House furnishings
Property taxes	Education
Transportation	Savings
Medical	Investment
Debt repayment	Other
Maintenance and repairs	Total discretionary
Life insurance	Total annual expenditures
Property and liability insurance	
Total fixed	

Source: Trust Department, Chase Manhattan Bank, Financial Planning Report.

YOUR SOURCES OF FUNDS IN RETIREMENT

In Chapter 3, some of your sources of funds for retirement are examined in general. In Chapters 4–13 an in-depth analysis of the major sources of funds for your retirement is presented. After you have reviewed these chapters you should be able to evaluate the feasibility of your retirement plan based on your expected sources of income/assets. One of the following three situations will exist:

1 You will not be able to retire when you desire and have sufficient income/assets to meet your retirement objectives.
2 You will be able to retire when you wish with sufficient income, but it will be tight. If inflation runs at a higher rate than anticipated, you may not have sufficient income to meet your objectives.
3 You will have more than sufficient assets/income to meet your retirement standards.

SITUATION 1—INSUFFICIENT ASSETS/INCOME

You are faced with a problem that has many possible alternatives to consider. You may be forced to accept some combination of these alternatives if your computations and assumptions have been accurate.

1 Retire at a later age.
2 Accept a smaller retirement income.
3 Modify your standard of living now so you can put aside more funds for retirement.
4 Change your investment approach. Rather than lowering your standard of living, you may want to make less conservative investments in the hopes of increasing your rate of return.
5 Obtain a second job to generate more assets that can be used for your retirement.
6 Plan to work part-time during your retirement.

These are personal decisions, and you must make them. Too many people don't realize until their retirement that they do not have sufficient assets to live in the manner they would like. The sooner you analyze your own situation and determine whether your initial retirement objectives can be met, the more flexibility you will have in examining these alternatives and selecting those that are best for you.

SITUATION 2—SUFFICIENT ASSETS/INCOME

Even if it appears that you will have sufficient assets/income to meet your retirement objectives, do not become too self-satisfied. You should regularly—at least once a year—reexamine the assumptions underlying your analysis to assure yourself that these assumptions are still valid. Has the rate of inflation changed? Do your assumptions regarding your sources of income still apply? Are you considering some of the options described in Situation 1 to protect yourself in case the inflation rate increases or the rate of return on some of your investments falls off in future years?

SITUATION 3—MORE THAN SUFFICIENT ASSETS/INCOME

Your situation is enviable. Since you do not have any problem in achieving your retirement objectives, you may want to reexamine your choice of investments. Perhaps you should consider more conservative investments to safeguard your position. You may want to consider increasing your standard of living now if you are not interested in building an estate for your dependents. You may also want to consult an attorney to discuss some of the estate planning alternatives outlined in Chapter 15.

SUMMARY

Most people do not plan sufficiently for their retirement. As a result they find that they do not have sufficient assets and income in their retirement years. A proper planning process involves the following steps:

1   Estimate your income requirements for retirement in today's dollars.

2   Determine the age at which you would like to retire.

3   Select an average inflation rate that you think is reasonable between now and the time you expect to retire. (A reasonable rate now would be somewhere between 8–10% per year.)

4   Convert your income requirements in today's dollars into income requirements at retirement age, taking inflation into consideration.

5   Identify your sources of income. See Chapters 4–13.

6   Compare the income/assets you expect to have at retirement with your requirements.

7   If your requirements fall short of your expected income, you should consider the alternatives discussed in this chapter.

8   If your requirements are met by your expected income, congratulations. However, you should continue to monitor your retirement plan and review your goals, assumptions, sources of income, and the inflation rate yearly.

3 Sources of Income for Your Retirement

You should identify all the sources and potential sources of income that you anticipate using during your retirement. Your alternatives include private pension plans, Social Security, Individual Retirement Arrangements (IRAs), self-employed retirement plans, life insurance and annuities, personal investments, and any other sources such as inheritances and anticipated gifts.

PRIVATE PENSION PLANS

One of the major sources of retirement income to employees in the United States is the private pension plan. No employer is obligated to establish private pension plans for the use of employees. However, competition among employers and strong unions have had the effect of promoting private pension plans in both large and small businesses throughout the country.

The Employee Retirement Income Security Act of 1974 (ERISA) ensures employees that they will receive the benefits promised by these private pension plans even in the event of corporate bankruptcy or merger. This act also ensures that you are provided the basic information you need to determine what your particular benefits are. Chapter 7 contains a detailed discussion of the provisions of ERISA and lists important questions and issues related to private pension plans.

If you currently work for an employer who sponsors a private pension plan, your employer should provide you with the information you need about your

11

eligiblity to receive pension income and how much income you can expect based on your years of service and income level.

Even if you are not satisfied working for your current employer, you may want to consider continuing to work for this employer until you have some pension rights (vesting). Under ERISA, you may be vested in as few as 5 years or as many as 15 years of qualified service, depending on the option your employer selects. You should know whether you are vested. If not, find out how much longer you must continue working for this employer before you are.

You may feel that the pension income you would eventually receive would not be worth very much when you retire because of inflation. You should consider however, that the employer may decide at some future date to increase pension payments. It is not inconceivable that federal legislation may in fact force employers to increase pension benefits because of inflation.

Another factor to consider before you leave your present employer is the pension plan of your new employer. For example you may be too old to work a sufficient number of years for your new employer to not receive a pension. In that case you may want to postpone changing employment until you do have some vesting rights with your present employer.

Private pension plans vary as to whether contributions from employees are mandatory, optional, or permitted at all. The taxable status of your private pension income is based on the extent of your own contribution to the plan. If you have made no contribution, all the retirement income you receive is taxable. You will not be taxed for any of the funds you contributed and later receive as pension income. You will be taxed for all employer contributions. You will also be taxed for any income that was earned on both your contribution and your employer's contribution when it is returned to you in the form of retirement income. A fuller explanation of the taxability of private pensions is given in Chapter 7.

SOCIAL SECURITY

You will be eligible to receive income from Social Security if you have worked the required length of time at a job covered by the Social Security law. Most workers are eligible for Social Security. However, most federal civilian employees and some state and local employees are covered by their own retirement programs instead.

Your eligibility for a Social Security retirement income is based on the number of work credits you accumulated under Social Security. Depending on the year you reach age 62, you need from 7¼ to 10 years of work credit to be eligible. (An in-depth discussion of Social Security is presented in Chapter 4, including a more detailed definition of work credits.) If you want to find out how many years of work credits you already have under Social Security, you can request a form from your local Social Security office. It can be mailed to you or you can pick it up.

The amount of your retirement check will depend on the following factors: your average earnings over a period of years; at what age you retire; the number of years you worked under Social Security; whether you have an eligible spouse or dependent child; and the impact of inflation.

One of the attractive features of Social Security retirement income is the inflation protection feature. Each year the administrators of Social Security review the Consumer Price Index. If it has gone up, your Social Security retirement income check is increased by the same percentage.

Since the retirement income you will eventually receive from Social Security will be based partly on inflation, to estimate your retirement income from Social Security you must assume an average rate of inflation until your retirement. In Chapter 9 an example is given to show you how to use tables to compute your retirement income making certain assumptions.

Social Security income is currently exempt from federal taxes since your contributions to Social Security are not tax deductible. However, the Social Security system is not sound from an actuarial standpoint. Congress may be forced to modify the Social Security system. A recurring proposal has been to tax Social Security income. If this change is incorporated into law, you will have to adjust your Social Security income to an after-tax basis for planning purposes.

INDIVIDUAL RETIREMENT ACCOUNTS (IRAs)

You are now eligible to establish an IRA account if you are self-employed or if you work for any employer, even if you are a participant in your employer's qualified retirement plan. The major advantage of the IRA program is that it allows you to set aside up to $2000 of earned income in a retirement program for yourself on a tax deferred basis. The amount that you set aside for retirement as well as the income you earn on your investment is not taxable until you start withdrawing funds at retirement, as early as age 59½ or as late as age 70½.

The major disadvantage of the IRA plan is that you are penalized severely if you withdraw funds prior to age 59½. An in-depth discussion of the IRA program is presented in Chapter 8.

There are many options available to you in selecting an investment program for your IRA funds. The rate of return you receive depends on the performance of the investments you select. Chapter 9 contains a detailed review of investment options.

When you withdraw funds from your IRA account, all of the in come is taxable since you have not paid any taxes on the funds you have invested.

SELF-EMPLOYED RETIREMENT ACCOUNTS (KEOGHs)

Individuals are eligible to establish Keogh accounts only if they are self-employed. In most respects Keogh plans are similar to IRA plans. The major difference is that with Keogh plans, individuals are allowed to put aside 15% of their earned income up to a maximum of $15000 per year. Keogh plans do have an important restriction. Self-employed individuals cannot establish a plan for themselves exclusively. If you set up a plan for yourself, you must also establish a plan for your employees. For this reason a number of self-employed individuals establish IRA plans rather than Keogh plans to avoid this problem. A detailed explanation of Keogh plans is presented in Chapter 11.

PERMANENT LIFE INSURANCE PLANS

Permanent life insurance plans encompass whole life insurance and endowment insurance. Both forms of insurance provide you with cash values that you can use during your lifetime. When you reach retirement age you may want to consider using the cash values in these policies to supplement your retirement income. However, once you use the funds from these policies they are no longer available for your insurance protection. A comprehensive discussion of insurance is contained in Chapter 5.

If you surrender a whole life insurance policy for cash, you must pay ordinary income tax for any cash you receive greater than the premiums you paid, less any dividends you received. If when your endowment policy matures you elect to receive a lump sum distribution, you must pay taxes on the difference between your cost (premiums less dividends) and what you receive.

ANNUITIES

Annuities can be used to supplement any other retirement income you expect. Annuities can be purchased with the proceeds from llife insurance plans, or they can be purchased with any other funds you have available. One of the attractive features about some annuities is that the insurance companies guarantee a specific rate of return for the rest of your life or, if you choose, the lives of you and your spouse. Annuities are discussed in detail in Chapter 6.

In general, annuities are taxable only to the extent that the amount you receive exceeds your initial contribution.

PERSONAL INVESTMENT PROGRAM

By following the procedure outlined in Chapter 2 you will derive a minimum income level that meets your retirement objectives. You can then itemize the income you expect from your private pension, Social Security, any personal pension programs (IRA/Keogh), insurance, and any annuities or other deferred compensation. If the sum of your expected income from these sources exceeds your minimum retirement objectives, you do not need an independent investment program for retirement. However, if you find there is a gap, you should consider setting aside an additional sum of money for a personal investment program. Chapters 12 and 13 contain an analysis of various investment alternatives, encompassing both the more traditional investment vehicles and other investment options that became more popular because of excellent growth patterns in the 1970's.

4 Social Security

The Social Security system can provide the following types of benefits: retirement income for eligible workers, disability income, survivor benefits, and hospital and medical insurance under Medicare.

Social Security legislation was enacted in 1935. Since that time there have been modifications in the laws to provide broader coverage. Initially, Social Security covered only the worker upon retirement. In 1939 the law was changed to pay survivors when the worker died.

In the 1950s coverage was expanded to include most self-employed persons, most state and local employees, household and farm employees, members of the armed forces, and members of the clergy. Today most jobs in the United States are covered by Social Security. In 1954 disability insurance was added to insure workers against loss of income caused by total disability. In 1965 Medicare was introduced, providing hospital and medical insurance to people 65 and over. In 1973 Medicare was made available to people under 65 who were entitled to disability checks for 2 or more consecutive years and to people with permanent kidney failure who need dialysis or kidney transplants.

In 1972 legislation was enacted providing automatic increases in Social Security benefits as the cost of living increases. This is especially important because of the high rate of inflation and because many private pension plans are not indexed to cost of living increases.

ELIGIBILITY

You qualify for benefits if you have worked a required minimum length of time at a job covered by Social Security regulations. You may also qualify if you are self-employed for a sufficient length of time. Railroad workers are covered jointly by Social Security and by their independent retirement system. Federal workers who are covered by their own civil service retirement program are not covered by Social Security on the basis of their earnings. However, they as well as other individuals not working under Social Security, may be protected as dependents of other workers.

ESTIMATING SOCIAL SECURITY RETIREMENT INCOME

The retirement income you receive from Social Security is a function of the following factors: the work credits you receive under Social Security, the age at which you retire, and your average earnings.

Work Credits

To get a Social Security retirement check, you must have credit for a certain amount of work under Social Security. The following chart shows how much credit you need:

If you reach 62 in	You need credit for this much work
1980	7¼ years
1981	7½ years
1983	8 years
1987	9 years
1991 or later	10 years

If you stop working under Social Security before you have this much credit, you are not entitled to retirement benefits. Any credit you have earned will be maintained under your Social Security number. You can add to your credits if you return to work in a job covered by Social Security. You can request a statement of your earnings and your work credits under Social Security by filling out a form, available at any Social Security office, requesting this information.

When You Can Receive Retirement Checks

You are eligible to get a full monthly check at age 65. However, you can elect to receive reduced payments as early as age 62, 63, or 64. Exhibit 4-1 illustrates the difference in benefits based on retirement at different ages.

Exhibit 4-1 Monthly retirement benefits (payable starting July 1977)

Average Yearly Earnings ($)	For Workers				For Dependents[a]				Family[b] Benefits
	Retirement at 65	At 64	At 63	At 62	Spouse at 65 or Child	At 64	At 63	At 62	
923 or less	114.30	106.70	99.10	91.50	57.20	52.50	47.70	42.90	171.50
1,200	147.10	137.30	127.50	117.70	73.60	67.50	61.40	55.20	220.70
2,600	216.00	201.60	187.20	172.80	108.00	99.00	90.00	81.00	324.00
3,000	236.40	220.70	204.90	189.20	118.20	108.40	98.50	88.70	361.40
3,400	253.50	236.60	219.70	202.80	126.80	116.30	105.70	95.10	408.30
4,000	278.10	259.60	241.10	222.50	139.10	127.60	116.00	104.40	475.30
4,400	297.90	278.10	258.20	238.40	149.00	136.60	124.20	111.80	528.10
4,800	315.40	294.40	273.40	252.40	157.70	144.60	131.50	118.30	575.30
5,200	331.60	309.50	287.40	265.30	165.80	152.00	138.20	124.40	622.20

5,600	347.90	324.80	301.60	278.40	174.00	159.50	145.00	130.50	645.10
6,000	364.50	340.20	315.90	291.60	182.30	167.20	152.00	136.80	668.60
6,400	380.80	355.50	330.10	304.70	190.40	174.60	158.70	142.80	692.10
6,800	398.20	371.70	345.20	318.60	199.10	182.60	166.00	149.40	715.70
7,200	418.70	390.80	362.90	335.00	209.40	192.00	174.50	157.10	740.70
7,600	437.10	408.00	378.90	349.70	218.60	200.40	182.20	164.00	764.90
8,000	453.10	422.90	392.70	362.50	226.60	207.80	188.90	170.00	792.90
8,400	462.80	432.00	401.10	370.30	231.40	212.20	192.90	173.60	809.90
8,800	474.20	442.60	411.00	379.40	237.10	217.40	197.60	177.90	829.80
9,200	484.50	452.20	419.90	387.60	242.30	222.20	202.00	181.80	847.80
9,400	488.60	456.10	423.50	390.90	244.30	224.00	203.60	183.60	854.80
9,600	492.50	459.70	426.90	394.00	246.30	225.80	205.30	184.80	861.90
9,800	498.00	464.80	431.60	398.40	249.00	228.30	207.50	186.80	871.30
10,000	502.00	468.60	435.10	401.60	251.00	230.10	209.20	188.30	878.50

[a]If a person is eligible for both a worker's benefit and a spouse's benefit, the check actually payable is limited to the larger of the two.
[b]The maximum amount payable to a family is generally reached when a worker and two family members are eligible.

Estimating Steps

There is an eight-step process to determine your retirement benefits:

1   Your retirement check is based on your average earnings over a period of
    years. The number of years to count depends on the year you were born
    according to the following table:

Year you were born	Years needed
1913	19
1914	20
1915	21
1916	22
1918	24
1920	26
1925	31
1930 or later	35*

*Maximum number of years that count. Write the number of years here _____ .

2   Fill in the following worksheet (Exhibit 4-2). Column A shows maximum
    earnings covered by Social Security. In column B list your earnings
    beginning with 1951. Write 0 for a year of no earnings. If you earned more
    than the maximum in any year, list only the maximum. Estimate your
    earnings for future years including any years you plan to work past 65. Stop
    with the year before you retire.

3   Cross off your list the years of your lowest earnings until the number of years
    left is equal to the number of years indicated in step 1. You may have years in
    which you did not have any earnings.

4   Add the earnings for the years left on your list. Write the total at the bottom
    of the worksheet, and indicate that total here. Total earnings: $ _____ .

5   Divide the total from step 4 by the number of years indicated in step 1. The
    result is your average yearly earnings covered by Social Security. Write that
    figure here. Average earnings: $ _____ .

6   Examine the benefit chart (Exhibit 4-1). Find the average yearly earnings

Exhibit 4-2 Social Security Work Sheet

Year	A	B
1951	3,600	
1952	3,600	
1953	3,600	
1954	3,600	
1955	4,200	
1956	4,200	
1957	4,200	
1958	4,200	
1959	4,800	
1960	4,800	
1961	4,800	
1962	4,800	
1963	4,800	
1964	4,800	
1965	4,800	
1966	6,600	
1967	6,600	
1968	7,800	
1969	7,800	
1970	7,800	
1971	7,800	
1972	9,000	
1973	10,800	
1974	13,200	
1975	14,100	
1976	15,300	
1977	16,500	
1978	17,700	
1979	22,900	
1980	25,900[a]	
Total		$

"The maximum amount of annual earnings that count for Social Security will rise automatically after 1981 as earnings levels increase. Because of this, the base in 1982 and later may be higher than $29,700

21

closest to your own, as computed in step 5. Write that figure here. Estimated earnings: $ _____ .

7 If you have an eligible spouse or child, examine Exhibit 4-1 and determine the dependent benefit you would be entitled to. Write that amount here. Dependent allowance: $ _____ .

8 Add the subtotals of steps 6 and 7. Compare that amount with the amount in the family benefits column in Exhibit 4-1. Record the total amount unless it is greater than the family benefits figure. If it is greater, record the figure in the family benefits column. Total family retirement benefit: $ _____ .

The amount indicated for the total family retirement benefit at the end of step 8 does not take into consideration the growth in Social Security benefits that will occur because of indexing based on the rise in the cost of living.

Some people think that if they have always earned the maximum amount covered by Social Security they will get the highest benefits shown on the charts published by Social Security. This is not necessarily so. The reason is that the maximum amount of earnings covered by Social Security was lower in past years than it is now. Your contributions in previous years are averaged with the higher contributions in recent years.

YOUR RETIREMENT OPTIONS

You have only a few options to choose from in the timing and amount of your retirement check. You can retire at age 62 (assuming you have sufficient work credits), 63, or 64. If you select one of those options your pension will be 80, 86⅔, and 93⅓% of your full benefits. That decision should be based on your own personal financial and health situation. Essentially you must decide whether the value of reduced payments at an earlier age is worth more than the value of a full pension at a later age. When you make this decision, if you are a man, you should also take into consideration the impact it will have on your wife's Social Security benefit check. When she reaches age 65 she will be entitled to 50% of your benefit. If you retire early, her check will also be affected. If you retire at age 62, for example, your wife's retirement check will be reduced 10%.

Another option you have is to continue working after age 65. Under the current law, you can earn up to $2760 without affecting your Social Security benefit. If you earn more than $2760, your benefit is reduced $100 for every $2 you earn. For example, if you earned $5000, your Social Security benefit would be reduced by $1120 (50% of ($5000 − $2760)). After you reach age 72 there is no penalty. You may earn as much as you can without affecting your Social Security retirement benefits.

DEPENDENT RETIREMENT BENEFITS

One of the significant ways in which Social Security differs from other pension programs is in respect to dependents. For example, a wife is eligible to receive pension benefits in addition to her husband's even if she did not work at all under Social Security. A wife is entitled to a pension check equal to 50% of her husband's if she is 65. She may elect to accept lower benefits if she wants to start receiving payments at age 62, 63, or 64. The younger she is when she requests a pension check the lower her monthly check will be. A wife is entitled to 50% of the amount of her husband's pension check even when under 65 if she has dependent children under 18 or dependent children over 18 who became disabled before age 22.

Benefits are payable to a dependent husband aged 60 or over or to a disabled widow or widower who is at least 50 years old.

Each unmarried child who is under 18 or a full-time student up to 22 is also eligible for a benefit equal to 50% of their father's. There is a maximum amount, however, that is payable to a family. If the sum of the individual components exceeds the maximum, only the maximum amount is paid to the family.

A divorced woman is entitled to benefits based on her former husband's earnings if the marriage lasted at least 10 years. Until recently there was a 20-year requirement. Accordingly, women who are considering dissolving a marriage that has lasted almost ten years should consider whether the additional compensation is worth prolonging the marriage.

If you receive a pension from government employment not covered by Social Security, the benefits you receive as a *dependent* will be reduced on a dollar for dollar basis for each dollar you receive from that pension. If you earn sufficient work credits working under Social Security, however, you would be entitled to both your government pension and your Social Security retirement pension. It is only the benefits you receive as a *dependent* that are affected by your government pension.

SURVIVOR BENEFITS

In the event of your death your dependents will receive monthly payments. Widows generally are not eligible to collect benefits unless they are 60 years old. If a widow requests retirement benefits at age 60 she would receive an allowance of 71.5% of the pension her husband would be receiving if he were alive. If she waits until she is 65 before requesting widow's benefits she would receive 100% of her husband's pension. Looking at the situation from another perspective, if the women were already receiving a 50% allowance, her husband's death would result in a 50% drop in family income. For example, assume a retired male was receiving $600 per month in retirement benefits and his wife was receiving $300 per month as a dependent. When he dies the wife would receive $600 per month.

A widow under 65 is eligible to receive 75% of the benefits her deceased husband would have been eligible (or was eligible) to recieve at age 65, if she is responsible for a young (under 18) or disabled child. Each dependent or disabled child is also eligible to receive 75% of the deceased father's benefit. The total of all these benefits cannot, however, exceed the maximum family allowable amount. Benefits are payable to surviving dependent parents or to a dependent widower who is at least 60 years old.

DISABILITY BENEFITS

The risk of disability is something everyone must face. When disability occurs, it may affect a family's financial security more than the retirement or even the death of a worker.

Disabled people who receive monthly benefits come from all walks of life: the 40-year-old salesman who has had a heart attack; the 23-year-old secretary sidelined for more than a year by an auto accident; the 53-year-old widow who is crippled with advanced arthritis; the retired or disabled worker's 32-year-old son who has been mentally retarded from birth. Each person who applies for disability benefits is considered for services by the vocational rehabilitation agency in his or her state.

Who Can Get Benefits Because of Disability?

The Social Security program provides disability protection in different situations. Monthly benefits can be paid to:

Disabled workers under 65 and their families.

Persons disabled before 22 who continue to be disabled. These benefits are payable as early as 18 when a parent (or grandparent under certain circumstances) receives Social Security retirement or disability benefits or when an insured parent dies.

Disabled widows and widowers and, under certain conditions, disabled surviving divorced wives of men who worked long enough under Social Security to receive Social Security benefits. These benefits are payable as early as 50.

A disabled person is eligible for Medicare after being entitled to disability payments for 24 consecutive months.

Application for Benefits Needed

Application for disability benefits must be completed before any payments can be made. For disabled persons unable to handle their own affairs the application may be made by his or her spouse, parent, other relative or friend, or legal guardian.

A Disabled Worker Needs Some Work Credits

If you are a worker and become severely disabled, you will be eligible for monthly benefits if you have worked under Social Security long enough and recently enough. The amount of work credits you need depends on your age when you become disabled:

Before 24   You need credit for 1½ years of work in the 3-year period ending when your disability begins.

24 through 30   You need credit for having worked half the time between the age of 21 and the time you become disabled.

31 or older   All workers disabled at 31 or older—except the blind—need the amount of credit shown in the following chart:
Five years of this credit must have been earned in the 10 years ending when a worker has become disabled. The years need not be continuous or in units of full years.

Persons Previously Entitled to Disability Benefits

The period in which workers were disabled is not counted in figuring the amount or recentness of work needed to be eligible for benefits.

   If you are disabled by blindness, you do not have to meet this requirement of recently covered work, but you do need credit for ¼ year of work for each year since 1950 or the year when you reached 21 if later, up to the year you became blind. A minimum of 1½ years of credit is needed.

When Is a Worker Disabled?

To be considered disabled under the Social Security law you must have a physical or mental condition that:

Prevents you from doing any substantial gainful work.

Exhibit 4-3   Work Credits for Disability Benefits

Born After 1929, Became Disabled at Age	Born Before 1930, Became Disabled Before 62 in	Years of Work Credit You Need
42 or younger	1971	5
44	1973	5½
46	1975	6
48	1977	6½
50	1979	7
52	1981	7
54	1983	8
56	1985	9
58	1987	9½
60	1989	10
62 or older	1991 or later	

Five years of this credit must have earned in the 10 years ending when a worker has become disabled. The years need not be continuous or in units of full years.

Is expected to last (or has lasted) for at least 12 months or is expected to result in death.

If you meet these requirements, you may be able to get payments even if your recovery from the disability is expected. The medical evidence from your physician or other sources will show the severity of your condition and the extent to which it prevents you from doing substantial gainful work. Your age, education, training, and work experience also may be considered in deciding whether you are able to work. If you can't do your regular work but can do other substantial gainful work, you will not be considered disabled.

Special Provisions for Blind People

A person whose vision is no better than 20/200 with glasses or who has a limited visual field of 20 degrees or less is considered blind under the Social Security law. If Social Security considers that you are blind and you have worked long enough, you are eligible for a disability "freeze" even if you are actually working. This means that your future benefits, which are figured from your average earnings, will not be reduced because you have low earnings or no earnings during those years in which you were disabled. If you are blind, 55 to 65 years old, and have worked long enough under Social Security, you can get cash disability benefits if you are unable to perform work requiring skills or abilities comparable to those required by the work you did regularly before you reached 55 or became blind, whichever is later. Benefits will not be paid, however, for any month in which you actually perform substantial gainful work.

People disabled because of blindness have a special measure of "substantial gainful activity." A person receiving benefits because of blindness is considered to be engaging in substantial gainful activity if his or her earnings exceed $375 a month (in 1979). The monthly measure will be higher in future years.

Dependents of Disabled Workers

While you are receiving benefits as a disabled worker, payments can also be made to certain members of your family. These family members include:

Your unmarried children under 18.

Your children 18−22 if they are unmarried and attending school full-time.

Your unmarried children 18 or older who were disabled before reaching 22 and

continue to be disabled. Stepchildren, adopted children, and, in certain circumstances, grandchildren also may qualify for benefits on your record.)

Your wife at any age if she has in her care a child under 18 or disabled who is
getting benefits based on your Social Security record.

Your wife 62 or older even if there are no children entitled to benefits.

Your husband 62 or older.

A child may be eligible on a grandparent's Social Security record only if the
child's parents are disabled or deceased and the child was living with the
grandparent at the time the grandparent qualified for benefits.

If You Also Receive Worker's Compensation

If you are a disabled worker under age 62 and are entitled to both Social Security
disability benefits and worker's compensation, the total monthly payments to you
and your family may not exceed 80% of your average monthly earnings before
you became disabled. Your full earnings, including any amounts above the
maximum creditable for Social Security, may be considered when your average
earnings are figured for this purpose. Social Security benefits must be reduced if
combined benefits from Social Security and worker's compensation would
otherwise be over this limit.

People Disabled Before Age 22

If you have an unmarried son or daughter 18 or older who became disabled
before 22 and is still disabled, he or she may start receiving disability benefits at
the following times:

When you start getting Social Security retirement or disability benefits.

At your death if you had enough Social Security work credits for the payment of
benefits to your survivors.

A person disabled before 22 needs no Social Security work credits to get
benefits. The payments, based on the earnings of a parent, may continuue for as
long as he or she is disabled and the parent's eligibility continues. The decision
whether a person has been disabled since childhood is made in the same way as
the decision whether a worker is disabled.

If a child with a severe medical condition is now receiving child's benefits scheduled to stop at age 18, the child or someone in the family should get in touch with the Social Security office a few months before the eighteenth birthday to see about continuing the benefits past 18 on the basis of disability.

If a disability first occurs between the ages of 18 and 22, an application should be filed at that time or later when benefits are payable on the Social Security work record of a parent.

The mother of a disabled son or daughter entitled to disability benefits may also qualify for benefits regardless of her age if she has the son or daughter in her care.

Disabled Widows or Widowers

If you are disabled and are the widow, widower, or (under certain circumstances) the surviving divorced wife of a person who worked long enough under Social Security, you may be able to get monthly benefits as early as age 50. The benefits will be permanently reduced, and the amount of the reduction will depend on the age at which benefits start. You need no work credits of your own to receive benefits based on the earnings of your deceased spouse.

A widow or widower may be considered disabled only if she or he has an impairment so severe that it ordinarily would prevent a person from working and is expected to last at least 12 months. Vocational factors such as age, education, and previous work experience cannot be considered in deciding whether a widow or widower is disabled. (They would be for a disabled worker.)

In general, you cannot receive these benefits unless your disability starts before your spouse's death or within 7 years after the death. However, if you receive benefits as a widow with children, you can be eligible if you become disabled before those payments end or within 7 years after they end. (This 7-year period protects the widow until she has a chance to earn enough work credits for disability protection on her own Social Security record.)

A disabled surviving divorced wife may receive benefits based on the earnings of her former husband only if their marriage lasted 10 years or longer.

When Benefits Are Payable

Benefits begin after a waiting period of 5 full calendar months. No benefits can be paid for these first 5 months of disability; therefore, the first payment is for the sixth full month. If you are disabled more than 6 full months before you apply, back benefits may be payable but are limited to the 12 months preceding the month you apply. If you have recovered from a disability that lasted 12 months or more but have not yet applied for benefits, you may still be eligible for some back payments. But if you wait longer than 14 months after you recover to apply, you will not be eligible for any back benefits.

An application for disability benefits can be filed after the death of a disabled worker. If the claim is approved, back payments may be made for some months preceding the death of the worker. An application for the back payment must be filed within 3 months after the worker's death. In addition, survivors benefits may be payable beginning the month the worker died.

There is no 5-month waiting period for people disabled before age 22 who are entitled to benefits on a parent's work record. Benefit to a person disabled before 22 can begin the month a parent's retirement or disability benefits start or the month an insured parent dies.

Your benefit payments may continue as long as you remain unable to work. If someone married while receiving benefits as a person disabled in childhood or as a disabled widow or widower, the benefits usually will stop. In some cases, however, they can be continued. You can get more information about these exceptions from your Social Security office.

Medicare for Disabled People

Certain disabled people under 65 are eligible for Medicare. They include disabled workers at any age, persons who became disabled before age 22, and disabled widows and widowers age 50 or over who have been entitled to disability checks for 2 consecutive years or more. Medicare protection ends when disability benefits ends. If a person has another period of disability later on, Medicare coverage can be resumed after he or she has been entitled to disability checks for another 2 consecutive years. For more information, ask at any Social Security office for a copy of *A Brief Explanation of Medicare*.

Medicare for People with Permanent Kidney Failure

People who need long-term dialysis treatment or a kidney transplant for permanent kidney failure can be covered by Medicare. People who have worked long enough under Social Security to be insured, people getting monthly benefits, and the wives or husbands and dependent children of insured people and beneficiaries will be eligible if they need maintenance dialysis or a kidney transplant. For more information, ask at any Social Security office for a copy of *Medicare for People Under 65 with Permanent Kidney Failure*.

Amounts of Monthly Payments

Benefits to workers disabled after 1978 and their dependents are based in part on earnings that have been adjusted to take account of increases in average wages since they were earned. The adjusted earnings are averaged together and a formula is applied to the adjusted average to compute the benefit rate. Monthly benefits for workers disabled in 1979 range from an estimated $12 to about $500. Monthly benefits to a worker and family range from $183 to about $900.

Disability Benefits and Other Social Security Benefits

Benefits because of disability are not paid in addition to other monthly Social Security benefits. If you become entitled to more than one monthly benefit at the same time, the amount you receive ordinarily will be equal to the larger of the benefits.

If you become disabled after you start receiving Social Security benefits, it may be to your advantage to switch over to benefits based on disability. For instance, if you start receiving reduced retirement benefits at age 62 and then become disabled at age 63, your benefit may be higher if you change to disability payments. If you were receiving reduced widow's or widower's benefits or a reduced retirement benefit before you became disabled, your disability benefits also will be reduced to take into account the number of months you received the other benefits. Even with this reduction, however, your disability benefits may be higher than the benefits you were receiving. The people in your Social Security office can give you the amount of the different benefits in this situation.

Effect of Work on Benefit Payments

If you receive benefits as a disabled worker, an adult disabled since childhood, or a disabled widow or widower, you are not subject to the general rule under which some benefits are withheld if you have substantial earnings. There are special rules, including medical consideration, for determining if any work you do might affect your disability payments.

If one of your dependents who is under 65 and not disabled works and earns more than $3480 in 1979, some of the dependent's benefits may be withheld. In general, $1 in benefits is withheld for each $2 over $3480. Different rules apply to dependents who are 65 or over.

The amount a pension can earn without having any benefits withheld will increase automatically in future years as the level of average wages rises.

The Disability Decision

When you apply for benefits because of disability, the Social Security office will send your claim to a disability determination services office in your state—usually associated with the vocational rehabilitation agency. That office will decide whether you are disabled under the law. A team of trained people in the state agency—a physician and a disability evaluation specialist—will consider all the facts in your file. They will request medical evidence from your doctor, hospital, clinic, or institution where you have been treated. If there is a charge for a medical report, you will be responsible for it.

Additional medical information may be needed to determine whether you are disabled under the law. If this information is not available in the records of your family physician, you may be asked to undergo additional medical examinations and tests at government expense.

MEDICARE

Medicare is a health insurance program for people 65 and older and some people under 65 who are disabled. It is a federal government agency for administering health care financing. Medicare has two parts: hospital insurance and medical insurance.

Medicare hospital insurance can help pay for medically necessary inpatient hospital care and, after a hospital stay, for inpatient care in a skilled nursing facility and for care in your home by a home health agency.

Medicare medical insurance can help pay for medically necessary doctor's services, outpatient hospital services, outpatient physical therapy and speech pathology services, and a number of other medical services and supplies not covered by the hospital insurance part of Medicare. Medical insurance also can help pay for necessary home health services when hospital insurance cannot pay for them.

Medicare does not pay the full cost of some covered services. As general health care costs rise, these amounts may increase. For people with very low incomes, the Medicaid program in their state may pay the amounts Medicare does not pay and may pay some health care expenses not covered by Medicare.

Medicare payments are handled by private insurance organizations under contract with the government. Organizations handling claims from hospitals, skilled nursing facilities, and home health agencies are called intermediaries. Organizations handling claims from doctors and other suppliers of services covered under the medical insurance part of Medicare are called carriers.

Your Medicare Card

Be sure to keep the Medicare health insurance card sent to you. The card shows the Medicare protection you have (hospital insurance, medical insurance, or both) and the date your protection started.

The card also shows your health insurance claim number. The claim number has nine digits and a letter. In some cases there will be another number after the letter. Be sure to put your full claim number on all Medicare claims and correspondence. If a husband and wife both have Medicare, they get separate cards and different claim numbers. Each must use the exact claim number shown on his or her card.

Important Things to Remember

1   Always show your Medicare card when you receive services that Medicare can help pay for.
2   Always write your health insurance claim number (including the letter) on any bills you send in and on any correspondence about Medicare.
3   Carry your card with you whenever you are away from home. If you ever lose it, ask the people in the Social Security office immediately for a new one.
4   Do not use your Medicare card before the effective date shown on the card.
5   Permanent Medicare cards made of metal or plastic, sold by some manufacturers, are not a substitute for your officially issued Medicare card.

Eligibility

Individuals who have worked long enough to receive retirement income benefits are automatically entitled to Medicare benefits at nominal costs for themselves and their dependents. Other elderly U.S. citizens can also participate in the Medicare program if they pay specified monthly costs. The cost of the medical insurance program was $9.60 per month in 1980. The cost of the hospital insurance program was $69.00 per month in 1980. To be eligible for the hospital insurance an individual must be covered by the medical insurance.

Hospital Insurance

Medicare hospital insurance helps pay for three kinds of care: (1) inpatient hospital care, and, when medically necessary after a hospital stay, (2) inpatient care in a skilled nursing facility, and (3) home health care.

There is a limit on how many days of hospital or skilled nursing facility care and how many home health visits Medicare can help pay for in each benefit period. However, your hospital insurance protection is renewed every time you start a new benefit period. Medicare hospital insurance will pay for most but not all of the services you receive in a hospital or skilled nursing facility or from a home health agency. There are covered services and noncovered services under each kind of care. Covered services are services and supplies that hospital insurance can pay for.

For benefit periods starting in 1980, your share of the costs of covered care under the hospital insurance part of Medicare will be:

For the first 60 days in the hospital, $180 (up from $160).

For the sixty-first through the ninetieth day in the hospital, $45 a day (up from $40).

For the 60 reserve days, $90 a day (up from $80).

For the twenty-first through the one-hundredth day in a skilled nursing facility, $22.50 a day (up from $20).

Medical Insurance

Medicare medical insurance can help pay for (1) doctor's services, (2) outpatient hospital care, (3) outpatient physical therapy and speech pathology services, (4) home health care, and (5) many other health services and supplies not covered by Medicare hospital insurance.

There is a basic payment rule under medical insurance. After you have $60 in reasonable charges for covered medical expenses in each calendar year, medical insurance will pay 80% of the reasonable charges for any additional covered services you receive during the rest of the year.

Your first $60 in covered expenses in each calendar year is called the medical insurance deductible. You need to meet this $60 deductible only once per calendar year. The deductible can be met by any combination of covered expenses. You do not have to meet a separate deductible for each different kind of covered service you might receive. There is also a special carryover rule that will help you if some or all of your medical expenses in the last 3 months of the year can be used to meet your deductible.

Charges

Under the law, medical insurance payments are based on "reasonable charges" for covered services and supplies. The Medicare carrier for your area determines the reasonable charges for covered services and supplies using a procedure prescribed in the Medicare law. Each year the carrier reviews the actual charges made by doctors and suppliers in your area during the previous year. Based on this review, new reasonable charges are put into effect about July 1 of each year.

The carrier determines reasonable charges by first calculating the customary charges (generally the most frequent charge) by each doctor and supplier for each separate service or supply furnished to patients in the previous calendar year.

Next, the carrier determines the prevailing charge for each covered service and supply. The prevailing charge is the amount high enough to cover the customary charges in three out of every four bills submitted in the previous year for each service and supply. However, increases in prevailing charges for doctor's services are limited from year to year by an "economic index" formula that relates doctors' fee increases to the actual increases in the cost of maintaining their practices and to raises in general earnings levels.

When a medical insurance claim is submitted, the carrier compares the actual charge shown on the claim with the customary and prevailing charges for that service or supply. The reasonable charge approved by the carrier will be either the customary charge, the prevailing charge, or the actual charge, whichever is lowest.

If your doctor's or supplier's actual charge is higher than the reasonable charge, this does not necessarily mean that his or her charges are unreasonable. Usually when the Medicare reasonable charge is lower than the actual charge, it is because your doctor or supplier recently raised his or her charge and it has not been in effect long enough to be included in Medicare's annual review. In other cases, of course, the actual charge may be higher than the reasonable charge because the doctor or supplier charges higher for the particular service or supply than most other doctors and suppliers in your area. Or the doctors in your area may have increased some of their charges by larger amounts than Medicare can recognize under the "economic index" formula in the law.

When a doctor or supplier accepts an assignment of the medical insurance payment, he or she agrees that the total charge to you for covered services will be the reasonable charge approved by the carrier. For this reason you may want to find out in advance whether the doctor or supplier will accept assignment.

Additional Information about Medicare

The Social Security administration publishes a free document, *Your Medicare Handbook,* which contains very detailed information concerning Medicare. You can either call your local office and ask them to mail you the handbook, or you can visit your local office and pick one up there. It contains information pertaining to your coverage, charges, and claims submittal.

ADDITIONAL INFORMATION/APPLYING FOR BENEFITS

You can get specific information about benefit checks either by calling a local Social Security office or going there in person. If you go to a local office it is recommended that you bring a copy of your latest W-2 form or a copy of your last federal income tax return if you are self-employed.

You *do not automatically* receive Social Security benefits when you become eligible for them. To receive any benefit, whether it is a retirement, disability, death or other benefit, you must apply at the nearest Social Security office. It is important to apply as soon as possible, since a delay in applying might cause you to lose some benefits. You can contact your local office to get advice on how early you should apply for benefits such as retirement, which you can predict in advance.

In applying for benefits you should bring—in addition to your W-2 or tax return—the following:

Your Social Security card or a record of your number.

Proof of your age: a birth certificate or a baptismal certificate made at or shortly after your birth.

Your marriage certificate if you are applying for benefits as a spouse.

Your children's birth certificates if you are applying for them.

Your Social Security office has many free booklets describing all the possible benefits available from Social Security. You can obtain these booklets by going to your local office. If you know which booklet you are interested in, you can call the local office and request that they mail you the booklet.

Most Social Security offices will also make speakers available at no cost if you have a group of sufficient size interested in a specific topic or topics. You can make arrangements for a speaker by calling your local office and giving them an indication of what kind of audience is to be addressed and the principal subjects you are interested in.

5 Life Insurance

In essence there are three major questions you should ask about your life insurance program as well as the programs of your family members.

1   How much insurance is needed?
2   What kind is required?
3   Where should it be purchased?

Your need for life insurance will undoubtedly change over time. For most individuals the need for life insurance is much greater in the early stages of working life when there may be young children and a nonworking spouse. As children become self-sufficient and when and if both husband and wife work, individual life insurance needs should be reexamined.

One of the most important decisions you should make regarding life insurance is whether you want it to serve as "pure" insurance or as a savings device. The problem with using life insurance as a device to save money is twofold:

1   There is the danger that, by placing an emphasis on savings, you are underinsured during critical periods of your life since you would be buying a more expensive form of policy with a lower face value than you would have if you bought "pure" insurance—that is, term insurance for the same premium dollar.
2   The rate of return you would obtain on this investment may not keep pace with inflation. You should not buy any insurance that builds up cash values for you until you have looked at alternative investment options.

38

DETERMINING THE AMOUNT OF LIFE INSURANCE YOU NEED

The following considerations should be taken into account when you determine your life insurance requirements.

Use of Funds

Liquid assets required for final expenses such as medical, funeral, and settling of estate.

Income during estate settlement period.

Educational expenses for youur children.

Income to cover continuing living expenses for your spouse.

Sources of Funds

The assets your dependents will obtain from your estate independent of your insurance program.

Independent income your dependents have or can obtain.

Assets your dependents now have.

Social Security coverage your dependents will have.

Other pension coverage your dependents will have.

Other inheritances expected for your dependents.

PERMANENT PLANS

Some forms of life insurance combine insurance and savings under one policy. This form of insurance is known as "permanent plan" insurance. The major distinctions between this form of insurance and term insurance is that with permanent plans the premiums are fixed, the policy generally covers a longer time period, and cash values, which can be used as collateral for loans, are built up over time. There are three basic forms of permanent plan insurance: whole life, limited payment life, and endowment policies.

Whole Life

Whole life insurance, also known as ordinary or straight life insurance, is the most common form of life insurance. The policy remains in force for an individual's lifetime as long as the premium is paid. The premium is constant, and the face amount of the policy is fixed. After the policy has been in force a few years, it has a cash value that increases each year. This cash value represents the savings accrued in the policy. At the policyholder's option, he or she can borrow against this cash value at an interest rate stipulated in the initial policy. The policyholder is obligated to pay interest to the insurance company only if he or she takes out a loan. If the policyholder dies while a loan is outstanding, however, the beneficiary would receive the face amount minus any outstanding loans.

Limited Payment Life

Limited payment life is similar to whole life, with the exception that payments are required for a limited time period only. For example, if a 40-year-old man wanted permanent insurance of $50,000 but did not want to pay premiums after age 65, he could take out a 25-year limited payment life policy with a face amount of $50,000. If he died before age 65, his beneficiary would receive $50,000. If he were alive at age 65, he would not have to continue to pay premiums to keep his policy in force. If he wished, he could also terminate the policy at age 65 and take the cash value accrued in the policy. The cash value would be less than $50,000. (The only time the cash value is equal to the face value of the policy is with an endowment policy.) Even though the cash value is less than $50,000, the cash value is still greater than it is for a comparable whole life policy. The premium for limited payment life is higher than the premium for whole life for the same face amount and age.

Endowment

The endowment policy also has a fixed face amount and a specified time period. If the policyholder dies within that time, the face amount is paid to the beneficiary. At the end of the specified time, if the policyholder is alive, the *entire* face amount is paid to the policyholder. Accordingly, premiums for endowment policies are much higher than straight life or limited payment life premiums.

Endowment policies should be used only if it is more important to save money than to obtain the cheapest form of insurance.

TERM INSURANCE

Term plans provide life insurance for a specific number of years that may vary from 1-year terms to more common periods of 5, 10, or 20 years. Most insurance companies do not write policies after age 65, although a few companies write policies up to age 70. A death benefit is payable should death result during a term period. If you live beyond the specific term you are insured for, you receive no benefits with this type of policy. You are buying "pure insurance" with no savings feature.

When one term ends and you renew the policy, your premiums are increased to reflect the fact that you are a bigger insurance risk because you are older. Some term plans give you the right to renew for another period when a term ends regardless of health. This is a very important consideration and should be clarified before you take out any term insurance.

Most term policies allow you to convert to a permanent plan such as whole life. You would be able to make this conversion normally only if you execute the option a few years before the expiration of the term period. If you execute the option within the required time period, you would not have to supply any health information or take a health examination. The premium you pay would be based on your age at the time you convert.

Term insurance that decreases in face value during the term of coverage is known as decreasing term insurance. This type of insurance is often used as mortgage protection insurance. When used for this purpose, the face amount of the policy is roughly equal to the amount of the mortgage, and the length of the term policy would be equal to the length of the mortgage contract.

Term insurance can be used effectively as part of a long-term retirement program. If individuals have enough term insurance during their working lives, they can develop independent investment programs with objectives to meet retirement needs. If individuals develop independent investment programs, coupled with other retirement benefits, they will not longer need insurance at retirement age.

TERM VERSUS PERMANENT

The choice of term versus permanent insurance should be a personal decision after you understand the essential differences between the two forms of insurance. The major advantages and disadvantages are summarized below.

Advantages of Term

Lower initial premium.

Can be used to meet temporary need.

Provides more coverage with fixed dollar amount when you might not be able to afford adequate coverage with permanent insurance.

Can provide flexibility by being convertible to permanent insurance.

Disadvantages of Term

Cannot be renewed after specified age.

Increased premium when renewed.

No buildup of cash values.

Advantages of Permanent Insurance

Cannot be canceled because of age.

Constant premium.

Buildup of cash values.

Increases in value accumulate tax-free.

Flexibility in treating dividends (e.g., lowering premium or purchasing more insurance).

Forced savings.

Disadvantages of Permanent Insurance

Higher initial premium.

Insurance buyer may have inadequate protection if he or she has only limited funds with which to purchase insurance.

Higher investment returns may be available elsewhere.

Not easy to compare expected return on investment in insurance to alternate investments.

Since insurance salespeople make more of a commission on permanent insurance, the sales approach can be biased.

PARTICIPATING VERSUS NONPARTICIPATING

Many types of life insurance are also classified as participating or nonparticipating. A policy providing payment of dividends is known as participating. A nonparticipating type pays no dividends.

Dividend payments usually begin after the policy has been in effect for 2 or 3 years. Dividends are derived from any excess investment earnings in addition to any part of your premium payments that are left after the company pays the current year's benefit to policyholders, pays its expenses, and sets aside reserves for future benefit payments. Since there is no guarantee that the company will have this excess, the dividend is not guaranteed. However, you can check an insurance company's previous dividend history. This is the best indication you have about expected dividends in the future.

The primary advantage of the nonparticipating policy is that because its costs are fixed the initial premium should be lower. Participating policies, however, enable you to benefit from any favorable experience. Its long run costs may be lower.

RIDERS

At the time an insurance policy is issued certain optional features are available at a lower cost than if purchased separately. They include the following:

Waiver of Premium   Provides that policy will be kept in force by the company without further payment of premiums if you become totally disabled before age 60 or 65.

Disability Income   Provides payment of a monthly income because of a total disability after an initial waiting period.

Accidental Death Benefit   Provides that two or three times the face amount of the policy will be paid if you die by accident prior to a specified age, usually 65.

Decreasing Term Rider   May be cheaper to buy decreasing term as a rider to an existing policy than to buy a separate policy.

Guaranteed Insurability   Gives you the option to buy a stated amount of additional insurance at specified intervals up to a maximum age without presenting evidence of insurability.

Cost of Living Rider   Enables the policy holder to purchase more insurance each year to help offset increasing insurance needs because of inflation.

Level Term Rider   Temporary coverage that may be attached to an existing permanent policy to provide a fixed amount of extra insurance for a fixed time period.

It is important to consider these rider options carefully when a policy is initially purchased, since it may not be possible to add them later or the cost may be prohibitive.

GROUP VERSUS INDIVIDUAL

For most people group insurance is cheaper than individual policy insurance. Group insurance is cheaper because of the lower administrative costs to the insurance company. The one major exception occurs when a younger individual is covered in a group having a much higher average age.

Group life insurance is normally available through employer groups, labor unions, trade associations, professional associations, credit unions, and other creditors. Group coverage differs from coverage under an individual policy in the following ways:

1 Insurance is obtained simply by being an eligible member of the group; usually no medical examination is required.
2 Separate policies are not issued, just a certificate and a booklet explaining the benefits. A single policy for the whole group is issued.
3 The cost is low because the coverage is term, the employer may pay part of the premium, and the administrative costs are lower.
4 The premium rate is based on the composition and experience of the group.
5 If your individual group membership or employment ends for any reason, you usually have the right—*for a limited period of time*—to convert to an individual life insurance policy. If the group or employer terminates the group policy, you may be entitled to certain conversion rights.

COMPARE COSTS—INTEREST-ADJUSTED METHOD

Insurance companies are not regulated to the extent that they must charge the same premiums for the same risk situation. Premiums vary between companies, and it is difficult for the layman to determine the cheapest policy, because not only do premiums vary, but so do dividends and the accumulation of cash values.

To compare insurance costs on the same basis, the interest-adjusted method of computing costs was developed. With the use of this method, an interest-adjusted cost index takes into consideration three basic variables: premiums, dividends, and cash value. The interest-adjusted method takes into consideration the time value of money. An interest rate is applied to all three cost variables over time, and these costs are then reduced to a single cost index number that allows comparison between companies.

There is no federal law requiring an insurance agent to volunteer information such as how the cost index of his or her company compares to other companies. A sophisticated insurance buyer would not purchase insurance from a company whose cost index was considerably higher than the industry average.

Cost indexes can be obtained through publications put out by A.M. Best & Company, Inc. and in some states through a state insurance department.

Periodicals such as *Changing Times* and *Consumers Report* frequently publish selected cost comparisons.

Cost indexes are developed for specific categories such as male, term, $20,000, age 30. Companies can have above average cost indexes for one type of policy and below average indexes for others. Therefore, it is important to determine the type and amount of insurance you require before completing a cost comparison.

BENEFICIARY

You should determine the appropriate beneficiary of your life insurance in coordination with your estate plan. If you plan to pass everything to your spouse then she or he should be the beneficiary. Minor children should be avoided as beneficiaries because of the required court supervision and expense.

Assignment of Life Insurance

If your estate will be of considerable size, you may wish to save estate taxes for your dependents by assigning your life insurance to someone else other than your spouse. The 1981 tax law allows you to pass unlimited assets to your spouse, free of estate tax. Therefore there is no advantage in assigning your policy to your spouse. When you assign your life insurance, you are giving up ownership of your policy. Upon your death the proceeds of the policy will not be included in your estate.

There are a few potential disadvantages associated with the assignment of policies. The new owner of the policy must demonstrate that she or he is paying the premiums. Otherwise the IRS can protest the ownership.

One of the major disadvantages of assignment is the loss of your flexibility. Once you assign the policy to someone else you cannot change the beneficiary of the policy. The policy is no longer yours. If you were forced to take out new insurance at an advanced age, you might find it more difficult to be insured, and the premiums would be higher for any permanent insurance.

In any event, you should plan carefully before you assign any life insurance, and you should do so only with competent legal and tax advice.

CHECKLIST OF IMPORTANT TIPS

1   Selecting a Plan

Your life insurance needs depend on your responsibilities, standard of living, sources of continuing income (such as your pension plan, savings, and investments), and the amount of life insurance coverage you may already have (such as group insurance through your job or union and Social Security survivors benefits).

Check to see if you can save money by qualifying for any group life insurance.

If you buy term insurance and your need for coverage will last beyond the term period, make sure the policy is renewable and/or convertible to a permanent policy.

You can choose a nonparticipating policy with a fixed cost or a participating policy that returns the unused part of the premium as a dividend so that cost will depend on the company's experience.

2   Comparison Shopping

It pays to shop for the right policy at the right price, but don't shop by price alone.

Prices for similar policies can vary substantially from company to company.

Beware of insurance programs that seem too good to be true and don't allow yourself to be pressured into a hasty decision.

Don't buy more than you can afford.

3   Selecting a Company and Agent

Know your agent and make sure the agent is licensed in your state.

Deal with a licensed company in your state.

4   Applying for a Policy

Make sure the information you give in the application is correct before you sign.

Know how long you will be paying premiums and whether they increase at a later date.

You can save money by choosing the right method of paying premiums.

You can save money by choosing the right amount of insurance when premium rates vary.

Ask about the various riders available at the time you buy the policy.

Know when the policy or rider coverage terminates.

Know if your policy has a cash value and, if so, what it will be.

If you are entitled to dividends, you can choose how they will be paid—carefully select the option that is best for you.

Know the settlement options and advantages of each to you and your beneficiary.

When buying the policy, you generally get a 10-day free examination period, and you can get immediate protection with a conditional receipt.

Your policy is incontestable after a specified time period; the company can't cancel your policy unless you fail to pay premiums.

5   As a Policyholder

If you have a life insurance policy, don't switch to another company without considering the consequences carefully.

It's never too late to update your policy—particularly when you retire.

Make sure your beneficiary knows about the policy and where it is kept.

Life insurance policies should be readily available; don't keep them in safety deposit boxes.

In addition to naming a beneficiary, name a contingent beneficiary.

If you can't pay premiums, try to save your insurance coverage through policy loans and nonforfeiture options rather than surrendering the policy for cash.

Review your dividend option from time to time.

Before you leave dividends on deposit with the company, compare the policy's interest rate with rate of return on other investments.

To get cash when you surrender your policy you must specifically ask for it.

If you have questions or complaints unanswered or unsatisfied by your company or agent, get in touch with your state insurance department.

6   As a Beneficiary

You shouldn't need a lawyer to collect benefits and you don't have to pay any fee to make a claim.

You may be entitled to a partial premium refund of the final premium in addition to the other policy proceeds.

Know where the policy is located and make sure your correct current address is known to the company. If you have not applied for policy proceeds within a stipulated time period after the insured's death, the money may be transferred to the state in accordance with the Abandoned Property Law.

If the policy gives you the right to select a settlement option, review the advantages of each carefully.

TAXABILITY OF INSURANCE

Estate and Inheritance Tax—Federal

When the decedent was the owner of the insurance policy, the value of the policy is included in the estate. The value of the policy is the face value less any loans outstanding against the policy. If the decedent owned someone else's insurance policy, the value of the policy is the cash surrender value of the policy. If the decedent was insured but the policies were owned by someone else, the value of these policies are not included in the estate. It must be clear, however, that the decedent did not have any incidence of ownership in these policies such as the right to convert the policy to another form of insurance, assign the policy, borrow cash values, or change the beneficiary.

Estate and Inheritance Tax—State

States generally tax on the same basis as the federal government in terms of ownership and value of insurance. However, there are unique differences between states. For example, some states exempt all insurance from taxation. Some states exempt insurance payable to a specific beneificary such as an individual or trust. Some states allow specific dollar amount exemptions.

Income Tax

Whole life insurance and term insurance proceeds are not subject to income taxes on the death of the insured, but if you turn in your whole life policy for its cash surrender value you may be subject to income taxes. You are subject to taxes if the amount of the cash surrender value and dividends exceed the premiums you have paid. Accordingly, before you surrender any policy you should first contact your life insurance agent to determine how much tax, if any, you would have to pay. You may want to consider other alternatives such as borrowing on the policy and/or postponing surrendering the policy until such time you are in a lower tax bracket.

The beneficiary of a policy can leave the proceeds of the policy with the insurance company to generate interest. That interest is subject to tax when it is received by the beneficiary. Any interest received above $1000 is taxable.

Gift Tax

If you assign your life insurance to someone, you may be subject to gift tax. As discussed in Chapter 15, there is now a unified tax that combines gift tax and estate tax. Whole life insurance is valued at the cash surrender value. That value is indicated on the life insurance policy. Term insurance does not have any cash value. Accordingly, no gift tax would be applicable.

You are allowed to give any individual up to $10,000 per year and not be subject to a gift tax. A long as you transfer a policy to an individual there is no gift tax on the premium you pay for that individual if your total gift to that party does not exceed $10,000 for that year. However, if you transfer the insurance to an irrevocable insurance trust, the premium will not qualify for the annual exclusion. The IRS will claim that the premium payment in this situation does not constitute a present interest but rather represents a future interest.

6 Annuities

An annuity is a contract issued by a life insurance company, that promises the purchaser a stream of income. Depending on the type of annuity, that stream can be for a specific time period or for life.

There are three specific types of annuities that should be clearly understood: deferred annuities, fixed annuities, and variable annuities.

Deferred annuities, which have become very popular lately, are annuities in which the payout to the purchaser does not begin until a future year after the purchase. The time that the payout will be initiated is determined by the buyer of the annuity. A purchaser of a deferred annuity can select either a variable or a fixed annuity.

A fixed annuity is a contract or agreement by which an insurance company accepts a sum of money and guarantees to pay a regular income for either a stated period or for life. With fixed annuties insurance companies guarantee a minimum rate of return. The insurance companies invest the proceeds from the sale of fixed annuities in long-term investments to ensure this minimum return.

A variable annuity is one in which income may vary depending on the performance of the investments made by the insurance company. Insurance companies introduced the concept of variable annuities to broaden their market by attracting investors more concerned with inflation than with a fixed return. The insurance companies place a portion of the annuity funds into investments such as common stocks, which, it is hoped, will provide a higher return in the long run than a fixed annuity. Variable annuities have not done well in general because of the poor performance of common stocks the last few years. Therefore, more fixed income annuities have been sold recently than variable annuities.

Since the late 1970s, there have been efforts to combine money market funds with insurance annuities in the form of variable annuities. Some well-known investment firms are participating in the development and marketing of these annuities, and it is likely that this form of variable annuity will become popular.

GROWTH IN POPULARITY OF DEFERRED ANNUITIES

Deferred annuities have become much more popular since the mid-1970s for three basic reasons. First, yields on annuities are much higher than they were a few years ago. It is not unusual for yields to be guaranteed for the first year or two at 9%, and up to 8.25% for the next 5 years.

The second major reason is the tax factor. Income from an initial investment compounds tax-free. Accordingly, deferred annuities provide an excellent tax shelter, which becomes magnified with high yields. There is a possibility that the government will challenge the tax-free status of annuities.

The third major factor is sales commission. Historically, annuities were sold directly by life insurance agents who received a front end load, or sales commission. This situation has changed as insurance companies have developed selling arrangements with Wall Street brokers. Under these arrangements, the broker receives a commission directly from the issuing insurance company. The annuity buyer does not pay a front end load. Since the broker receives a higher percentage sales commission than he or she would for a stock transaction, there is an incentive to promote the sale of deferred annuities. Some of the brokerage firms now selling annuities are: Dean Witter Reynolds; Merrill Lynch, Pierce, Fenner & Smith; E.F. Hutton; Blythe Eastman; Paine Webber; Jackson & Curtis; Bache Halsey Stuart Shields; and Shearson Loeb Rhoades.

ADVANTAGES OF DEFERRED ANNUITIES

Tax Deferral of Income

The investment you make is with after-tax dollars. That principal is not taxed again. Any gains are taxed as ordinary income but not until you withdraw the funds. If your withdrawal takes place after retirement your tax bracket normally will be lower than it is during your working years. Accordingly, you will be paying less taxes. Moreover, your income and dividends will be reinvested tax-free until you start withdrawing funds.

Safety of Principal

If you invest in a fixed deferred annuity, you will always get your principal investment back if you leave your investment intact for a minimum number of years. Only if you cash in your annuity within the first several years after your initial investment would you not receive the full amount of your investment. In that case you would incur "surrender charges," discussed in more detail later in this chapter.

High Income

Yields can be high. The yields of a deferred annuity will fluctuate over the time you own it. Normally, the yield will be fixed for a limited time, and yields will vary depending on market conditions. When interest rates go up in general, yields on annuities will go up, and vice versa.

Sales Charges

If you purchase annuities from a stockbroker, normally you would not pay any sales commission. The insurance company pays the broker a sales commission. If you purchase an annuity directly from an insurance agent, you normally would pay a front end sales commission.

DISADVANTAGES OF DEFERRED ANNUITIES

Surrender Charges

In general you will be allowed to take out only a certain percentage of the value of your annuity each year for the first several years without penalty. For example, one plan allows you to take out 6% of the value of your annuity each year without charge. If you take out more than 6% you will be charged a 5% penalty for the amount you withdraw above the 6% allowable. Although the penalties vary between funds, there will generally be a penalty unless you have paid a sales commission initially.

State Tax

States can assess a state premium tax on any annuity sold. This tax is assessed against the gross value of the annuity purchased and can be as much as $25 per $1000.

Protection from Inflation

Deferred annuities may give you some protection against inflation when interest rates are high. When interest rates drop, however, it is not likely that the return on your investment will exceed the rate of inflation. The rate guaranteed on a lifetime basis generally has been much lower than inflation rates in the United States. The rates guaranteed for the first few years are higher than the rates of the lifetime guarantees, but you cannot count on getting that rate of return if interest rates fall.

Service

If you purchase an annuity from a stockbroker, you may find that you do not get the same personalized service you would get from an insurance agent. Brokers are used to dealing with clients on the phone in a relatively brisk manner since their normal stock and bond transactions are executed rapidly. If a broker specializes in annuities, that situation may not be the case. It is in your best interest to deal with a broker and brokerage firm that has made commitment to stay in the annuity business.

Inflexibility

You normally will not be able to switch your assets out of the annuity into another form of investment in the first several years without penalty. Therefore, you lose some flexibility. If interest rates fall, for example, you may feel that the rate of return you are receiving from the annuity is not adequate, but you cannot switch without being penalized with surrender charges.

Rate Changes

If interest rates go up higher rates are guaranteed for the new annuity purchases but not for previously bought annuities. Therefore, if interest rates increase substantially, the most recent annuity purchasers have the better contracts.

DIFFERENCES BETWEEN VARIABLE AND FIXED ANNUITIES

Form of Investment

Historically, insurance companies have invested a significant percent of their assets from variable annuities in common stocks. This is in contrast to the handling of assets from fixed annuities, which insurance companies usually invest in long-term bonds.

    This historical pattern is changing. Some of the newer variable annuities have their money invested in money market funds—that is, short-term, highly liquid, low-risk investments. If short-term yields remain attractive in comparison to long-term bond yields and returns on common stock investments, this type of annuity may prove even more attractive and popular.

Guaranteed Minimum Rate at which Funds Accumulate

Variable annuities generally offer no minimum rate at which funds accumulate. This is to be expected since common stock prices fluctuate. Fixed annuities do guarantee a minimum rate. Insurance companies can guarantee these minimum rates by purchasing bond portfolios with a mixture of maturities.

Sales Charges/Surrender Charges

In general, most insurance companies sell their variable annuities through their sales force. In that case, you can expect to pay a front end sales commission. If you pay a sales commission, you probably would not have to pay any surrender charges when you sell your annuity.

Some insurance companies have begun to sell variable annuities through other financial organizations in the same way that fixed annuities are offered for sale through stockbrokers. The insurance company pays the sales commission directly to the financial institution selling the fund. The annuity buyer would not pay a sales commission directly. In this situation, however, there would almost always be a surrender charge similar to that imposed on fixed annuity purchases. In other words,there is no free ride whether you purchase variable annuities or fixed annuities. Either you pay a front end sales commission or you incur a surrender charge if you withdraw funds within the first several years. You pay the equivalent of a sales charge in either situation.

Guaranteed Monthly Annuity

With fixed annuities the insurance company will always guarantee a minimum monthly annuity payment per $1000 of accumulated value. This minimum payment guaantee will vary between funds. It is important for you to select an insurance company that guarantees as high a rate as its competitiors.

With variable annuities you may have the option to select either a fixed payout with a monthly guarantee or a variable payout. If you select a variable payout, you will have a guaranteed rate for a minimum amount of time. After that your payments would depend on the performance of the portfolio your funds are invested in. Whether you decide to select a variable monthly payout should depend on the risks you can accept.

If you are concerned with protection from inflation, you can consider a variable payout, recognizing that your payout will fluctuate and may be less than the guaranteed monthly annuity. If you do select the variable payout option, you should certainly examine the track record of the insurance company in terms of its return on variable payouts. A.M. Best & Company, Inc. is an excellent source of information for comparing performances of life insurance companies for different types of policies.

Use of Mutual Funds

Some insurance companies use mutual funds for their variable annuities. These mutual funds can be common stock funds, bond funds, money market funds, and so forth. The insurance company allows the variable annuity buyer to switch from one fund to another with only a nominal charge. In this situation, you should be evaluating the historical performances of the mutual fund that the insurance company is utilizing. Chapter 12 discusses in detail investments in mutual funds and identifies reliable sources for reviewing past performance.

If the insurance company invests your money in a mutual fund you will not get the same rate of return you would get if you invested in the fund directly. The service charge you pay the insurance company would reduce the fee by approximately 1%. However, if you invested in the fund directly, you would not be receiving the tax deferral you obtain because of your investment in the annuity.

There is a tax disadvantage if the insurance company invests in a mutual fund that declares long-term capital gains. Although insurance companies can defer taxes on interest income, dividends, and short-term capital gains, it cannot defer taxes on long-term capital gains. This amounts to double taxation because the insurance company pays taxes at its capital gains tax rate, and you will pay taxes at ordinary income rates when you start receiving your monthly payments.

KEY QUESTIONS TO ASK REGARDING ANNUITIES

1   What Are the Guaranteed Monthly Annuity Payments per $1000 of Accumulated Value?

These guaranteed payments will vary with each issuer. You should compare the guarantees among the various issuers before you select an offering company.

2   What Is the Rate Currently Being Paid to Annuity Owners?

Although an insurance company is obligated to pay a specific minimum, the company can pay a higher rate. If two companies offer the same minimum guarantee but one company consistently pays a higher rate, you should select the company that has been paying the higher rate.

3   What Is the Guaranteed Minimum Rate at Which Funds Accumulate?

Some companies will guarantee one rate for the first year and another rate afterward. Other companies will guarantee an initial rate for 2 years or longer and guarantee another rate after that time period. The subsequent rate is generally lower.

4   What Is the Sales Commission as a Percent of the Initial Investment?

There may be no sales commission if your purchase the annuity through a stockbroker. If you purchase an annuity from a life insurance agent you will probably be paying a front end sales commission.

5   What Is the Surrender Cost of Redemption?

In the early years after you have purchased an annuity you generally cannot cash in your fixed annuity without paying a surrender charge. This charge is computed as a percent of the accumulated value of the annuity, will vary between issuers, and normally will not be charged after 6 or 7 years. During the first 6 or 7 years, however, the surrender cost can be as high as 10%. Accordingly, after you purchase an annuity it becomes rather expensive to sell it since you will be penalized heavily for at least a number of years.

6   Does Your State Tax Annuities?

State laws vary as far as taxing annuities. Before you purchase one, find out if your state has a premium tax. The tax can be as high as $25 per $1000.

7   Are There Any Other State Laws That Are Specifically Related to Annuities?

Yes. For example, some states allow a minimum guarantee of only 1 year for fixed annuities.

8   Which Securities Firms Sell Annuities?

Although this is not a complete list, the following firms have sales personnel who can sell annuities to you: Dean Witter Reynolds; Merrill Lynch, Pierce, Fenner & Smith; Shearson, Loab Rhoades; Bache Halsey Stuart Shields; Blyth Eastman Dillon; Paine Webber; and A.G. Edwards.

Your sales agent, whether an insurance agent or stockbroker, should be able to answer these questions for you.

IRAS AND KEOGH

If you are eligible to establish a Keogh or an IRA account (see Chapters 8 and 11), you can select many investment options, including annuity options. If you choose and IRA or Keogh option, the amount you contribute is tax deductible on your federal, state, and local tax returns. When you start receiving your annuity payments, all of the distribution becomes taxable at ordinary income rates. Under the existing federal laws on Keoghs and IRAs your payments are restricted to upper limits based on your income levels. For example, for defined contribution Keogh plans, the maximum contribution you can make each year is the lower of $15,000 per year or 15% of your earned income. For IRA plans the maximum is $2000 per year.

If you establish annuity plans independent of Keogh or IRA, you do not have any limitation in terms of maximum contributions permitted. The funds you put into the plan are after-tax dollars. You receive no tax advantage when you place funds in the annuity initially. When you start receiving annuity payments, however, you will not pay any income tax on the funds you established the annuity with. You will be taxed only on the income that was earned from your initial investments.

There may be advantages for you in using both IRA and Keogh plans independent of annuity plans. As pointed out in Chapter 9, there are many investments that you can make within the IRA/Keogh structure that have more advantages than annuities. However, since there are limitations to how much money you can contribute to IRA and Keogh plans, you may wish to contribute the maximum amount you can to a IRA/Keogh and establish independent annuity plans for any other funds you have available to obtain tax-free accumulations.

ANNUITY PAYMENT OPTIONS

There are numbers of options available to you when you are ready to receive annuity payments. The major options and their advantages and disadvantages follow.

Lifetime Annuity, One Annuitant

With this option you receive payments for the rest of your life. This option would be desirable if you do not have a surviving spouse or if your surviving spouse would have sufficient assets after your death and would not require this annuity income. For example, if a man had a great deal of life insurance of which his wife was the beneficiary, he could select this option knowing that the life insurance proceeds would provide his spouse with an adequate income after his death.

Uniform Joint and Survivor Annuities

You receive payments for the rest of your life, and the same payment is received by the other annuitant if he or she survives you. This type of annuity is useful if you are concerned with providing income to another party such as your spouse. The annuity paid is based on the combined life expectancies of both parties. For example, if your wife is much younger than you, the annuity would be less than it would be if she were older than you. Before you select this type of option consider whether the annuitant will need the annuity after you die. If your life insurance and other assets are sufficient, you may not need this type of annuity.

Limited Time Period

You receive payment until your death or until the end of a specified time period, whichever comes first. You would consider this type of annuity if you were less concerned with income after a certain period. For example, if you knew that in 10 years you would be receiving a certain sum of money, you could establish an annuity ending in 10 years to maximize your income during the period in which you require the most income.

Annuity with Stepped-up Payments

You receive a small payment for a specified number of years, after which you receive larger payments. You would use this type of annuity when you expect a reduction in other income at a certain time or if you want some protection from anticipated inflation.

Annuity with Stepped-Down Payments

You receive larger payments for a specified number of years, after which you receive smaller payments. You would use this type of annuity when you anticipate other income or a lump sum distribution at a certain time in the future. Normally, this type of plan would be used if an individual retired early and expected pension payments at a future date.

Joint Annuity with Lower Survivor Payment

Payment is at one level while both annuitants are alive. When one of the annuitants dies, the survivor receives a smaller payment for the rest of his or her life. This type of annuity should be considered in association with an insurance program if the survivor otherwise would not have sufficient income. A major question is whether the reduction in pension would be greater than the anticipated reduction in living expenses.

TAXABLE STATUS OF ANNUITIES

Tax Status When You Did Not Contribute (Method 1)

The tax status of your annuity is based on your contribution. If your employer made all of the contributions and you did not report them, you must report all your payments as ordinary income.

Tax Status When You Have Investment—3-Year Rule (Method 2)

You have an investment in the annuity if you have made a contribution to the annuity or if your employer made the contribution for you, which you reported as taxable income.

If within 3 years of the first payment to you, the total payments will be equal to or greater than your investment, you do not have to report the payments as taxable ordinary income until the payments exceed your contributions.

Tax Status—General Rule (Method 3)

The following rules apply for annuities that are not variable, do not have guaranteed payments, and are not subject to the 3-year rule just discussed.

Compute Your Investment in the Annuity Contract

First you must determine your total investment. This includes your contributions and employer contributions that you reported as income on your tax returns. From this total cost subtract the following:

Any premiums refunded, rebates, or dividends you received before the annuity starting date.

Any additional premium paid for double indemnity or disability.

Amounts you received under the contract before the annuity starting date that are not taxable.

The value of a refund feature.

Expected Return

The expected return is the total amount you will receive or expect to receive under the contract. If the payments are to be made to you for life, your expected return is computed by multiplying the amount of the annual payment by a factor based on your life expectancy as of the annuity starting date. These factors are listed in the actuarial tables (Exhibits 6-1, 6-2, 6-3 and 6-4) that follow. (Actuarial tables are prepared by the Internal Revenue Service and are updated as required. These are from the November 1980 publication, number 575, *Pension and Annuity Income,* which is available free from the Internal Revenue Service.)

If your annuity payments were for the rest of your life or until the expiration of a specified period, you would compute expected return utilizing Exhibit 6-4.

Example

Harry Smith, aged 60, will receive $3000/year for 10 years, or until he dies. The multiple indicated in the exhibit for male, 60, 10-year term is 8.9. The expected return is $26,700 ($3000 × 8.9).

If your annuity payments were for a single life annuity, you would utilize Exhibit 6-1 to compute expected return. If the annuity covered two parties in a joint and survivor annuity, you would utilize Exhibit 6-2.

If you are to receive payments for a fixed number of years, compute your expected return by multiplying your annual payments by the number of years you are entitled to receive them.

Exhibit 6-1 Ordinary Life Annuities—One Life—Expected Return Multiples

Ages		Multiples	Ages		Multiples	Ages		Multiples
Male	Female		Male	Female		Male	Female	
6	11	65.0	41	46	33.0	76	81	9.1
7	12	64.1	42	47	32.1	77	82	8.7
8	13	63.2	43	48	31.2	78	83	8.3
9	14	62.3	44	49	30.4	79	84	7.8
10	15	61.4	45	50	29.6	80	85	7.5
11	16	60.4	46	51	28.7	81	86	7.1
12	17	59.5	47	52	27.9	82	87	6.7
13	18	58.6	48	53	27.1	83	88	6.3
14	19	57.7	49	54	26.3	84	89	6.0
15	20	56.7	50	55	25.5	85	90	5.7
16	21	55.8	51	56	24.7	86	91	5.4
17	22	54.9	52	57	24.0	87	92	5.1
18	23	53.9	53	58	23.2	88	93	4.8
19	24	53.0	54	59	22.4	89	94	4.5
20	25	52.1	55	60	21.7	90	95	4.2
21	26	51.1	56	61	21.0	91	96	4.0
22	27	50.2	57	62	20.3	92	97	3.7
23	28	49.3	58	63	19.6	93	98	3.5
24	29	48.3	59	64	18.9	94	99	3.3
25	30	47.4	60	65	18.2	95	100	3.1
26	31	46.5	61	66	17.5	96	101	2.9
27	32	45.6	62	67	16.9	97	102	2.7
28	33	44.6	63	68	16.2	98	103	2.5
29	34	43.7	64	69	15.6	99	104	2.3
30	35	42.8	65	70	15.0	100	105	2.1
31	36	41.9	66	71	14.4	101	106	1.9
32	37	41.0	67	72	13.8	102	107	1.7
33	38	40.0	68	73	13.2	103	108	1.5
34	39	39.1	69	74	12.6	104	109	1.3
35	40	38.2	70	75	12.1	105	110	1.2
						106	111	1.0
36	41	37.3	71	76	11.6	107	112	.8
37	42	36.5	72	77	11.0	108	113	.7
38	43	35.6	73	78	10.5	109	114	.6
39	44	34.7	74	79	10.1	110	115	.5
40	45	33.8	75	80	9.6	111	116	0

Exhibit 6-2 Ordinary Joint Life and Last Survival Annuities—Two Lives—Expected Return Multiples

Ages	Male	35	36	37	38	39	40	41	42	43	44	45	46	47
Male	Female	40	41	42	43	44	45	46	47	48	49	50	51	52
35	40	46.2	45.7	45.3	44.8	44.4	44.0	43.6	43.3	43.0	42.6	42.3	42.0	41.8
36	41	45.7	45.2	44.8	44.3	43.9	43.5	43.1	42.7	42.3	42.0	41.7	41.4	41.1
37	42	45.3	44.8	44.3	43.8	43.4	42.9	42.5	42.1	41.8	41.4	41.1	40.7	40.4
38	43	44.8	44.3	43.8	43.3	42.9	42.4	42.0	41.6	41.2	40.8	40.5	40.1	39.8
39	44	44.4	43.9	43.4	42.9	42.4	41.9	41.5	41.0	40.6	40.2	39.9	39.5	39.2
40	45	44.0	43.5	42.9	42.4	41.9	41.4	41.0	40.5	40.1	39.7	39.3	38.9	38.6
41	46	43.6	43.1	42.5	42.0	41.5	41.0	40.5	40.0	39.6	39.2	38.8	38.4	38.0
42	47	43.3	42.7	42.1	41.6	41.0	40.5	40.0	39.6	39.1	38.7	38.2	37.8	37.5
43	48	43.0	42.3	41.8	41.2	40.6	40.1	39.6	39.1	38.6	38.2	37.7	37.3	36.9
44	49	42.6	42.0	41.4	40.8	40.2	39.7	39.2	38.7	38.2	37.7	37.2	36.8	36.4
45	50	42.3	41.7	41.1	40.5	39.9	39.3	38.8	38.2	37.7	37.2	36.8	36.3	35.9
46	51	42.0	41.4	40.7	40.1	39.5	38.9	38.4	37.8	37.3	36.8	36.3	35.9	35.4
47	52	41.8	41.1	40.4	39.8	39.2	38.6	38.0	37.5	36.9	36.4	35.9	35.4	35.0

Ages	Male	48	49	50	51	52	53	54	55	56	57	58	59	60
Male	Female	53	54	55	56	57	58	59	60	61	62	63	64	65
35	40	41.5	41.3	41.0	40.8	40.6	40.4	40.3	40.1	40.0	39.8	39.7	39.6	39.5
36	41	40.8	40.6	40.3	40.1	39.9	39.7	39.5	39.3	39.2	39.0	38.9	38.8	38.6
37	42	40.2	39.9	39.6	39.4	39.2	39.0	38.8	38.6	38.4	38.3	38.1	38.0	37.9
38	43	39.5	39.2	39.0	38.7	38.5	38.3	38.1	37.9	37.7	37.5	37.3	37.2	37.1
39	44	38.9	38.6	38.3	38.0	37.8	37.6	37.3	37.1	36.9	36.8	36.6	36.4	36.3
40	45	38.3	38.0	37.7	37.4	37.1	36.9	36.6	36.4	36.2	36.0	35.9	35.7	35.5
41	46	37.7	37.3	37.0	36.7	36.5	36.2	36.0	35.7	35.5	35.3	35.1	35.0	34.8
42	47	37.1	36.8	36.4	36.1	35.8	35.6	35.3	35.1	34.8	34.6	34.4	34.2	34.1
43	48	36.5	36.2	35.8	35.5	35.2	34.9	34.7	34.4	34.2	33.9	33.7	33.5	33.3
44	49	36.0	35.6	35.3	34.9	34.6	34.3	34.0	33.8	33.5	33.3	33.0	32.8	32.6
45	50	35.5	35.1	34.7	34.4	34.0	33.7	33.4	33.1	32.9	32.6	32.4	32.2	31.9
46	51	35.0	34.6	34.2	33.8	33.5	33.1	32.8	32.5	32.2	32.0	31.7	31.5	31.3
47	52	34.5	34.1	33.7	33.3	32.9	32.6	32.2	31.9	31.6	31.4	31.1	30.9	30.6
48	53	34.0	33.6	33.2	32.8	32.4	32.0	31.7	31.4	31.1	30.8	30.5	30.2	30.0
49	54	33.6	33.1	32.7	32.3	31.9	31.5	31.2	30.8	30.5	30.2	29.9	29.6	29.4
50	55	33.2	32.7	32.3	31.8	31.4	31.0	30.6	30.3	29.9	29.6	29.3	29.0	28.8
51	56	32.8	32.3	31.8	31.4	30.9	30.5	30.1	29.8	29.4	29.1	28.8	28.5	28.2
52	57	32.4	31.9	31.4	30.9	30.5	30.1	29.7	29.3	28.9	28.6	28.2	27.9	27.6
53	58	32.0	31.5	31.0	30.5	30.1	29.6	29.2	28.8	28.4	28.1	27.7	27.4	27.1
54	59	31.7	31.2	30.6	30.1	29.7	29.2	28.8	28.3	27.9	27.6	27.2	26.9	26.5
55	60	31.4	30.8	30.3	29.8	29.3	28.8	28.3	27.9	27.5	27.1	26.7	26.4	26.0
56	61	31.1	30.5	29.9	29.4	28.9	28.4	27.9	27.5	27.1	26.7	26.3	25.9	25.5
57	62	30.8	30.2	29.6	29.1	28.6	28.1	27.6	27.1	26.7	26.2	25.8	25.4	25.1
58	63	30.5	29.9	29.3	28.8	28.2	27.7	27.2	26.7	26.3	25.8	25.4	25.0	24.6
59	64	30.2	29.6	29.0	28.5	27.9	27.4	26.9	26.4	25.9	25.4	25.0	24.6	24.2
60	65	30.0	29.4	28.8	28.2	27.6	27.1	26.5	26.0	25.5	25.1	24.6	24.2	23.8

Exhibit 6-2 *(Continued)*

Ages														
	Male	61	62	63	64	65	66	67	68	69	70	71	72	73
Male	Female	66	67	68	69	70	71	72	73	74	75	76	77	78
35	40	39.4	39.3	39.2	39.1	39.0	38.9	38.9	38.8	38.8	38.7	38.7	38.6	38.6
36	41	38.5	38.4	38.3	38.2	38.2	38.1	38.0	38.0	37.9	37.9	37.8	37.8	37.7
37	42	37.7	37.6	37.5	37.4	37.3	37.3	37.2	37.1	37.1	37.0	36.9	36.9	36.9
38	43	36.9	36.8	36.7	36.6	36.5	36.4	36.4	36.3	36.2	36.2	36.1	36.0	36.0
39	44	36.2	36.0	35.9	35.8	35.7	35.6	35.5	35.5	35.4	35.3	35.3	35.2	35.2
40	45	35.4	35.3	35.1	35.0	34.9	34.8	34.7	34.6	34.6	34.5	34.4	34.4	34.3
41	46	34.6	34.5	34.4	34.2	34.1	34.0	33.9	33.8	33.8	33.7	33.6	33.5	33.5
42	47	33.9	33.7	33.6	33.5	33.4	33.2	33.1	33.0	33.0	32.9	32.8	32.7	32.7
43	48	33.2	33.0	32.9	32.7	32.6	32.5	32.4	32.3	32.2	32.1	32.0	31.9	31.9
44	49	32.5	32.3	32.1	32.0	31.8	31.7	31.6	31.5	31.4	31.3	31.2	31.1	31.1
45	50	31.8	31.6	31.4	31.3	31.1	31.0	30.8	30.7	30.6	30.5	30.4	30.4	30.3
46	51	31.1	30.9	30.7	30.5	30.4	30.2	30.1	30.0	29.9	29.8	29.7	29.6	29.5
47	52	30.4	30.2	30.0	29.8	29.7	29.5	29.4	29.3	29.1	29.0	28.9	28.8	28.7
48	53	29.8	29.5	29.3	29.2	29.0	28.8	28.7	28.5	28.4	28.3	28.2	28.1	28.0
49	54	29.1	28.9	28.7	28.5	28.3	28.1	28.0	27.8	27.7	27.6	27.5	27.4	27.3
50	55	28.5	28.3	28.1	27.8	27.6	27.5	27.3	27.1	27.0	26.9	26.7	26.6	26.5
51	56	27.9	27.7	27.4	27.2	27.0	26.8	26.6	26.5	26.3	26.2	26.0	25.9	25.8
52	57	27.3	27.1	26.8	26.6	26.4	26.2	26.0	25.8	25.7	25.5	25.4	25.2	25.1
53	58	26.8	26.5	26.2	26.0	25.8	25.6	25.4	25.2	25.0	24.8	24.7	24.6	24.4
54	59	26.2	25.9	25.7	25.4	25.2	25.0	24.7	24.6	24.4	24.2	24.0	23.9	23.8
55	60	25.7	25.4	25.1	24.9	24.6	24.4	24.1	23.9	23.8	23.6	23.4	23.3	23.1
56	61	25.2	24.9	24.6	24.3	24.1	23.8	23.6	23.4	23.2	23.0	22.8	22.6	22.5
57	62	24.7	24.4	24.1	23.8	23.5	23.3	23.0	22.8	22.6	22.4	22.2	22.0	21.9
58	63	24.3	23.9	23.6	23.3	23.0	22.7	22.5	22.2	22.0	21.8	21.6	21.4	21.3
59	64	23.8	23.5	23.1	22.8	22.5	22.2	21.9	21.7	21.5	21.2	21.0	20.9	20.7
60	65	23.4	23.0	22.7	22.3	22.0	21.7	21.4	21.2	20.9	20.7	20.5	20.3	20.1
61	66	23.0	22.6	22.2	21.9	21.6	21.3	21.0	20.7	20.4	20.2	20.0	19.8	19.6
62	67	22.6	22.2	21.8	21.5	21.1	20.8	20.5	20.2	19.9	19.7	19.5	19.2	19.0
63	68	22.2	21.8	21.4	21.1	20.7	20.4	20.1	19.8	19.5	19.2	19.0	18.7	18.5
64	69	21.9	21.5	21.1	20.7	20.3	20.0	19.6	19.3	19.0	18.7	18.5	18.2	18.0
65	70	21.6	21.1	20.7	20.3	19.9	19.6	19.2	18.9	18.6	18.3	18.0	17.8	17.5
66	71	21.3	20.8	20.4	20.0	19.6	19.2	18.8	18.5	18.2	17.9	17.6	17.3	17.1
67	72	21.0	20.5	20.1	19.6	19.2	18.8	18.5	18.1	17.8	17.5	17.2	16.9	16.7
68	73	20.7	20.2	19.8	19.3	18.9	18.5	18.1	17.8	17.4	17.1	16.8	16.5	16.2
69	74	20.4	19.9	19.5	19.0	18.6	18.2	17.8	17.4	17.1	16.7	16.4	16.1	15.8
70	75	20.2	19.7	19.2	18.7	18.3	17.9	17.5	17.1	16.7	16.4	16.1	15.8	15.5
71	76	20.0	19.5	19.0	18.5	18.0	17.6	17.2	16.8	16.4	16.1	15.7	15.4	15.1
72	77	19.8	19.2	18.7	18.2	17.8	17.3	16.9	16.5	16.1	15.8	15.4	15.1	14.8
73	78	19.6	19.0	18.5	18.0	17.5	17.1	16.7	16.2	15.8	15.5	15.1	14.8	14.4

Exhibit 6-2 (Continued)

Ages													
Male	Male	74	75	76	77	78	79	80	81	82	83	84	85
Male	Female	79	80	81	82	83	84	85	86	87	88	89	90
35	40	38.6	38.5	38.5	38.5	38.4	38.4	38.4	38.4	38.4	38.4	38.3	38.3
36	41	37.7	37.6	37.6	37.6	37.6	37.5	37.5	37.5	37.5	37.5	37.5	37.4
37	42	36.8	36.8	36.7	36.7	36.7	36.7	36.6	36.6	36.6	36.6	36.6	36.6
38	43	36.0	35.9	35.9	35.9	35.8	35.8	35.8	35.8	35.7	35.7	35.7	35.7
39	44	35.1	35.1	35.0	35.0	35.0	34.9	34.9	34.9	34.9	34.8	34.8	34.8
40	45	34.3	34.2	34.2	34.1	34.1	34.1	34.1	34.0	34.0	34.0	34.0	34.0
41	46	33.4	33.4	33.3	33.3	33.3	33.2	33.2	33.2	33.2	33.1	33.1	33.1
42	47	32.6	32.6	32.5	32.5	32.4	32.4	32.4	32.3	32.3	32.3	32.3	32.3
43	48	31.8	31.8	31.7	31.7	31.6	31.6	31.5	31.5	31.5	31.5	31.4	31.4
44	49	31.0	30.9	30.9	30.8	30.8	30.8	30.7	30.7	30.7	30.6	30.6	30.6
45	50	30.2	30.1	30.1	30.0	30.0	29.9	29.9	29.9	29.8	29.8	29.8	29.8
46	51	29.4	29.4	29.3	29.2	29.2	29.2	29.1	29.1	29.0	29.0	29.0	28.9
47	52	28.7	28.6	28.5	28.5	28.4	28.4	28.3	28.3	28.2	28.2	28.2	28.1
48	53	27.9	27.8	27:8	27.7	27.6	27.6	27.5	27.5	27.5	27.4	27.4	27.4
49	54	27.2	27.1	27.0	26.9	26.9	26.8	26.8	26.7	26.7	26.6	26.6	26.6
50	55	26.4	26.3	26.3	26.2	26.1	26.1	26.0	26.0	25.9	25.9	25.8	25.8
51	56	25.7	25.6	25.5	25.5	25.4	25.3	25.3	25.2	25.2	25.1	25.1	25.0
52	57	25.0	24.9	24.8	24.7	24.7	24.6	24.5	24.5	24.4	24.4	24.3	24.3
53	58	24.3	24.2	24.1	24.0	23.9	23.9	23.8	23.7	23.7	23.6	23.6	23.5
54	59	23.6	23.5	23.4	23.3	23.2	23.2	23.1	23.0	23.0	22.9	22.9	22.8
55	60	23.0	22.9	22.8	22.7	22.6	22.5	22.4	22.3	22.3	22.2	22.2	22.1
56	61	22.3	22.2	22.1	22.0	21.9	21.8	21.7	21.6	21.6	21.5	21.5	21.4
57	62	21.7	21.6	21.5	21.3	21.2	21.1	21.1	21.0	20.9	20.8	20.8	20.7
58	63	21.1	21.0	20.8	20.7	20.6	20.5	20.4	20.3	20.2	20.2	20.1	20.0
59	64	20.5	20.4	20.2	20.1	20.0	19.9	19.8	19.7	19.6	19.5	19.4	19.4
60	65	19.9	19.8	19.6	19.5	19.4	19.3	19.1	19.0	19.0	18.9	18.8	18.7
61	66	19.4	19.2	19.1	18.9	18.8	18.7	18.5	18.4	18.3	18.3	18.2	18.1
62	67	18.8	18.7	18.5	18.3	18.2	18.1	18.0	17.8	17.7	17.7	17.6	17.5
63	68	18.3	18.1	18.0	17.8	17.6	17.5	17.4	17.3	17.2	17.1	17.0	16.9
64	69	17.8	17.6	17.4	17.3	17.1	17.0	16.8	16.7	16.6	16.5	16.4	16.3
65	70	17.3	17.1	16.9	16.7	16.6	16.4	16.3	16.2	16.0	15.9	15.8	15.8
66	71	16.9	16.6	16.4	16.3	16.1	15.9	15.8	15.6	15.5	15.4	15.3	15.2
67	72	16.4	16.2	16.0	15.8	15.6	15.4	15.3	15.1	15.0	14.9	14.8	14.7
68	73	16.0	15.7	15.5	15.3	15.1	15.0	14.8	14.6	14.5	14.4	14.3	14.2
69	74	15.6	15.3	15.1	14.9	14.7	14.5	14.3	14.2	14.0	13.9	13.8	13.7
70	75	15.2	14.9	14.7	14.5	14.3	14.1	13.9	13.7	13.6	13.4	13.3	13.2
71	76	14.8	14.5	14.3	14.1	13.8	13.6	13.5	13.3	13.1	13.0	12.8	12.7
72	77	14.5	14.2	13.9	13.7	13.5	13.2	13.0	12.9	12.7	12.5	12.4	12.3
73	78	14.1	13.8	13.6	13.3	13.1	12.9	12.7	12.5	12.3	12.1	12.0	11.8
74	79	13.8	13.5	13.2	13.0	12.7	12.5	12.3	12.1	11.9	11.7	11.6	11.4
75	80	13.5	13.2	12.9	12.6	12.4	12.2	11.9	11.7	11.5	11.4	11.2	11.0
76	81	13.2	12.9	12.6	12.3	12.1	11.8	11.6	11.4	11.2	11.0	10.8	10.7
77	82	13.0	12.6	12.3	12.1	11.8	11.5	11.3	11.1	10.8	10.7	10.5	10.3
78	83	12.7	12.4	12.1	11.8	11.5	11.2	11.0	10.7	10.5	10.3	10.1	10.0
79	84	12.5	12.2	11.8	11.5	11.2	11.0	10.7	10.5	10.2	10.0	9.8	9.6
80	85	12.3	11.9	11.6	11.3	11.0	10.7	10.4	10.2	10.0	9.7	9.5	9.3
81	86	12.1	11.7	11.4	11.1	10.7	10.5	10.2	9.9	9.7	9.5	9.3	9.1
82	87	11.9	11.5	11.2	10.8	10.5	10.2	10.0	9.7	9.4	9.2	9.0	8.8
83	88	11.7	11.4	11.0	10.7	10.3	10.0	9.7	9.5	9.2	9.0	8.7	8.5
84	89	11.6	11.2	10.8	10.5	10.0	9.8	9.5	9.3	9.0	8.7	8.5	8.3
85	90	11.4	11.0	10.7	10.3	10.0	9.6	9.3	9.1	8.8	8.5	8.3	8.1

Exhibit 6-2 *(Continued)*

Ages						
	Male	86	87	88	89	90
Male	Female	91	92	93	94	95
35	40	38.3	38.3	38.3	38.3	38.3
36	41	37.4	37.4	37.4	37.4	37.4
37	42	36.5	36.5	36.5	36.5	36.5
38	43	35.7	35.7	35.6	35.6	35.6
39	44	34.8	34.8	34.8	34.8	34.8
40	45	33.9	33.9	33.9	33.9	33.9
41	46	33.1	33.1	33.1	33.0	33.0
42	47	32.2	32.2	32.2	32.2	32.2
43	48	31.4	31.4	31.4	31.3	31.3
44	49	30.6	30.5	30.5	30.5	30.5
45	50	29.7	29.7	29.7	29.7	29.7
46	51	28.9	28.9	28.9	28.9	28.9
47	52	28.1	28.1	28.1	28.1	28.0
48	53	27.3	27.3	27.3	27.3	27.2
49	54	26.5	26.5	26.5	26.5	26.5
50	55	25.8	25.7	25.7	25.7	25.7
51	56	25.0	25.0	24.9	24.9	24.9
52	57	24.3	24.2	24.2	24.2	24.1
53	58	23.5	23.5	23.4	23.4	23.4
54	59	22.8	22.7	22.7	22.7	22.7
55	60	22.1	22.0	22.0	22.0	21.9
56	61	21.4	21.3	21.3	21.3	21.2
57	62	20.7	20.6	20.6	20.6	20.5
58	63	20.0	19.9	19.9	19.9	19.8
59	64	19.3	19.3	19.2	19.2	19.2
60	65	18.7	18.6	18.6	18.5	18.5
61	66	18.1	18.0	17.9	17.9	17.9
62	67	17.4	17.4	17.3	17.3	17.2
63	68	16.8	16.8	16.7	16.7	16.6
64	69	16.2	16.2	16.1	16.1	16.0
65	70	15.7	15.6	15 5	15.5	15.4
66	71	15.1	15.0	15.0	14.9	14.8
67	72	14.6	14.5	14.4	14.4	14.3
68	73	14.1	14.0	13.9	13.8	13.8
69	74	13.6	13.5	13.4	13.3	13.2
70	75	13.1	13.0	12.9	12.8	12.7
71	76	12.6	12.5	12.4	12.3	12.2
72	77	12.1	12.0	11.9	11.8	11.8
73	78	11.7	11.6	11.5	11.4	11.3
74	79	11.3	11.2	11.1	11.0	10.9
75	80	10.9	10.8	10.7	10.5	10.5
76	81	10.5	10.4	10.3	10.2	10.1
77	82	10.2	10.0	9.9	9.8	9.7
78	83	9.8	9.7	9.5	9.4	9.3
79	84	9.5	9.3	9.2	9.1	8.9
80	85	9.2	9.0	8.9	8.7	8.6
81	86	8.9	8.7	8.6	8.4	8.3.
82	87	8.6	8.4	8.3	8.1	8.0
83	88	8.3	8.2	8.0	7.9	7.7
84	89	8.1	7.9	7.8	7.6	7.5
85	90	7.9	7.7	7.5	7.4	7.2
86	91	7.7	7.5	7.3	7.1	7.0
87	92	7.5	7.3	7.1	6.9	6.8
88	93	7.3	7.1	6.9	6.7	6.6
89	94	7.1	6.9	6.7	6.5	6.4
90	95	7.0	6.8	6.6	6.4	6.2

Exhibit 6-3 Percent Value of Refund Feature

Ages   Duration of guaranteed amount

Male	Fe-male	1 year	2 years	3 years	4 years	5 years	6 years	7 years	8 years	9 years	10 years	11 years	12 years	13 years
		Percent	*Percent*	*Percent*	*Percent*	*Percent*	*Percent*	*Percent*	*Percent*	*Percent*	*Percent*	*Percent*	*Percent*	*Percent*
35	40	----	----	----	1	1	1	1	1	2	2	2	2	2
36	41	----	----	----	1	1	1	1	1	2	2	2	2	3
37	42	----	----	1	1	1	1	1	2	2	2	2	3	3
38	43	----	----	1	1	1	1	1	2	2	2	2	3	3
39	44	----	----	1	1	1	1	2	2	2	2	3	3	3
40	45	----	----	1	1	1	1	2	2	2	3	3	3	4
41	46	----	----	1	1	1	1	2	2	2	3	3	3	4
42	47	----	----	1	1	1	2	2	2	3	3	3	4	4
43	48	----	1	1	1	1	2	2	2	3	3	4	4	4
44	49	----	1	1	1	1	2	2	3	3	3	4	4	5
45	50	----	1	1	1	2	2	2	3	3	4	4	5	5
46	51	----	1	1	1	2	2	3	3	3	4	4	5	5
47	52	----	1	1	1	2	2	3	3	4	4	5	5	6
48	53	----	1	1	2	2	2	3	3	4	5	5	6	6
49	54	----	1	1	2	2	3	3	4	4	5	5	6	7
50	55	----	1	1	2	2	3	3	4	5	5	6	7	7
51	56	----	1	1	2	3	3	4	4	5	6	6	7	8
52	57	1	1	2	2	3	3	4	5	5	6	7	8	8
53	58	1	1	2	2	3	4	4	5	6	7	7	8	9
54	59	1	1	2	2	3	4	5	5	6	7	8	9	10
55	60	1	1	2	3	3	4	5	6	7	8	8	9	10
56	61	1	1	2	3	4	4	5	6	7	8	9	10	11
57	62	1	1	2	3	4	5	6	7	8	9	10	11	12
58	63	1	2	2	3	4	5	6	7	8	9	10	12	13
59	64	1	2	3	4	5	6	7	8	9	10	11	12	14
60	65	1	2	3	4	5	6	7	8	10	11	12	13	15
6'	66	1	2	3	4	5	6	8	9	10	12	13	14	16
62	67	1	2	3	4	6	7	8	10	11	12	14	15	17
63	68	1	2	4	5	6	7	9	10	12	13	15	16	18
64	69	1	3	4	5	7	8	9	11	13	14	16	17	19
65	70	1	3	4	6	7	9	10	12	13	15	17	19	20
66	71	1	3	4	6	8	9	11	13	14	16	18	20	22
67	72	2	3	5	6	8	10	12	14	15	17	19	21	23
68	73	2	3	5	7	9	11	13	14	16	18	21	23	25
69	74	2	4	6	7	9	11	13	16	18	20	22	24	26
70	75	2	4	6	8	10	12	14	17	19	21	23	26	28
71	76	2	4	6	9	11	13	15	18	20	22	25	27	29
72	77	2	5	7	9	12	14	16	19	21	24	26	29	31
73	78	2	5	7	10	12	15	18	20	23	25	28	30	33
74	79	3	5	8	11	13	16	19	22	24	27	30	32	35
75	80	3	6	8	11	14	17	20	23	26	29	31	34	37
76	81	3	6	9	12	15	18	21	24	27	30	33	36	39
77	82	3	7	10	13	16	20	23	26	29	32	35	38	41
78	83	4	7	11	14	17	21	24	28	31	34	37	40	43
79	84	4	8	11	15	19	22	26	29	33	36	39	42	45
80	85	4	8	12	16	20	24	27	31	34	38	41	44	47
81	86	4	9	13	17	21	25	29	33	36	40	43	46	49
82	87	5	9	14	18	23	27	31	35	38	42	45	48	51
83	88	5	10	15	19	24	28	33	37	40	44	47	50	53
84	89	5	11	16	21	26	30	34	38	42	46	49	52	55
85	90	6	11	17	22	27	32	36	41	44	48	51	55	57
86	91	6	12	18	24	29	34	38	43	47	50	54	57	59
87	92	7	13	19	25	31	36	40	45	49	52	56	59	61
88	93	7	14	21	27	32	38	42	47	51	55	58	61	63
89	94	8	15	22	28	34	40	45	49	53	57	60	63	65
90	95	8	16	23	30	36	42	47	51	55	59	62	65	67

Exhibit 6-3 *(Continued)*

Ages		Duration of guaranteed amount											
Male	Female	14 years	15 years	16 years	17 years	18 years	19 years	20 years	21 years	22 years	23 years	24 years	25 years
		Percent	*Percent*	*Percent*	*Percent*	*Percent*	*Percent*	*Percent*	*Percent*	*Percent*	*Percent*	*Percent*	*Percent*
35	40	3	3	3	4	4	4	5	5	5	6	6	7
36	41	3	3	4	4	4	5	5	5	6	6	7	7
37	42	3	3	4	4	4	5	5	6	6	7	7	8
38	43	3	4	4	4	5	5	6	6	7	7	8	8
39	44	4	4	4	5	5	6	6	7	7	8	8	9
40	45	4	4	5	5	6	6	7	7	8	8	9	9
41	46	4	5	5	6	6	7	7	8	8	9	9	10
42	47	5	5	5	6	6	7	8	8	9	9	10	11
43	48	5	5	6	6	7	8	8	9	9	10	11	12
44	49	5	6	6	7	7	8	9	9	10	11	12	12
45	50	6	6	7	7	8	9	9	10	11	12	12	13
46	51	6	7	7	8	9	9	10	11	12	12	13	14
47	52	7	7	8	9	9	10	11	12	12	13	14	15
48	53	7	8	8	9	10	11	12	12	13	14	15	16
49	54	8	8	9	10	11	11	12	13	14	15	16	17
50	55	8	9	10	11	11	12	13	14	15	16	17	18
51	56	9	10	10	11	12	13	14	15	16	17	18	20
52	57	9	10	11	12	13	14	15	16	17	18	20	21
53	58	10	11	12	13	14	15	16	17	19	20	21	22
54	59	11	12	13	14	15	16	17	18	20	21	22	24
55	60	11	13	14	15	16	17	18	20	21	22	24	25
56	61	12	13	15	16	17	18	20	21	22	24	25	27
57	62	13	14	16	17	18	20	21	22	24	25	27	28
58	63	14	15	17	18	19	21	22	24	25	27	28	30
59	64	15	16	18	19	21	22	24	25	27	28	30	31
60	65	16	18	19	20	22	24	25	27	28	30	32	33
61	66	17	19	20	22	23	25	27	28	30	32	33	35
62	67	18	20	22	23	25	27	28	30	32	33	35	37
63	68	20	21	23	25	26	28	30	32	33	35	37	39
64	69	21	23	24	26	28	30	32	33	35	37	39	41
65	70	22	24	26	28	30	32	33	35	37	39	41	42
66	71	24	26	28	29	31	33	35	37	39	41	43	44
67	72	25	27	29	31	33	35	37	39	41	43	45	46
68	73	27	29	31	33	35	37	39	41	43	45	47	48
69	74	28	30	33	35	37	39	41	43	45	47	48	50
70	75	30	32	34	37	39	41	43	45	47	49	50	52
71	76	32	34	36	39	41	43	45	47	49	51	52	54
72	77	34	36	38	41	43	45	47	49	51	53	54	56
73	78	35	38	40	43	45	47	49	51	53	55	56	58
74	79	37	40	42	45	47	49	51	53	55	57	58	60
75	80	39	42	44	47	49	51	53	55	57	58	60	62
76	81	41	44	46	49	51	53	55	57	59	60	62	63
77	82	43	46	48	51	53	55	57	59	61	62	64	65
78	83	45	48	50	53	55	57	59	61	62	64	65	67
79	84	48	50	53	55	57	59	61	63	64	66	67	68
80	85	50	52	55	57	59	61	63	64	66	67	69	70
81	86	52	54	57	59	61	63	65	66	68	69	70	72
82	87	54	56	59	61	63	65	66	68	69	71	72	73
83	88	56	58	61	63	65	66	68	70	71	72	73	74
84	89	58	60	63	65	67	68	70	71	73	74	75	76
85	90	60	62	65	67	68	70	71	73	74	75	76	77
86	91	62	64	66	68	70	72	73	74	75	76	77	--------
87	92	64	66	68	70	72	73	74	76	77	78	--------	--------
88	93	66	68	70	72	73	75	76	77	78	--------	--------	--------
89	94	68	70	72	73	75	76	77	78	--------	--------	--------	--------
90	95	70	72	73	75	76	77	79	--------	--------	--------	--------	--------

Exhibit 6-4 Temporary Life Annuities—One Life—Expected Return Multiples

Ages		Temporary period—maximum duration of annuity									
		Years									
Male	Female	1	2	3	4	5	6	7	8	9	10
0 to 8	0 to 13	1.0	2.0	3.0	4.0	5.0	6.0	7.0	8.0	8.9	9.9
9	14	1.0	2.0	3.0	4.0	5.0	6.0	7.0	8.0	8.9	9.9
10	15	1.0	2.0	3.0	4.0	5.0	6.0	7.0	8.0	8.9	9.9
11	16	1.0	2.0	3.0	4.0	5.0	6.0	7.0	8.0	8.9	9.9
12	17	1.0	2.0	3.0	4.0	5.0	6.0	7.0	8.0	8.9	9.9
13	18	1.0	2.0	3.0	4.0	5.0	6.0	7.0	8.0	8.9	9.9
14	19	1.0	2.0	3.0	4.0	5.0	6.0	7.0	8.0	8.9	9.9
15	20	1.0	2.0	3.0	4.0	5.0	6.0	7.0	8.0	8.9	9.9
16	21	1.0	2.0	3.0	4.0	5.0	6.0	7.0	8.0	8.9	9.9
17	22	1.0	2.0	3.0	4.0	5.0	6.0	7.0	8.0	8.9	9.9
18	23	1.0	2.0	3.0	4.0	5.0	6.0	7.0	8.0	8.9	9.9
19	24	1.0	2.0	3.0	4.0	5.0	6.0	7.0	8.0	8.9	9.9
20	25	1.0	2.0	3.0	4.0	5.0	6.0	7.0	8.0	8.9	9.9
21	26	1.0	2.0	3.0	4.0	5.0	6.0	7.0	8.0	8.9	9.9
22	27	1.0	2.0	3.0	4.0	5.0	6.0	7.0	8.0	8.9	9.9
23	28	1.0	2.0	3.0	4.0	5.0	6.0	7.0	8.0	8.9	9.9
24	29	1.0	2.0	3.0	4.0	5.0	6.0	7.0	7.9	8.9	9.9
25	30	1.0	2.0	3.0	4.0	5.0	6.0	7.0	7.9	8.9	9.9
26	31	1.0	2.0	3.0	4.0	5.0	6.0	7.0	7.9	8.9	9.9
27	32	1.0	2.0	3.0	4.0	5.0	6.0	7.0	7.9	8.9	9.9
28	33	1.0	2.0	3.0	4.0	5.0	6.0	7.0	7.9	8.9	9.9
29	34	1.0	2.0	3.0	4.0	5.0	6.0	6.9	7.9	8.9	9.9
30	35	1.0	2.0	3.0	4.0	5.0	6.0	6.9	7.9	8.9	9.9
31	36	1.0	2.0	3.0	4.0	5.0	6.0	6.9	7.9	8.9	9.9
32	37	1.0	2.0	3.0	4.0	5.0	6.0	6.9	7.9	8.9	9.9
33	38	1.0	2.0	3.0	4.0	5.0	6.0	6.9	7.9	8.9	9.9
34	39	1.0	2.0	3.0	4.0	5.0	5.9	6.9	7.9	8.9	9.8
35	40	1.0	2.0	3.0	4.0	5.0	5.9	6.9	7.9	8.9	9.8
36	41	1.0	2.0	3.0	4.0	5.0	5.9	6.9	7.9	8.9	9.8
37	42	1.0	2.0	3.0	4.0	5.0	5.9	6.9	7.9	8.8	9.8
38	43	1.0	2.0	3.0	4.0	5.0	5.9	6.9	7.9	8.8	9.8
39	44	1.0	2.0	3.0	4.0	4.9	5.9	6.9	7.9	8.8	9.8
40	45	1.0	2.0	3.0	4.0	4.9	5.9	6.9	7.8	8.8	9.7
41	46	1.0	2.0	3.0	4.0	4.9	5.9	6.9	7.8	8.8	9.7
42	47	1.0	2.0	3.0	4.0	4.9	5.9	6.9	7.8	8.8	9.7
43	48	1.0	2.0	3.0	4.0	4.9	5.9	6.9	7.8	8.8	9.7
44	49	1.0	2.0	3.0	4.0	4.9	5.9	6.8	7.8	8.7	9.7
45	50	1.0	2.0	3.0	3.9	4.9	5.9	6.8	7.8	8.7	9.6
46	51	1.0	2.0	3.0	3.9	4.9	5.9	6.8	7.8	8.7	9.6
47	52	1.0	2.0	3.0	3.9	4.9	5.9	6.8	7.7	8.7	9.6
48	53	1.0	2.0	3.0	3.9	4.9	5.9	6.8	7.7	8.6	9.5
49	54	1.0	2.0	3.0	3.9	4.9	5.8	6.8	7.7	8.6	9.5
50	55	1.0	2.0	3.0	3.9	4.9	5.8	6.8	7.7	8.6	9.5
51	56	1.0	2.0	3.0	3.9	4.9	5.8	6.7	7.7	8.6	9.4
52	57	1.0	2.0	3.0	3.9	4.9	5.8	6.7	7.6	8.5	9.4
53	58	1.0	2.0	2.9	3.9	4.9	5.8	6.7	7.6	8.5	9.3
54	59	1.0	2.0	2.9	3.9	4.8	5.8	6.7	7.6	8.4	9.3
55	60	1.0	2.0	2.9	3.9	4.8	5.8	6.7	7.5	8.4	9.2
56	61	1.0	2.0	2.9	3.9	4.8	5.7	6.6	7.5	8.4	9.2
57	62	1.0	2.0	2.9	3.9	4.8	5.7	6.6	7.5	8.3	9.1
58	63	1.0	2.0	2.9	3.9	4.8	5.7	6.6	7.4	8.3	9.1
59	64	1.0	2.0	2.9	3.9	4.8	5.7	6.5	7.4	8.2	9.0
60	65	1.0	2.0	2.9	3.8	4.8	5.6	6.5	7.3	8.1	8.9
61	66	1.0	2.0	2.9	3.8	4.7	5.6	6.5	7.3	8.1	8.8
62	67	1.0	2.0	2.9	3.8	4.7	5.6	6.4	7.2	8.0	8.8
63	68	1.0	2.0	2.9	3.8	4.7	5.6	6.4	7.2	7.9	8.7

[1] See footnote at end of table.

70

Exhibit 6-4 *(Continued)*

Ages		Temporary period—maximum duration of annuity									
		years									
Male	Female	1	2	3	4	5	6	7	8	9	10
64	69	1.0	1.9	2.9	3.8	4.7	5.5	6.3	7.1	7.9	8.6
65	70	1.0	1.9	2.9	3.8	4.6	5.5	6.3	7.1	7.8	8.5
66	71	1.0	1.9	2.9	3.8	4.6	5.4	6.2	7.0	7.7	8.4
67	72	1.0	1.9	2.9	3.7	4.6	5.4	6.2	6.9	7.6	8.3
68	73	1.0	1.9	2.8	3.7	4.6	5.4	6.1	6.8	7.5	8.2
69	74	1.0	1.9	2.8	3.7	4.5	5.3	6.1	6.8	7.4	8.0
70	75	1.0	1.9	2.8	3.7	4.5	5.3	6.0	6.7	7.3	7.9
71	76	1.0	1.9	2.8	3.7	4.5	5.2	5.9	6.6	7.2	7.8
72	77	1.0	1.9	2.8	3.6	4.4	5.2	5.8	6.5	7.1	7.6
73	78	1.0	1.9	2.8	3.6	4.4	5.1	5.8	6.4	7.0	7.5
74	79	1.0	1.9	2.8	3.6	4.3	5.0	5.7	6.3	6.8	7.3
75	80	1.0	1.9	2.7	3.5	4.3	5.0	5.6	6.2	6.7	7.1
76	81	1.0	1.9	2.7	3.5	4.2	4.9	5.5	6.1	6.5	7.0
77	82	1.0	1.9	2.7	3.5	4.2	4.8	5.4	5.9	6.4	6.8
78	83	1.0	1.9	2.7	3.4	4.1	4.7	5.3	5.8	6.2	6.6
79	84	1.0	1.8	2.7	3.4	4.1	4.7	5.2	5.7	6.1	6.4
80	85	1.0	1.8	2.6	3.4	4.0	4.6	5.1	5.5	5.9	6.2
81	86	1.0	1.8	2.6	3.3	3.9	4.5	5.0	5.4	5.7	6.0
82	87	1.0	1.8	2.6	3.3	3.9	4.4	4.8	5.2	5.6	5.8
83	88	.9	1.8	2.6	3.2	3.8	4.3	4.7	5.1	5.4	5.6
84	89	.9	1.8	2.5	3.2	3.7	4.2	4.6	4.9	5.2	5.4
85	90	.9	1.8	2.5	3.1	3.6	4.1	4.5	4.8	5.0	5.2
86	91	.9	1.8	2.5	3.1	3.6	4.0	4.3	4.6	4.8	5.0

Ages		Temporary period—maximum duration of annuity									
		Years									
Male	Female	11	12	13	14	15	16	17	18	19	20
0 to 8	0 to 13	10.9	11.9	12.9	13.9	14.9	15.8	16.8	17.8	18.8	19.7
9	14	10.9	11.9	12.9	13.9	14.9	15.8	16.8	17.8	18.8	19.7
10	15	10.9	11.9	12.9	13.9	14.9	15.8	16.8	17.8	18.8	19.7
11	16	10.9	11.9	12.9	13.9	14.9	15.8	16.8	17.8	18.8	19.7
12	17	10.9	11.9	12.9	13.9	14.9	15.8	16.8	17.8	18.8	19.7
13	18	10.9	11.9	12.9	13.9	14.9	15.8	16.8	17.8	18.8	19.7
14	19	10.9	11.9	12.9	13.9	14.9	15.8	16.8	17.8	18.8	19.7
15	20	10.9	11.9	12.9	13.9	14.9	15.8	16.8	17.8	18.7	19.7
16	21	10.9	11.9	12.9	13.9	14.8	15.8	16.8	17.8	18.7	19.7
17	22	10.9	11.9	12.9	13.9	14.8	15.8	16.8	17.8	18.7	19.7
18	23	10.9	11.9	12.9	13.9	14.8	15.8	16.8	17.8	18.7	19.7
19	24	10.9	11.9	12.9	13.9	14.8	15.8	16.8	17.7	18.7	19.7
20	25	10.9	11.9	12.9	13.9	14.8	15.8	16.8	17.7	18.7	19.7
21	26	10.9	11.9	12.9	13.8	14.8	15.8	16.8	17.7	18.7	19.6
22	27	10.9	11.9	12.9	13.8	14.8	15.8	16.7	17.7	18.7	19.6
23	28	10.9	11.9	12.9	13.8	14.8	15.8	16.7	17.7	18.7	19.6
24	29	10.9	11.9	12.9	13.8	14.8	15.8	16.7	17.7	18.6	19.6
25	30	10.9	11.9	12.8	13.8	14.8	15.7	16.7	17.7	18.6	19.6
26	31	10.9	11.9	12.8	13.8	14.8	15.7	16.7	17.6	18.6	19.5
27	32	10.9	11.9	12.8	13.8	14.8	15.7	16.7	17.6	18.6	19.5
28	33	10.9	11.8	12.8	13.8	14.7	15.7	16.6	17.6	18.5	19.5
29	34	10.9	11.8	12.8	13.8	14.7	15.7	16.6	17.6	18.5	19.4
30	35	10.9	11.8	12.8	13.7	14.7	15.6	16.6	17.5	18.4	19.4
31	36	10.8	11.8	12.8	13.7	14.7	15.6	16.5	17.5	18.4	19.3
32	37	10.8	11.8	12.7	13.7	14.6	15.6	16.5	17.4	18.4	19.3

[1] See footnote at end of table.

Exhibit 6-4 *(Continued)*

Ages		Temporary period—maximum duration of annuity									
		years									
Male	Female	11	12	13	14	15	16	17	18	19	20
33	38	10.8	11.8	12.7	13.7	14.6	15.6	16.5	17.4	18.3	19.2
34	39	10.8	11.8	12.7	13.6	14.6	15.5	16.4	17.4	18.3	19.2
35	40	10.8	11.7	12.7	13.6	14.6	15.5	16.4	17.3	18.2	19.1
36	41	10.8	11.7	12.7	13.6	14.5	15.4	16.3	17.2	18.1	19.0
37	42	10.8	11.7	12.6	13.6	14.5	15.4	16.3	17.2	18.1	18.9
38	43	10.7	11.7	12.6	13.5	14.4	15.3	16.2	17.1	18.0	18.9
39	44	10.7	11.6	12.6	13.5	14.4	15.3	16.2	17.1	17.9	18.8
40	45	10.7	11.6	12.5	13.5	14.4	15.2	16.1	17.0	17.8	18.7
41	46	10.7	11.6	12.5	13.4	14.3	15.2	16.1	16.9	17.8	18.6
42	47	10.6	11.6	12.5	13.4	14.3	15.1	16.0	16.8	17.7	18.5
43	48	10.6	11.5	12.4	13.3	14.2	15.1	15.9	16.7	17.6	18.4
44	49	10.6	11.5	12.4	13.3	14.1	15.0	15.8	16.7	17.5	18.3
45	50	10.5	11.4	12.3	13.2	14.1	14.9	15.7	16.6	17.4	18.1
46	51	10.5	11.4	12.3	13.2	14.0	14.8	15.7	16.5	17.2	18.0
47	52	10.5	11.4	12.2	13.1	13.9	14.7	15.6	16.3	17.1	17.8
48	53	10.4	11.3	12.2	13.0	13.8	14.7	15.4	16.2	17.0	17.7
49	54	10.4	11.3	12.1	12.9	13.8	14.6	15.3	16.1	16.8	17.5
50	55	10.3	11.2	12.0	12.9	13.7	14.5	15.2	16.0	16.7	17.4
51	56	10.3	11.1	12.0	12.8	13.6	14.3	15.1	15.8	16.5	17.2
52	57	10.2	11.1	11.9	12.7	13.5	14.2	14.9	15.6	16.3	17.0
53	58	10.2	11.0	11.8	12.6	13.4	14.1	14.8	15.5	16.1	16.8
54	59	10.1	10.9	11.7	12.5	13.2	14.0	14.6	15.3	15.9	16.5
55	60	10.1	10.9	11.6	12.4	13.1	13.8	14.5	15.1	15.7	16.3
56	61	10.0	10.8	11.5	12.3	13.0	13.7	14.3	14.9	15.5	16.1
57	62	9.9	10.7	11.4	12.2	12.8	13.5	14.1	14.7	15.3	15.8
58	63	9.8	10.6	11.3	12.0	12.7	13.3	13.9	14.5	15.0	15.5
59	64	9.8	10.5	11.2	11.9	12.5	13.2	13.7	14.3	14.8	15.3
60	65	9.7	10.4	11.1	11.7	12.4	13.0	13.5	14.0	14.5	15.0
61	66	9.6	10.3	11.0	11.6	12.2	12.8	13.3	13.8	14.2	14.7
62	67	9.5	10.2	10.8	11.4	12.0	12.5	13.1	13.5	14.0	14.3
63	68	9.4	10.0	10.7	11.3	11.8	12.3	12.8	13.2	13.7	14.0
64	69	9.3	9.9	10.5	11.1	11.6	12.1	12.5	13.0	13.3	13.7
65	70	9.1	9.8	10.3	10.9	11.4	11.9	12.3	12.7	13.0	13.3
66	71	9.0	9.6	10.2	10.7	11.2	11.6	12.0	12.4	12.7	13.0
67	72	8.9	9.5	10.0	10.5	10.9	11.3	11.7	12.0	12.3	12.6
68	73	8.7	9.3	9.8	10.3	10.7	11.1	11.4	11.7	12.0	12.2
69	74	8.6	9.1	9.6	10.0	10.4	10.8	11.1	11.4	11.6	11.8
70	75	8.4	8.9	9.4	9.8	10.2	10.5	10.8	11.0	11.2	11.4
71	76	8.3	8.7	9.2	9.6	9.9	10.2	10.4	10.7	10.9	11.0
72	77	8.1	8.6	8.9	9.3	9.6	9.9	10.1	10.3	10.5	10.6
73	78	7.9	8.3	8.7	9.0	9.3	9.6	9.8	9.9	10.1	10.2
74	79	7.7	8.1	8.5	8.8	9.0	9.2	9.4	9.6	9.7	9.8
75	80	7.6	7.9	8.2	8.5	8.7	8.9	9.1	9.2	9.3	9.4
76	81	7.4	7.7	8.0	8.2	8.4	8.6	8.7	8.8	8.9	9.0
77	82	7.1	7.5	7.7	7.9	8.1	8.3	8.4	8.5	8.5	8.6
78	83	6.9	7.2	7.4	7.6	7.8	7.9	8.0	8.1	8.2	8.2
79	84	6.7	7.0	7.2	7.3	7.5	7.6	7.7	7.7	7.8	7.8
80	85	6.5	6.7	6.9	7.1	7.2	7.3	7.3	7.4	7.4	7.4
81	86	6.3	6.5	6.6	6.8	6.9	6.9	7.0	7.0	7.1	--------
82	87	6.0	6.2	6.4	6.5	6.5	6.6	6.7	6.7	--------	
83	88	5.8	6.0	6.1	6.2	6.2	6.3	6.3	--------		
84	89	5.6	5.7	5.8	5.9	5.9	6.0	--------			
85	90	5.3	5.5	5.5	5.6	5.6	--------				
86	91	5.1	5.2	5.3	5.3	--------					

[1] See footnote at end of table.

Exhibit 6-4 (Continued)

Ages		Temporary period maximum duration of annuity									
		Years									
Male	Female	21	22	23	24	25	26	27	28	29	30
0 to 8	0 to 13	20.7	21.7	22.7	23.6	24.6	25.6	26.5	27.5	28.4	29.4
9	14	20.7	21.7	22.7	23.6	24.6	25.5	26.5	27.5	28.4	29.4
10	15	20.7	21.7	22.7	23.6	24.6	25.5	26.5	27.5	28.4	29.4
11	16	20.7	21.7	22.6	23.6	24.6	25.5	26.5	27.4	28.4	29.3
12	17	20.7	21.7	22.6	23.6	24.6	25.5	26.5	27.4	28.4	29.3
13	18	20.7	21.7	22.6	23.6	24.6	25.5	26.5	27.4	28.4	29.3
14	19	20.7	21.7	22.6	23.6	24.5	25.5	26.4	27.4	28.3	29.3
15	20	20.7	21.6	22.6	23.6	24.5	25.5	26.4	27.4	28.3	29.2
16	21	20.7	21.6	22.6	23.6	24.5	25.5	26.4	27.3	28.3	29.2
17	22	20.7	21.6	22.6	23.5	24.5	25.4	26.4	27.3	28.2	29.2
18	23	20.7	21.6	22.6	23.5	24.5	25.4	26.3	27.3	28.2	29.1
19	24	20.6	21.6	22.5	23.5	24.4	25.4	26.3	27.2	28.1	29.1
20	25	20.6	21.6	22.5	23.5	24.4	25.3	26.3	27.2	28.1	29.0
21	26	20.6	21.5	22.5	23.4	24.4	25.3	26.2	27.1	28.0	28.9
22	27	20.6	21.5	22.5	23.4	24.3	25.3	26.2	27.1	28.0	28.9
23	28	20.6	21.5	22.4	23.4	24.3	25.2	26.1	27.0	27.9	28.8
24	29	20.5	21.5	22.4	23.3	24.2	25.2	26.1	27.0	27.8	28.7
25	30	20.5	21.4	22.3	23.3	24.2	25.1	26.0	26.9	27.8	28.6
26	31	20.5	21.4	22.3	23.2	24.1	25.0	25.9	26.8	27.7	28.5
27	32	20.4	21.3	22.3	23.2	24.1	25.0	25.8	26.7	27.6	28.4
28	33	20.4	21.3	22.2	23.1	24.0	24.9	25.8	26.6	27.5	28.3
29	34	20.3	21.2	22.1	23.0	23.9	24.8	25.7	26.5	27.4	28.2
30	35	20.3	21.2	22.1	23.0	23.8	24.7	25.6	26.4	27.2	28.1
31	36	20.2	21.1	22.0	22.9	23.8	24.6	25.5	26.3	27.1	27.9
32	37	20.2	21.1	21.9	22.8	23.7	24.5	25.4	26.2	27.0	27.8
33	38	20.1	21.0	21.9	22.7	23.6	24.4	25.2	26.0	26.8	27.6
34	39	20.0	20.9	21.8	22.6	23.5	24.3	25.1	25.9	26.7	27.4
35	40	20.0	20.8	21.7	22.5	23.3	24.2	25.0	25.7	26.5	27.2
36	41	19.9	20.7	21.6	22.4	23.2	24.0	24.8	25.6	26.3	27.0
37	42	19.8	20.6	21.5	22.3	23.1	23.9	24.6	25.4	26.1	26.8
38	43	19.7	20.5	21.4	22.2	23.0	23.7	24.5	25.2	25.9	26.6
39	44	19.6	20.4	21.2	22.0	22.8	23.6	24.3	25.0	25.7	26.4
40	45	19.5	20.3	21.1	21.9	22.6	23.4	24.1	24.8	25.5	26.1
41	46	19.4	20.2	21.0	21.7	22.5	23.2	23.9	24.6	25.2	25.9
42	47	19.3	20.1	20.8	21.6	22.3	23.0	23.7	24.3	25.0	25.6
43	48	19.2	19.9	20.7	21.4	22.1	22.8	23.4	24.1	24.7	25.3
44	49	19.0	19.8	20.5	21.2	21.9	22.6	23.2	23.8	24.4	25.0
45	50	18.9	19.6	20.3	21.0	21.7	22.3	22.9	23.5	24.1	24.6
46	51	18.7	19.4	20.1	20.8	21.5	22.1	22.7	23.2	23.8	24.3
47	52	18.6	19.3	19.9	20.6	21.2	21.8	22.4	22.9	23.4	23.9
48	53	18.4	19.1	19.7	20.4	21.0	21.5	22.1	22.6	23.1	23.5
49	54	18.2	18.9	19.5	20.1	20.7	21.2	21.7	22.2	22.7	23.1
50	55	18.0	18.7	19.3	19.8	20.4	20.9	21.4	21.9	22.3	22.7
51	56	17.8	18.4	19.0	19.6	20.1	20.6	21.1	21.5	21.9	22.3
52	57	17.6	18.2	18.7	19.3	19.8	20.2	20.7	21.1	21.5	21.8
53	58	17.4	17.9	18.5	19.0	19.4	19.9	20.3	20.7	21.0	21.3
54	59	17.1	17.7	18.2	18.7	19.1	19.5	19.9	20.2	20.6	20.8
55	60	16.9	17.4	17.9	18.3	18.7	19.1	19.5	19.8	20.1	20.3
56	61	16.6	17.1	17.5	18.0	18.4	18.7	19.0	19.3	19.6	19.8
57	62	16.3	16.8	17.2	17.6	18.0	18.3	18.6	18.9	19.1	19.3
58	63	16.0	16.5	16.9	17.2	17.6	17.9	18.1	18.4	18.6	18.8
59	64	15.7	16.1	16.5	16.8	17.1	17.4	17.7	17.9	18.1	18.2
60	65	15.4	15.8	16.1	16.4	16.7	17.0	17.2	17.4	17.5	17.7
61	66	15.1	15.4	15.7	16.0	16.3	16.5	16.7	16.9	17.0	17.1
62	67	14.7	15.0	15.3	15.6	15.8	16.0	16.2	16.3	16.4	16.5
63	68	14.4	14.6	14.9	15.1	15.3	15.5	15.7	15.8	15.9	16.0
64	69	14.0	14.3	14.5	14.7	14.9	15.0	15.2	15.3	15.3	15.4
65	70	13.6	13.8	14.1	14.2	14.4	14.5	14.6	14.7	14.8	14.9
66	71	13.2	13.4	13.6	13.8	13.9	14.0	14.1	14.2	14.2	14.3
67	72	12.8	13.0	13.2	13.3	13.4	13.5	13.6	13.7	13.7	13.7
68	73	12.4	12.6	12.7	12.8	12.9	13.0	13.1	13.1	13.2	13.2
69	74	12.0	12.1	12.3	12.4	12.4	12.5	12.6	12.6	12.6	12.6
70	75	11.6	11.7	11.8	11.9	12.0	12.0	12.0	12.1	12.1	12.1
71	76	11.2	11.3	11.3	11.4	11.5	11.5	11.5	11.6	11.6	
72	77	10.7	10.8	10.9	10.9	11.0	11.0	11.0	11.0		
73	78	10.3	10.4	10.4	10.5	10.5	10.5	10.5			
74	79	9.9	9.9	10.0	10.0	10.1	10.1				
75	80	9.5	9.5	9.6	9.6	9.6					
76	81	9.1	9.1	9.1	9.1						
77	82	8.6	8.7	8.7							
78	83	8.2	8.3								
79	84	7.8									

The multiples in this table are not applicable to annuities for a term certain; for such cases see sec. 1.72-5(c) of the Income Tax Regulations.

Compute Taxable Portion of Annuity

Divide your investment by your expected return. The resulting percent is your "exclusion percentage." This portion of your annuity is considered nontaxable by the IRS.

Example

You are receiving $10,000 for life from your annuity. You invested $100,000. Your expected return is $150,000. Your exclusion percentage is 67%. Accordingly, 67% of your pension is tax-free and 33% is taxable.

Variable Annuities

The following rules apply to variable annuities. If you are receiving payments under a variable annuity contract and will recover your cost within 36 months after the date you receive the first payment, you whould use the 3-year rule (Method 2).

To determine whether you will recover your cost of a variable annuity within 36 months, multiply the amount of the first periodic payment you receive by the number of periodic payments you will receive within 36 months. If this amount added to any payment of accrued installments received in a lump sum equals or exceeds your cost, you must use the 3-year rule.

If you do not qualify for the 3-year rule, you would use the general rule (Method 3). The amount of each payment that is not taxed is computed by dividing your investment, adjusted for any refund features, by the number of periodic payments you expect to receive.

To determine the total number of payments, multiply the number of payments to be made each year by the number of years you will receive payments if the annuity is for a definite period. If the annuity is for life, you would determine the number of payments from the appropriate IRS table.

Example

Your total investment was $30,000. Your expected life is 15 years (from table) at the time annuity payments start. Therefore, the amount of your payment excluded from taxation is $2000 (30,000 ÷ 15)/year. If your first payment is $2500, you would include $500 ($2500 − 2000) in your gross income.

If your payment is less than the amount you can exclude from your taxes, when you receive your next payment, you may choose to recalculate the nontaxable portion.

Example

Assume you could exclude $2000 per year, but your first payment was only $1500. You would have $500 available as a credit. Assume you had 10 years of payments remaining. Divide the credit ($500) by the number of remaining payments (10) for an additional $50 exclusion. Thus the total taxable exclusion would be $2050 ($2000 + $50).

Refund Feature

Your annuity has a refund feature when these three conditions exist:

1 The expected return depends wholly or partly on the continued life of one or more persons.
2 The contract provides payments to a beneficiary or the estate of an annuitant after the death of the annuitant.
3 The payments are in the nature of a refund of what was paid for the annuity contract.

If your annuity does contain a refund feature, you must reduce your investment in the contract for tax purposes by the present value of the refund feature. The amount of this present value can be computed from the IRS present value table (Exhibit 6-3). The company that sold the annuity can also provide the present value.

Death Benefit Exclusion

If you are the beneficiary of a deceased employee or former employee, the pension or annuity you receive may qualify for a death benefit exclusion. This exclusion is limited to $5000 and generally applies to the amount by which the present value of the survivor annuity exceeds the larger of:

The employee's total regular contribution to the plan.

The amount the employee possessed a nonforfeitable right to receive. The maximum total exclusion is $5000 regardless of the number of employers paying death benefits or the number of beneficiaries.

Disability Pensions

If you retired on disability and at the time of your retirement you were permanently and totally disabled, you may exclude all or part of your disability payments as disability income up to the earliest of the following dates:

The beginning of the tax year in which you become age 65.

The beginning of the tax year for which you make an irrevocable election not to claim the disability income exclusion.

The date on which you reach mandatory retirement age.

After you have reached this date, you may not exclude amounts you receive as disability income, but you may exclude these amounts as a recovery of your annuity costs under applicable annuity rules.

SWISS ANNUITIES AND INSURANCE

One of the major problems of investing in an annuity now is inflation. For a fixed dollar amount that you turn over to an insurance company, that company will offer you a guaranteed rate of return on your investment. The insurance company cannot, however, guarantee that the return will keep pace with inflation in the United States. Since the Swiss franc has done much better historically than the U.S. dollar, there is reason to consider purchasing annuities and insurance from Swiss insurance companies whose proceeds would be paid in Swiss francs rather than U.S. dollars.

There are two primary reasons to consider investing in a Swiss rather than an American insurance company. The first is the performance of the Swiss franc. A comparison of the two currencies from 1970 to 1979 shows that the Swiss franc has increased in value 2½ times against the dollar. The major question is whether we can expect this trend to continue. As long as the annual rate of inflation in the United States continues at 10% or more and in Switzerland at only 4%, it is unlikely that the dollar will recover strongly with respect to the Swiss franc.

The other major reason for investing in a Swiss insurance company is diversification. In other sections of the book, the advantages of diversified investments such as gold, silver, or diamonds is discussed. For the same reasons that an investor should not place all assets in one type of investment, an investor should also consider the risk of placing all assets in one currency.

Investments through Swiss Insurance Companies

Swiss insurance companies, unlike banks, are not restricted and can accept deposits in any amount. Neither the initial deposit nor the interest earned is subject to any Swiss taxes if the investor does not live in Switzerland.

Swiss insurance companies offer three types of investments: savings plans, annuities, and ordinary life and term insurance.

Savings Plans

There are two savings plans available with different investment objectives. The first, the Swiss Capital Accumulator (SCA), is designed for investors who want to accumulate Swiss francs over an extended time by making annual deposits. It is designed for younger families with a need for high insurance and the need to build up assets.

Here is how it works.* If, for example, a man aged 35 decides to deposit 5000 Swiss francs per year for 15 years, he will be *guaranteed* by the insurance company a cash value of 81,000 Swiss francs at age 50. In addition, at current dividend rates, he will earn approximately 15,000 Swiss francs in tax-free dividends, making a total of 96,000 Swiss francs. In addition to the interest and dividends, the value of the investment will increase even more if the Swiss franc continues to outperform the dollar. Furthermore, the investor is protected by the insurance coverage of approximately 80,000 Swiss francs at the beginning, which increases to 90,000 Swiss francs in the last year. The investor with an SCA will have accumulated about the same amount of money as he would have in a Swiss bank account. In view of the fact that the investor has insurance coverage as well, the SCA has a definite advantage over a Swiss bank account.

The other savings plan, called the Swiss Capital Preservation Account (CPA), is for investors who want to make a lump sum or single deposit and let it grow. It is ideal for a middle-aged investor who has already accumulated some

---

*Information reprinted by permission from International Insurance Specialists, P.O. Box 949, 1211 Geneva 3, Switzerland.

capital and is concerned about preservation and growth. To show you how it works, let us take a man now aged 45 who plans to retire at age 60. He decides to make a deposit of 100,000 Swiss francs for 15 years. His *guaranteed* maturity value is approximately 142,000 Swiss francs, a sum for which he is immediately insured. In addition, his account is credited with tax-free dividends, which at the current rate will amount to approximately 25,000 Swiss francs so that the total value of his investment upon maturity will be 167,000 Swiss francs.

Fifteen years sounds like a long time so let us see what sort of flexibility the investor has. First, he can close the account at any time for its cash value. If he decides to do so in the first year, he suffers a penalty in the form of a loss of approximately 3%. By the third year, the cash value is approximately 103% of what he paid in. In the fifth year it is approximately 112%, and in the tenth year approximately 136%, including dividends. This alternative has advantages over an investment in a bond denominated in Swiss francs. If for example, Swiss interest rates rise, the price of the bonds you buy *today* will drop. With a CPA you do not run this risk. You are, in fact, guaranteed an increase in the value of your investment because if interest rates go up the dividends paid by the insurance company will go up as well.

The investor in either savings plan has additional flexibility—he can borrow up to 90% against the cash value at any time, presently at an annual rate of 4½%. If he loses faith in the Swiss franc for some reason and believes, for instance, that gold will be the best investment for the next few years, he can borrow against the account from the insurance company, transfer the borrowed funds to his bank, and instruct the bank to buy gold for him. Borrowing against the account does not affect the insurance coverage.

A possibly important additional feature of these savings plans is that under Swiss law they cannot be attached in case of bankruptcy if the beneficiaries are members of the family.

Swiss Annuities

Swiss annuities have a tremendous appeal all over the world because they have substantially outpaced the rise in the cost of living in the United States and other countries. If, for example, your retirement income had been 4300 Swiss francs in 1970 (then 1000 dollars), you would of course still be getting 4300 Swiss francs today, but that would now be equal to approximately 2638 dollars. To maintain the same purchasing power in 1978 that 1000 dollars had in 1970, you would need 1678 dollars. Since your Swiss annuity pays you 2638 dollars, you would be actually ahead in purchasing power by more than 50%.

Swiss annuities can be divided into two categories: immediate annuities and deferred annuities. In the case of an immediate annuity, you make a single deposit today and your annuity payments are 3 months, 6 months, or a year later, depending on whether you choose to draw your income for life on a quarterly, semiannual, or annual basis. In the case of a deferred annuity, you make a single deposit today or begin making annual deposits today and decide now or at some future date when you would like to begin receiving annuity payments.

In addition, annuities come with a variety of options that affect the amount of money paid to you. The Retirement Income Annuity with refund (RIA) and the Joint Income Annuity (JIA) both have payments guaranteed for a certain number of years regardless of how long the two annuitants live.

The RIA is purchased in the name of a single annuitant and offers maximum flexibility. First, the "with refund" option means that in case of the death of the annuitant any unused portion of the single deposit is refunded to the beneficiariees. If the investor lives longer than "average," the total amount he or she receives in the form of annuity payments will substantially exceed the initial deposit. Your investment is returned either in the form of a life income or in the form of a lump sum to the beneficiaries. Second, it is the only annuity that can be surrendered completely if for some reason you want your money back. The penalty in the first year is 3−5% depending on the insurance company issuing the contract and declines at the rate of about ½% per year thereafter.

If, for example, a woman aged 55 who decides to deposit 100,000 Swiss francs in an RIA—that is, a single annuity with refund—decides to start drawing her retirement income immediately, her *guaranteed annual income for life* is 5455 Swiss francs, which, with dividends at the current rate, increases to 5955 Swiss francs. If she starts at age 60, the guaranteed annual income is 6878 Swiss francs, which, with dividends, increases to 7582 Swiss francs. If she postpones drawing her life income until 65, her guaranteed annual income for life is 9464 Swiss francs, which, with dividends, increases to 10,536 Swiss francs.

The older you are, the higher your return. Calculating your annuity income as a return on your initial deposit, you can figure for your lifetime:

You start at age (male)	Return from the annuity itself	Return including the increase for the last 8 years in the value of the Swiss franc against the U.S. dollar
55	6.4%	20.4%
60	7.3%	21.3%
65	8.5%	22.5%
70	10.1%	24.1%
75	12.4%	26.4%

Whereas a single annuity covers one person, a Joint Income Annuity covers two—for example, a husband and wife. If you are looking for maximum security for you and your spouse, you should take out a joint annuity. However, the "with refund" option where the unused portion is refu.ded to your beneficiaries is not available in a joint annuity. This is not as big a problem as it may appear at first glance because payments can be specified for enough years to make sure that the payments at least equal your investment. The annuity should be written with an option that guarantees payments as "certain" for 10, 15, 20 or any other number of years so that the original investment is recovered in any event. This means that in case of the premature death of both annuitants the designated beneficiaries will receive payments equal to the remaining years of the option.

Ordinary Life and Term Insurance

Swiss insurance companies offer ordinary life and term policies that are essentially the same as policies issued by U.S. insurance companies. The essential difference is that the Swiss policies are denominated in Swiss francs.

Life Insurance Companies in Switzerland

There are only 21 life insurance companies in Switzerland. Three of them are nonSwiss, which leaves 18, and of these only eight are active in the international market. Swiss insurance companies are strictly supervised by the Swiss Federal Insurance Commission and must comply with a very strict code of practice. Under this code, Swiss insurance companies can invest their assets only in Switzerland and only in Swiss government obligations, Swiss real estate and mortgages, obligations of Swiss governmental agencies, and shares of Swiss companies (up to 5%). Never in the history of Swiss life insurance (over 120 years) has a company been forced to cease its activities nor has one ever failed to meet its obligations to policy holders. Moreover, Swiss insurance accounts are confidential. No insurance company will give information to a third party. This is why the confidentiality of a Swiss insurance account is often compared to that of a Swiss bank account.

7 Your Private Pension Plan and Erisa

If you work for an employer who has established a private pension plan in which you are or will be a participant, it is absolutely necessary that you learn as much as possible about the plan. Although the 1974 Pension Reform Law provides many safeguards regarding private pensions, you have the responsibility to learn how your employer's pension plan affects you. The Reform Law does not make all private pension plans alike by any means. You should become familiar with the Reform Law and, more important, learn as much about your pension plan as possible. The information is readily available. All you have to do is request it. The major portion of this chapter is devoted to identifying the major issues and questions you should be concerned about regarding your pension.

Most pension plans do not provide any automatic protection for you against inflation after retirement. Therefore, you should not overestimate the value of your private pension. The amount you expect to get in today's dollars may look adequate. The question you must ask is how adequate will it be if inflation continues at 10% per year or higher.

Many of the questions in this chapter were raised in the book *You and Your Pension*, by Kate Blackwell and Ralph Nader. Although the Pension Reform Law was passed after that book was published, the questions are still important.

ELIGIBILITY

Each employer can establish different rules on when you are eligible to receive a pension. For example, an employer may not start counting years of service until you reach a certain age or until you have been employed for a minimum length of time. Make sure you know the answers to the following questions regarding your

81

eligibility: How many years must you work for your employer before you qualify for a pension? How old must you be to collect benefits? How is a "break-in service" defined? Could a layoff eliminate your chances of receiving a benefit? What total of years of "credited service" must you have? Must these years be continuous or may they be broken by a leave or layoff? Must you be a member of a union or union local at retirement to get the benefits you have earned? What must you do to collect your benefit rights if you quit your job before retirement age? What must you do before you retire to apply?

VESTING RIGHTS

You become vested with an employer after you have worked a specified minimum length of time. At that point you have earned specified pension rights that cannot be taken away from you even if you quit your job or are terminated. The Reform Law specifies that employers can select one of three options for employees: (1) full vesting after 10 years of employment, (2) vesting of 25% of accrued benefits after 5 years with an increase each year until full vesting occurs after 15 years on the job, or (3) the "rule of 45"—providing 50% vesting after an employee's age and years of service total 45 and increasing vesting by 10% per year until 100% vesting has occurred. If you have 10 years of service, you are 50% vested. You should determine which of the three options your employer has selected.

   Do not make the assumption that once you are fully vested you should change jobs because you would receive the maximum pension retirement check. That is not so. Your retirement check will be computed in most cases based on *total* years of service in addition to salary information. If your pension is based on total years of service, your retirement check will be larger if your years of service exceed the minimum required for full vesting.

CONTRIBUTIONS

Under the Pension Reform Law your employer must provide you with answers to the following questions about contributions: How much does your employer contribute to the plan? How are these contributions computed? Are you allowed to contribute? If so, are your contributions mandatory or voluntary? What happens to your contributions if you die or leave the company before retirement? Can you withdraw your own contributions prior to retirement?

If you are allowed to make voluntary contributions to the plan, you should take into consideration the following factors. Your contributions, up to $2000 may be tax deductible because of the 1981 tax legislation. The interest or dividends that accumulate from your contributions will probably not be taxable until you withdraw these funds at retirement. This will give you a tax shelter until that time. This advantage must be weighed against the return you could receive by investing these funds elsewhere. You must be careful to take into consideration the tax aspects or alternative investments. If you are in a high tax bracket now, you should look carefully at the after-tax return you are getting on your investments and compare that to the return you expect to make if you contribute voluntarily to a company pension plan.

Another factor to consider is the "forced savings" aspect of contributions to a pension plan. Think about the self-discipline you must establish to contribute consistently to an alternative investment program. Many people believe they will contribute regularly to a self-imposed investment program but fail to do so. Individuals who know they do not have the required self-discipline recognize the need for retirement savings, and are satisfied with the rate of return offered through contributory pension plans should seriously consider making contributions through their employer sponsored plans.

BENEFITS

The Reform Law specifies that your employer must inform you whether all your compensation is counted in computing your benefits. You must be told when benefit payments begin and how they will be paid. You must also be told when you would not be eligible to receive benefits.

Look for answers to the following questions: How is your benefit computed? (Make sure you understand all the variables that are used in the computation.) Is it based on total years worked as well as salary? What will be your benefit if you work until mandatory retirement age? Do benefits accrue at the same rate regardless of length of service? (For example, some companies encourage employees to leave or retire early by using a formula adding fewer benefits after a specified length of service.) What benefits are promised if you get laid off or are fired tomorrow? Are benefits tied to Social Security compensation? (Many plans use Social Security payments as part of their compensation formula. In that way, if Social Security payments are increased the employer's contribution is reduced. The law does, however, place a limit on the percent of Social Security payments that can be used in the formula.) Will the years you worked before a plan was started count if the benefit is based on the years you have worked?

What benefits, if any, will you receive if you retire early or if you become disabled? This is a very important question, and you should give it careful attention. Too many employees have insufficient disability insurance. If your employer does not provide you with adequate disability coverage, you should consider obtaining independent coverage. This topic is covered in more detail in Chapter 4.

Does the plan have any provision to increase postretirement benefits based on increases in the cost of living? The Reform Law does not address this issue. Most employers who do increase postretirement benefits do so on a voluntary basis. You cannot expect employers to be able to increase pension benefits continually to keep pace with inflation. Those employers who have been generous in this way have increased their payments so that retirees' pension checks have increased approximately one-third of true living increases. Even if you work for an employer who has been generous in the past, you certainly should not count on any automatic increases when you plan your retirement.

SURVIVOR BENEFITS

Under the Pension Reform Law a plan must provide a joint and survivor option. The survivor benefit must not be less than 50% of the benefit payable to the retiree. The joint and survivor option applies unless the employee elects not to participate.

If you select a survivor option, your retirement benefit will be somewhat reduced during your lifetime, but your spouse, if he or she outlives you, will continue to receive pension benefits from your employer after your death. If you do not select a survivor option, after you die your spouse will not receive a pension from your employer. Your decision regarding the survivor option should be made taking into consideration the following factors:

Other income you will receive during your retirement.

Income your spouse would receive after your death if you did not select a survivor option.

The standard of living you could maintain if you accepted a survivor option.

The extent to which your pensions and your spouse's pensions are indexed to cost of living increases.

INSURANCE

Under the Pension Reform Law private pensions are insured by the Pension Benefit Guarantee Corporation located in Washington, D.C. This insurance protects pension holders and their survivors in the event that the pension plan is inadequately funded. The corporation will pay up to $750 per month in retirement benefits.

TAX STATUS

If your pension is completely paid for by your employer and you do not report your employer's contributions as income on your tax return, you must report all pension payments you receive as ordinary income.

8 Individual Retirement Arrangements (IRAs)

The major purpose of the Individual Retirement Arrangements (IRA) portion of the Pension Reform Law was to provide a tax sheltered retirement plan for individuals who are not covered by qualified employer sponsored retirement plans such as pension, profit sharing, stock bonus, or annuity plans.

In 1981 tax legislation was passed by Congress which broadened eligibility requirements. Starting in 1982 individuals covered by qualified plans as well as those who are not will be eligible to contribute up to $2000 per year in one or more approved investments. The major advantage of the plan is that the portion of income contributed to the plan as well as the income from the investment will not be taxed until funds are withdrawn at retirement, after age 59½.

There are several potential disadvantages, however. With the sole exception of disability, there are severe tax penalties if funds are withdrawn prematurely—that is, before age 59½. Moreover, there can be other penalties associated with premature withdrawal of funds that vary depending on the form of investment chosen.

In addition to the premature withdrawal penalties, there can be other penalties if excess contributions are made or if insufficient withdrawals are made after retirement is reached.

In general, however, the benefits of IRA accounts seem to outweigh the potential penalties for those eligible individuals who do not have to withdraw contributions prior to retirement age.

ELIGIBILITY

The eligibility requirements to establish IRA accounts were expanded significantly by the tax law passed in 1981. Prior to the passage of this law, you were eligible to establish an IRA in any given tax year only if you were self-employed or worked for someone else full- or part-time but were not an active participant in any of the following types of programs established by an employer:

A qualified pension, profit-sharing, or stock bonus plan of an employer.

A qualified annuity plan of an employer.

A qualified bond purchase plan of an employer.

A government retirement plan.

An annuity contract purchased by certain tax exempt organizations or public schools.

A qualified plan for self-employed individuals (HR-10 or Keogh Plan).

Based on the 1981 tax law, effective in 1982, individuals who are covered by an employer's pension plan will also be eligible to establish IRA accounts for the first time. If an employee contributes to an employer-sponsored pension plan, these contributions can be tax deductible with the same upper limit constraints as IRA accounts.

INITIATING AN IRA

To initiate an IRA, a written agreement, contract, or purchase application must be executed. These documents are generally available for the various sponsors of the different types of IRA investments discussed in Chapter 9. The agreement or contract and associated disclosure material must contain the conditions for establishing and maintaining the IRA account.

CONTRIBUTIONS

If you qualify to set up an IRA account, starting in 1982, you may contribute up to $2000 of your compensation. If you contribute less than $2000 to an employer-sponsored IRA pension plan, you can establish an independent IRA account and contribute the difference between $2000 and what you contribute to your employer's plan. If your contributions to an employer-sponsored pension plan are not tax deductible, then you can establish an independent IRA plan and contribute up to $2000 of your compensation. Prior to 1982 you could contribute up to $1500 or 15% of your earnings, whichever was less.

Compensation includes wages, salaries, or professional fees, as well as other amounts received for personal services actually rendered. It does not include income from items such as interest, dividends, or rentals from real estate. It is not necessary to contribute money to the IRA every year or to make the same contribution each year.

Example

Henry Roberts earns $40,000 in 1981. He also receives $2000 in interest income.

Compensation eligible	$40,000
Maximum contribution (the lesser of $1500 or 15% of $40,000 = $6000)	$1,500

Example

Robin Smith earns $5000 in 1982.

Compensation eligible	$5,000
Maximum contribution	$2,000

Example

Joan Taylor earns $50,000 in 1983. She contributes $1000 to her company's pension plan, which is now tax deductible. She wants to establish an independent IRA.

Compensation eligible	$50,000
Maximum contribution	$2,000
Contribution through company plan	$1,000
Maximum contribution to independent IRA	$1,000

Contributions can be made up to but not including the year in which an individual reaches age 70½. The amount contributed is deductible for income tax purposes. The deduction is made from gross income so that it is available whether deductions are itemized or the zero bracket (standard) deduction is used.

MARRIED COUPLE OPTIONS

If you and your spouse are individually eligible to set up an IRA account, two IRA accounts can be established. Starting in 1982, each of you can contribute up to $2000, per year to each of the IRA accounts.

If one spouse is eligible to establish an IRA and the other spouse has no compensation, separate IRA accounts can be established for each spouse. Utilizing this option, the maximum combined contribution to the two IRAs was increased to $2250 in 1982; previously the maximum was $1750.

The 1981 tax law relaxed the previous restrictions regarding splitting income between two spousal IRAs. Starting in 1982, spouses can allocate the maximum contribution, $2250, into the two IRA accounts in whatever manner they wish.

Example

Mr. J. Jones, income,	$20,000
Mrs. J. Jones, nonworking spouse	$ 0
Maximum contribution	$ 2,250
Mrs. J. Jones, IRA account	$ 2,000
Mr. J. Jones, IRA account	$ 250

One of the major factors you should consider, when you decide how to allocate funds into two IRA accounts, is the age differential between you and your spouse. If you plan to withdraw funds as early as possible without penalty, you should consider allocating more funds into the account of the older spouse. The earliest age you can withdraw funds without penalty is 59½.

The status of a nonworking spouse with respect to his or her IRA account can change. Assume that a spouse who previously did not work becomes employed. Both spouses are eligible to establish IRA accounts, and two regular IRA accounts can be established. The status of the account of the nonworking spouse is changed from a nonworking spouse IRA account to a regular IRA account.

The upper limit for subsequent contributions to each plan is based on the income earned by each IRA participant.

Example

Mr. John Smith, income, 1983	$ 5,000
Mrs. Mary Smith, income, 1983	$25,000
Mr. Smith's maximum contribution	$ 2,000
Mrs. Smith's maximum contribution	$ 2,000

In the tax year that you reach age 70½, you can no longer contribute to either your IRA or your nonworking spouse's IRA account.

ADVANTAGES

There are two major advantages associated with IRA accounts:

1 All contributions made to IRA accounts, in accordance with the eligibility and contribution rules discussed in this chapter, are tax deductible from gross income in the tax year that contributions are made. Taxes are not payable on this contribution until withdrawals are made at retirement age. Distributions made at retirement age, starting at age 59½, are taxable as ordinary income. Accordingly, if your income at retirement is less than your income was during your working years, your income tax is reduced. Moreover, the income tax is postponed until you retire.

2 All income earned on contributions made to the plan accumulate tax-free until distributions are made at retirement age. If you start contributing to an IRA early in your working life, you will have the benefit of many years of tax-free earnings until you start withdrawing funds. When these withdrawals are made, they are taxed as ordinary income. They are not eligible for capital gains treatment.

DISADVANTAGES/RESTRICTIONS

There are several restrictions associated with the use of IRA accounts that you must consider before you open an IRA account. Specifically, there are three major areas of restrictions that can lead to significant penalties: (1) premature withdrawal of funds; (2) insufficient withdrawals; and (3) excess contributions.

Premature Withdrawals

Once you open an IRA account, you will be penalized if you withdraw any funds prior to age 59½ unless you become disabled. To begin with, there are two tax penalties. Individuals withdrawing funds from their IRA accounts prior to reaching age 59½ are subject to a 10% tax on the amount of the withdrawals. They must also pay income tax on the amount of the withdrawals.

Example

Henry Smith, 50 years old, withdraws $1000 from his IRA account in 1979. His income places him in the 40% tax bracket. He has now incurred a tax penalty of $100 (10% of $1000) and must report $1000 in income on his federal return, thus paying an additional $400 in federal taxes.

In addition to the tax penalties there may be other penalties for early withdrawal based on the form of IRA investment chosen. For example, assume that an individual opens an IRA account at a bank and his contributions are used as payments toward a certificate of deposit (CD) with a maturity longer than 1 year. If a withdrawal is made prior to retirement age before the certificate matured, the IRA holder would forfeit 180 days of interest.

IRA plan holders could also incur early withdrawal penalties with other types of investments. Specifically, these investments include annuities, insurance—investment combinations, and CDs. These penalties are discussed in more detail in Chapter 9. Since there is now a variety of IRA investments to choose from, you should make sure you understood fully the early withdrawal penalties associated with any investment alternative you consider.

Insufficient Withdrawal

There are a number of options that you as an IRA account holder can exercise after age 59½ for distribution of your IRA account. Amounts contributed to an IRA must be initiated before the end of the year in which you reach age 70½. With some of these options there is a minimum distribution that must be made; otherwise an excise tax penalty will be imposed.

An underdistribution is the excess of the minimum payout required for the year over the amount actually paid. There is a 50% excise tax on the underdistribution. The tax is paid by the recipient of the distribution.

Example

John Roberts, aged 65, should have received a minimum of a $1000 distribution in 1979. He received only $500. His excise tax for the year is $250 (50% of $500).

If it is shown that the underdistribution was because of a reasonable error and reasonable steps are being taken to correct the situation, the 50% excise tax may be waived for the taxable year.

Excess Contribution

An excess contribution is the portion of a contribution over the amount that can be deducted. This results when you contribute more than the lesser of $2000 ($2250 if nonworking spouse is also covered). There is a 6% excise tax on excess contributions.

Example

John Smith, single, earns $5000 in 1982. He contributes $2750 to an IRA account. Mr. Smith is entitled to contribute a maximum of $2000 to his IRA account. Accordingly, $750 ($2750 − $2000) is an excess contribution. Mr. Smith would incur an excise tax penalty of $45 (6% of $750).

The 6% excise tax is a cumulative tax in that the penalty must be paid for each year the excess amount is left in the IRA account.

If you make an excessive contribution it should be withdrawn, as well as any earnings based on it, no later than the time that your tax returns must be filed (including extensions). In this way, you avoid paying the 6% excise tax. Any earnings from the excess contribution are subject to the 10% penalty on premature distributions even if the excess contributions are withdrawn prior to the due date for filing a tax return.

DISTRIBUTIONS

Distributions without penalty can be initiated after age 59½. Distributions must start before the end of the tax year in which you reach age 70½. The following options are available for distribution of funds:

The total amount of the IRA account can be distributed in 1 year.

Periodic payments can be made over

Your life.

The joint lives of you and your spouse.

A fixed period not exceeding your life expectancy.

A fixed period not exceeding the joint life expectancy of you and your spouse.

When you start withdrawing funds at retirement age, the distributions you receive are taxable as ordinary income. Since you were allowed a tax deduction for all contributions and earnings, all of the distributions you receive are taxable. None of the distributions are eligible for capital gains treatment. You may compute your tax liability using the regular income averaging provisions if you qualify for income averaging.

Beneficiaries

If you die before receiving the complete amount included in your IRA, the amount left in the IRA must either (1) be distributed to your beneficiary within 5 years after your death; or (2) be applied to purchase an immediate annuity for the beneficiary payable over the life of, or for a period not exceeding the life expectancy of the beneficiary.

Such an annuity is not required if you and your spouse were receiving prior distributions based on your life expectancies. In those circumstances, distributions may continue beyond 5 years.

Estate Tax

For individuals who die after 1976, the value of an annuity receivable by a beneficiary is excluded from the decedent's gross estate. The annuity must provide a series of substantially equal periodic payments to the beneficiary for life or for a period of at least 36 months after the decedent's death.

Gift Tax

Since December 31, 1976, distributions payable to a beneficiary after your death are not treated as a gift and are not subject to a gift tax.

Divorce

Transfers of IRAs from one spouse to another because of a divorce decree are nontaxable. Effective from the date of transfer, the IRA is considered to be the IRA of the spouse who received it.

SIMPLIFIED EMPLOYEE PENSION PLANS (SEPP)

The requirements of employers who establish and maintain qualified pension plans can be complex and expensive. The Simplified Employee Pension Plan (SEPP) was established so that employers can use IRAs rather than qualified pension plans. If an employer does establish a SEPP, then each employee who has reached age 25 and has worked during at least 3 of the preceding 5 years must be included in the plan.

Through 1981, the employer could contribute up to $7500 or 15% of employee compensation, whichever is less. Starting in 1982, the maximum contribution will be $15,000. The amount that the employer contributes must be included in your income. You in turn can deduct this contribution from your gross income. The employer's contributions must be made under a written allocation formula. The formula cannot discriminate in favor of any class of employee.

Contributions by the employer to a SEPP are fully vested and are subject to the same regulations as other IRA accounts. The employer cannot restrict you from withdrawing funds held in your accounts. You would, however, be subject to the same penalties of other IRA plans for early withdrawals.

If the amount of the employer's contribution is less than the amount you could contribute under the regular IRA rules—up to $2000 of your compensation—you can contribute the difference and take a deduction for the contribution.

Example

Joan Robinson's total compensation, 1982	$20,000
Employer's contribution to SEPP (maximum $2000)	$ 1,000
Joan Robinson's personal contribution (optional) ($2000 − $1000)	$ 1,000

You are not barred from SEPP even if you are covered by a qualified plan, government plan, or tax sheltered annuity. You could not, however, make individual contributions to the IRA in this situation.

FILING REQUIREMENTS

Your allowable deduction for contributions to your IRA is entered on Form 1040. You may use the worksheet contained in the 1040 instructions to assist you in computing your allowable deduction.

If you owe one of the IRA penalty taxes, for instance, excess contributions, premature distributions, prohibited transactions, or underdistributions, you must fill out Form 5329. You must also enter the total amount of IRA tax due on Form 1040. Form 5329 should be filed as an attachment to Form 1040.

If you do not have sufficient income to require filing an income tax return, you should file Form 5329 with the Internal Revenue Service at the same time and place you would have filed Form 1040. A check or money order payable to the IRS should be included.

Periodic payments from an IRA should be reported by the plan sponsor on Form W-2P. Payments that result in a total distribution of your IRA are reported by your sponsor on Form 1099R. All taxable distributions you receive should be reported on Form 1040.

Plan sponsors are required to provide you with a full account of your IRA by June 30 following the end of your tax year. When you make a contribution between January 1 and the due date for filing your return, you should specify which tax year the contribution is for. Unless you specify the year, the sponsor may assume the contribution is for the year in which it is received.

SUMMARY

The IRA account now provides an effective tax shelter for all employees because of the 1981 tax law. There are a wide range of investment alternatives with varying degrees of risk, yield, and potential capital appreciation. These alternatives are discussed in detail in Chapter 9.

Even if you do not contribute to your employer's qualified retirement plan, you may be eligible to set up an IRA account later. If you receive a lump sum distribution from that qualified plan because of termination of employment or because of discontinuation of the plan, you will be able to establish an IRA at that time. Those options are explored in Chapter 10.

A major potential problem associated with an IRA account is the risk of having to withdraw funds prior to retirement. Unless you become disabled, there are significant penalties if you withdraw funds prior to age 59½.

You must also be aware of the *nontax penalties* for changing investments or withdrawing funds both prior to and after retirement age. Once an IRA is established, you may transfer funds from one IRA form of investment into another after 1 year without tax penalty. This may be desirable if you become dissatisfied with the earnings of your initial investment. However, the nontax penalties of switching from your initial investment must be considered. These penalties will vary with the form of investment, and can be severe for certificates of deposit, annuities, and other insurance–investment combinations.

If your spouse does not work, you should consider opening two IRA accounts, one for each of you. There is a twofold advantage in this: (1) the maximum annual tax deduction is larger ($2250 rather than $2000) and (2) if either you or your spouse becomes disabled, the funds in one account can be withdrawn without a tax penalty.

In general, Keoghs and IRAs have many potential advantages if you avoid poor investment choices and penalties. Examine your investment alternatives carefully, and select one that will meet your major investment objectives and yet give you the flexibility to change investments without incurring penalties if your objectives change or if the performance of your initial investment does not meet your expectations.

9 IRA/Self-Employed (Keogh) Investment Alternatives

There are many investment alternatives available for use in your IRA/Keogh investment program. When the Pension Reform Law was passed in 1974, the number of investment alternatives available was limited. The most common investment alternatives were annuity contracts and endowments offered by insurance companies; savings accounts or certificates of deposit offered by banks, savings and loan associations, and credit unions; and individual retirement bonds offered by the U.S. government.

Since the mid-1970s other investment alternatives have become more readily available. These include mutual fund investments, common stock, and other investments managed by a brokerage firm or bank.

Before you select an investment vehicle, it is important to determine your primary investment objectives. What is most important for you: safety of principal, high income, flexibility, or growth potential? Exhibit 9-1 illustrates the estimated ratings of possible investments with respect to these and other criteria.

INFORMATION YOU SHOULD RECEIVE FROM SELLER

Before you establish an IRA/Keogh Plan, you should obtain the answers to the following questions from the seller of the plan:

1   Am I guaranteed the return of the amount of my investment and its earnings? If so, by whom? If not, am I guaranteed a specified amount, and how much will it be?

Exhibit 9-1 Investment Criteria and Comparisons

	IRA Investment Form								
Criteria	Endowment	Annuity	Savings Account	Stock Brokers Account	Saving Certificate (CD)	Money Market Fund	Mutual Fund (General)	Gold/Silver[1] Diamonds	Retirement Bonds
High income	Fair/Good	Fair/Good	Low	Variable	Fair/Good	Good	Variable		Fair
Risk	Low	Low	Low	Variable	Low	Low	Variable		None
Growth potential of capital	None	None	None	Variable	None	None	Variable		None
Administrative costs	High	High	None/Low	Nominal	None/Low	Nominal	Nominal		None
Flexibility	Low	Low	High	High	Low	High	High		High
Front end sales commisions	High	High	None	Medium	None	None	No-Load-None; Load-Medium		None
Study required to make initial selection	High	High	Low	High	Low	Medium	High		Low
Monitoring requirement on your part	Medium	Medium	Low	High	Low	Medium	High		Low

[1]Gold, silver, diamonds and art objects cannot be purchased for IRA or Keogh accounts after 12/31/81.

2   Is there a guaranteed rate of return on my investment? If so, what is it? For how long a period is the rate guaranteed? Will future investments in that same IRA receive the same guarantees?

3   Does the rate of return depend on investment performance? If so, how has the seller's investment performance been in the past years and how does this compare with general market indicators such as the New York Stock Exchange, Dow Jones, or Standard & Poors 500 averages? (If the investment is a mutual fund, review comparative performance and the fund's investment goals.) You can obtain mutual fund comparative data in *Investment Companies Services,* published by Wiesenberger Services, Inc., which you can find in a public library or at your broker's office.

4   What is the total amount of the fees, commissions, administrative costs, or charges of any sort deducted from the amount I invest or from the earnings of the IRA?

5   How much would I receive if I were to withdraw all the funds from my IRA at the end of any of its 5 years? How much would I receive at the ages of 60, 65, and 70? The seller of an IRA is required to give you these figures if the amount of your investment is guaranteed or if the expected value over the years can be figured reasonably. If the future value of your investment cannot now be calculated, the seller of an IRA is required to give you a statement in nontechnical language of any and all charges used to determine the net amount actually invested for you. This includes all charges deducted from your contributions, the method for determining the earnings on your investment, and any charges on those earnings.

The seller of an IRA is also required to give you the following information:

The eligibility requirements for an IRA.

The limitations on contributions.

The taxes on excess contributions.

Penalty taxes on premature distribution.

Penalties for borrowing from your IRA or using it as security for a loan.

This information must be provided no later than the seventh day preceding the establishment of an IRA. If the purchaser is permitted to revoke the IRA within 7 days of its establishment with a full return of money paid, the disclosure statement need not be furnished until the date of the establishment of the IRA. If the written terms of the IRA are amended, you are entitled to a written statement of the changes.

INSURANCE ALTERNATIVES

Many life insurance companies offer endowment contracts that combine insurance protection with a retirement savings program. The portion of your payment to the insurance company associated with insurance is not deductible from your taxes. That cost can amount to $300 annually. You may contribute the difference between your maximum allowable deduction and the amount allocated to the retirement savings portion of the endowment contract to a different IRA plan.

Example

Earnings, 1979	$30,000
Maximum allowable deduction	$ 1,500
Endowment contract premium	$ 1,500
Insurance cost (included in premium)	$ 300
Amount that can be contributed to another IRA plan	$ 300

One of the most difficult problems in evaluating insurance plans is calculating the expected return on your contribution. You should determine if there is a guaranteed rate of return and, if so, what it is. There are large differences in the investment performances of insurance companies for similar types of plans. You should ask the insurance sales agent for documentation that the investment performance of his or her company compares favorably with other insurance companies.

You may wish to do an independent study yourself. A source to consider is *Best's Review,* published monthly and yearly. You should also contact your state insurance department. Many state insurance departments have valuable information, available to you at no cost, that compares the cost/return on various types of insurance offerings. Insurance company costs and return on investment normally do not change dramatically. Therefore, you should select an insurance company only if it has an excellent history of low costs and high returns.

There can be significant differences among insurance plan offerings for other items such as front end fees, cost of early termination, commission, and administrative costs. By law, this information must be provided to you. You should review this type of data carefully, not only for insurance plans but for all plans you are considering.

IRA plans sponsored by insurance companies will not be easy for you to analyze. Do not consider any insurance IRA unless the agent has satisfactorily answered the questions and addressed the issues discussed in this chapter. Then you will be in a better position to compare the important investment factors of the insurance plan you are considering with other alternatives.

In general, life insurance plans do not compare favorably with other investment options for many investment criteria (see Exhibit 9-1). Insurance company plans for financially sound companies receive a high relative score on safety of principal. For many other criteria, however, such as flexibility, commissions and fees, minimum costs for early withdrawal, and growth potential, most insurance plans would not compare favorably with other options available to you.

ANNUITIES

An annuity is an agreement in which an insurance company provides you with a regular periodic income for a specified period or for life in return for a sum of money you give to the insurance company. There are three basic annuity options: fixed, flexible premium, and variable.

Fixed annuities are annuities in which you provide a fixed amount of money to the insurance company for a specific amount of time. This type of annuity can no longer be used as an IRA investment specifically because of the conflicts that can arise if the required annuity payment exceeds the maximum that an individual can contribute in any year.

Flexible Premium Annuity

A flexible premium annuity is an annuity in which your payment to the insurance company can vary each year. The return paid to you by the insurance company is based on the amount of money you contributed and the rate of return that the insurance company pays to you.

In the initial agreement the company will specify a guaranteed rate that can be as low as 3½, even though a much higher rate can be advertised. If interest rates remain high, you may receive more than the guaranteed rate, but a higher rate than the one specified in your agreement is not guaranteed.

When you evaluate annuities, just as you considered insurance investment options, you should consider carefully sales commissions, administrative cost, and early termination penalties. If you start an annuity contract and terminate the plan after a year or two, you will normally suffer heavy penalties.

You should also recognize that a quoted rate of return is based on the amount of your contribution that remains *after* fees and commissions. Accordingly, if you contribute $1000 and the initial sales commission is 40%, the guaranteed rate of return would be applied to $600, not $1000.

Variable Annuity

A variable annuity is one in which the insurance company invests your contributions in stocks or bonds in an attempt to keep pace with inflation. The ultimate return on your investment is based on the investment judgment of the insurance company. The insurance company may specify a minimum guaranteed rate in your contract.

In principal, the variable annuity looks good because you may be protected somewhat from inflation. Unfortunately, insurance companies have not had a very long history with variable annuities. Accordingly, it will be very difficult for you to select an insurance company that has an established track record.

If you establish a variable annuity plan and become dissatisfied with the insurance company's performance, it will be expensive to switch to another IRA form.

If you believe that investment in common stocks or bonds is a desirable inflation hedge, you should consider other IRA alternatives such as established mutual funds or the use of brokerage firms. You should compare closely differences in commissions, fees, as well as history of investment performance (see Exhibit 9-1).

STOCKS AND BONDS

You can purchase stocks and bonds directly from brokers if you use a trustee such as a bank or other qualified trustee. Some brokers have been active in this field by advertising and setting up their own trustee relationship for the use of their clients. The major advantage of this approach is that you and your broker have a wide variety of investments to select from.

Unfortunately, there seem to be many disadvantages. Since the amount of your contributions each year is limited by law, you would normally purchase odd lots, thus paying higher prices. You would also have to pay a minimum commission to the broker for each transaction. Moreover, you would have to pay trustee fees as well as brokerage commissions.

One alternative to consider is to build up assets in an alternate IRA until the asset base is sufficient to minimize odd lot fees and broker commissions. In addition, with a larger asset base you would be able to diversify your investments more effectively.

SAVINGS ACCOUNTS

You can establish an IRA savings account with a bank, savings and loan association, or credit union. The major advantage is flexibility. You can switch from a savings account to another IRA after 1 year without a tax or bank penalty. The major disadvantage is the rate of return. The current rates of 5−5¼% from banks and savings and loan associations are not attractive. Some credit unions sponsor IRAs and pay somewhat higher interest rates than banks. You must be eligible to join the credit union, however.

The interest rates available from banks and credit unions normally will not compare favorably with the rates available on long-term certificates of deposit at banks. When interest rates are generally high, the rates will not compare favorably with the returns available from money market mutual funds either. From a long-term viewpoint, savings accounts are not good vehicles for IRAs. They should be used primarily in specialized short-term situations. For example, you may be undecided about the type of IRA you want in the long run, but you know you want to establish an IRA program. You can contribute funds to a savings account IRA for 1 year while you are evaluating other IRA alternatives. In this situation you receive your tax credit, a minimum return on your investment, and can switch to another IRA after 1 year without penalty.

CERTIFICATES OF DEPOSIT (CD)

The major advantage of certificates of deposit is the high fixed interest rate. The rate is much higher than the rate for savings accounts. The specific rate, which can be higher than 10%, depends on the amount invested and the term of the certificate, which can be from 6 months to 8 years. Rates will vary among banks.

The primary disadvantage of the time deposit is that if you withdraw your funds prior to the certificate's maturity, you are penalized. Some financial institutions will not release the funds prior to the end of the initially agreed on period. For time deposits with maturities of 1 year or less, the minimum penalty for early withdrawal is the loss of 3 month's simple interest. For time deposits with maturities of over 1 year, the minimum penalty is the loss of 6 month's simple interest. Since June 2, 1980, a rule requires financial institutions to reduce the principal amount of the deposit in the event that the loss of interest in penalty fees exceeds the interest earned up to the date of withdrawal.

Another important factor related to flexibility is that the Bank *does not* have to release the funds allocated if the CD has not matured. The choice is up to the individual bank. Some banks have chosen to refuse to allow IRA holders to withdraw funds prior to maturity. You should discuss this factor with the bank and ask them what their policy is. You should specifically ask if they have ever refused a depositor funds under these circumstances. If they have refused, find another bank. The vast majority of banks will allow early withdrawals (subject to penalties).

Some institutions use each new deposit to calculate the date on which the *entire amount* can be withdrawn without penalty. This type of calculation can result in penalties of up to $50,000 in lost interest depending on how the agreement is written. You must read the agreement carefully. Agreements vary among financial institutions. You should select an institution that does not extend the term for all funds deposited. If you must withdraw some funds from your IRA before a CD matures, you certainly do not want to pay any penalties for funds deposited in a different CD.

Once the CD matures, you can rollover the funds into another IRA without penalty. If you do not exercise that option, a new CD is created with a new maturity. For example, assume you have an 8-year CD for $1000. If you do not transfer the funds out of the IRA at maturity, you have an 8-year extension to the CD. If you then want to withdraw funds you again would be subject to the early withdrawal penalties.

Some institutions charge fees. Do not select an institution that charges fees unless you feel they offer you flexibility or services that other institutions do not.

There are differences between the IRS and banking regulations with respect to penalties for early withdrawal of funds. For example, the IRS imposes penalties if an IRA holder withdraws funds prior to age 59½, unless he or she is disabled. The banks' penalties are independent of the IRS. Even if an individual becomes physically disabled and could avoid IRS penalties, he or she could not avoid early withdrawal penalties from the bank unless the CD has matured. The banking regulations permit funds to be withdrawn without penalty only if an individual is considered mentally incompetent.

The banks can, at *their option*, after the investor reaches age 59½, permit funds to be withdrawn without penalty if the CD has not matured. The bank does not have to specify in advance whether they will execute this option. Therefore, you must understand what the bank's policy is before you initiate any withdrawals from an non-matured CD, even if you have reached retirement age.

There is a conflict between IRS penalties and bank penalties in other circumstances. For example, assume an individual establishes a CD which mature prior to age 59½. If she withdraws the principal and interest, she avoids bank penalties but does have IRS penalties. If she decides to leave the funds in the bank and start a new CD, she avoids the IRS penalty but may face a bank penalty if she withdraws the funds after age 59½ but before the new CD matures. One way to avoid this type of problem is to rollover the matured CD to another investment form such as a no-load mutual fund, a government bond, or a passbook savings account.

In summary, CDs are complicated. Make sure you understand the bank's agreement before you initiate an IRA. Once you have established one, consider your options carefully as your CDs mature.

MUTUAL FUNDS

A mutual fund traditionally was a medium through which money was invested in a diversified selection of stocks and bonds. Mutual funds have recently been initiated that specialize in precious metals and commodities. Many mutual funds offer IRA and Keogh plans.

A major problem in using mutual funds is selection. There will be a wide variation in performance between the best and worst mutual fund during a specific span of time. To complicate the selection problem further, a fund may perform very well for one time period and poorly for other time periods. Each year, in August or Setpember, *Forbes* publishes a history of performance of the larger funds for the previous 12 months and for prior periods.

Some mutual funds charge a sales commission of up to 8.5%. Some funds, called no-loads, are sold directly from the fund itself and charge no sales commission. You can get a directory of the major no-load funds for $1 by writing to No Load Mutual Fund Association, Inc., Valley Forge, Pennsylvania 19481. You can also call directly at (215) 783-7600 or (212) 661−8030. You should buy a fund that charges a sales commission only if you are satisfied that its expected performance will be sufficiently better than the best no-load funds that charge no commission. All funds charge management fees averaging ½ of 1% of assets per year. This is not a high fee if the performance is good. Some funds charge a nominal fee for share redemption.

There are some funds, called money market or money funds, which invest only in high quality market instruments maturing in 1 year or less. These funds, although not federally insured, carry relatively little risk of loss of principal since short-term instruments fluctuate very little in value. When short-term interest rates are high, the rate of return will exceed 10% for most funds.

Short-term interest rates do fluctuate, however, and investors who initially invest in money market funds should monitor the treasury bill rate, which is the "bell-wether" of short-term rates. That rate is published in the major financial newspapers daily. Most funds have toll-free telephone numbers that you can use to determine what rate your money is earning. Thus as long as interest rates are high, you can keep your money in the money market funds. You can switch to other alternatives if interest rates fall.

Many large mutual funds sponsor money market and other funds such as common stock funds. These give you the flexibility of switching without penalty from one fund to another in that mutual fund family, even if your holding period is less than 1 year. Federal law specifies that funds cannot be rolled over from one IRA account to another without penalty unless the investment has been made for at least 1 year.

If you simply change your investment from one mutual fund to another with the *same mutual fund family*, the IRS does not consider it a rollover. You cannot, however, switch from one mutual fund to another in a different family without penalty before the 1-year waiting period. You always have the flexibility after 1 year to switch from a mutual fund investment to any other IRA investment form.

There are administrative fees associated with mutual fund investments. These fees are usually nominal, but the fee will vary with the fund.

In summary, there are many advantages of mutual fund IRAs. You have a wide selection of investment objectives to choose from. Administrative fees are low. There are no commissions if you select a no-load fund. You have much flexibility, especially if you select a fund that includes many funds in its family. You can rollover your mutual fund IRAs into other IRA forms without penalty after the federally mandated 1-year period.

The major disadvantage is the selection process. Since there are so many funds to select from, you have to do your homework properly. You must first determine your investment objectives and then select an established fund with a good track record consistent with your investment objectives.

Another disadvantage is the monitoring process. You cannot simply make your selection and not follow up on it. You must monitor progress, and if the performance of the fund is poor you should consider switching your funds either to another fund or to a different form of IRA when you can do so without penalty.

Although you must do some homework and some monitoring, the advantages of mutual funds as an IRA alternative are considerable. You should not select another form of IRA without giving this investment vehicle some consideration.

RETIREMENT BONDS

The U.S. government issues retirement bonds for both Keogh and IRA accounts. They are available in denominations of $50, $100, and $500. The law currently provides an interest rate of 8% per year compounded semiannually. These rates are adjusted periodically to reflect changes in interest rates. There are no administrative fees for retirement bonds. If you hold these bonds less than 1 year they earn no interest. After you reach age 70½ they do not earn interest. You can transfer from bonds to any type of IRA after 1 year with no penalty. You *cannot*, however, rollover bonds in *Keogh* plans into other forms of investment. The major advantages of these bonds in IRA accounts are safety of principal, no fees, and flexibility in transferring to other investment options. The major disadvantage is the relatively low interest rate in relation to the rate of inflation.

These bonds are not recommended for Keogh plans because of the restriction pertaining to rollovers.

SELF-DIRECTED ACCOUNTS

During the late 1970s many banks and financial organizations offered their services as trustees for self-directed accounts. The purpose of these accounts was to give IRA and Keogh investors the flexibility to select a wide variety of investments. During the 1970s many investors utilized these accounts to invest in gold, silver, diamonds, and fine art objects. In the late 1970s and early 1980s there was no legal restriction prohibiting the purchase of these investments for IRA/Keogh plans.

The 1981 tax law specifically excluded the purchase of gold, silver, diamonds, stamps, art works and other collectibles for Keogh/IRA plans in 1982 and thereafter. The law does not indicate that investments already made have to be liquidated. This amendment was undoubtedly included to assist the savings and loan industry regain some of the assets it had lost in the late 1970s and early 1980s to the money market funds and other popular investments. The amendment does not prevent you from purchasing mutual funds, offering Keogh/IRA plans, which specialize in the type of asset you would like to invest in.

The following banks will act as custodians for Keogh or IRA accounts in which you select your investments: First Citizens Bank & Trust Company of South Carolina; Central Bank, Oakland, California; Clayton Trust Co., St. Louis, Missouri; Lafayette Bank & Trust Co., Bridgeport, Connecticut; and Lincoln Trust Co., Denver, Colorado. Some brokerage firms, such as Merrill Lynch Pierce Fenner & Smith, Inc., also offer self-directed accounts. The administrative fees vary among banks and brokerage firms.

SUMMARY

There are many investment alternatives available for you to choose from for your IRA or Keogh plans. You must first establish your investment objectives and then determine which alternatives are consistent with them.

Although CDs are the most popular form of investment, these plans are not flexible and should be used only if you are reasonably sure you are going to hold the CD to maturity. You must also make sure you understand the provisions of the CD agreement, and in the case of early withdrawals make sure that you are penalized only on the amount you withdraw and not on the total of *all* deposits you have made to other CDs.

Insurance related plans are also inflexible, have high commissions and fees, and generally have a low rate of return. It is unlikely that the value of this form of investment will keep pace with inflation.

The no-load money market funds are attractive when interest rates are high. Fees are low, and there are no sales commissions. You have flexibility after 1 year to switch to other investment vehicles without penalty. Within the same mutual fund family, you can rollover your funds many times a year, subject to restrictions of the individual mutual fund.

In addition to the money market mutual funds, there are other categories of mutual funds that you can select, and there are many funds within each category. You should be able to find a fund that meets your investment objectives. The other advantages are low initial fees (for no-load funds) and flexibility. The major potential problem is selecting the fund. There are many funds, and performances of funds can vary from one time period to the next by significant percentages. Accordingly, fund selection is not that easy. This problem can be minimized somewhat by utilizing more than one fund and by switching out of funds that perform poorly. There are generally no special penalties for switching out of funds as long as your investment is left in for at least 1 year.

In general you must select an IRA investment using essentially the same criteria you would use for any other investment you would make. The difference is that you must also consider the potential tax and nontax penalties when you decide to withdraw funds.

If you don't think you are going to keep funds in an IRA until age 59½, you should not even initiate one. The tax penalties will be prohibitive. The nontax penalties vary with each form of investment and can be substantial. You must make sure you understand these potential penalties *before* you initiate an IRA/Keogh plan.

10 IRA Rollovers

A rollover contribution is a transfer of your retirement savings from one type of investment into another covered under an IRA. The initial investment could be derived from another form of IRA, or it could result from a lump sum distribution from an employer with whom you had a qualified pension plan or profit-sharing plan.

TIMING REQUIREMENTS

You are now permitted to make a rollover contribution from one IRA to another without reporting the distribution in gross income as long as the rollover occurs within 60 days after the date of the distribution.

Prior to 1978 you were allowed only one rollover every 3 years. The regulations have been changed so that you can now make a rollover contribution from one IRA to another once each year as long as each rollover is more than 1 year apart. (As indicated in the discussion of IRA investment alternatives in Chapter 9, if you choose an investment company that has more than one mutual fund in its family, you may be able to switch from one mutual fund to another within that mutual fund family many times during a year, subject to the restrictions of the sponsoring mutual fund.)

Although federal laws allow you to rollover your IRA funds once a year without federal penalty, there may be other penalties depending on your initial investment selection choice. Penalties could result in transfers from the following types of IRA investments: life insurance, annuities, and certificates of deposit. These penalties are explained in detail in Chapter 9.

Since there can be substantial penalties in switching from one investment to another, it is very important for you to determine the amount of assets that you will be able to rollover into a new IRA after penalties. If there is a substantial penalty, you should reconsider whether you wish to rollover your funds at all.

For certain types of IRA accounts certain times are more effective than others to consider rollovers. For example, if your initial IRA investment was in certificates of deposit, the best time to switch would be after the certificate matures. For insurance and annuity programs your fees are generally higher in the first year or so. A rollover after only 1 year would be expensive. If you initially invested in a money market mutual fund you should consider switching out after 1 year if short-term rates have fallen substantially. For government bond IRA's there is no rollover penalty after 1 year.

PROPERTY DISTRIBUTION

Property distributed from one IRA to another must be rolled over within 60 days from the date it was received. The *same* property must be rolled over. In other words, you cannot sell the property and submit a different asset form into the new IRA.

CHANGE IN TRUSTEESHIP

The funds in your IRA account can be transferred from one trustee to another. This is not considered a rollover as long as none of the funds are distributed to you. Because this transfer is not a rollover, the 1-year waiting period does not apply.

TRANSFERS TO ENDOWMENT CONTRACTS

You may wish to convert your IRA plan to an endowment contract. The trustee or custodian of your existing IRA plan can use the assets from your IRA to purchase an endowment contract. This will be treated as a rollover.

If your purchase any life insurance, the sum of money used for life insurance protection must be included as gross income for income tax purposes. However, there would not be a 10% federal penalty on premature distributions.

TRANSFER OF LUMP SUM DISTRIBUTIONS

If you receive a lump sum distribution from your employer's qualified plan, you have the option to rollover some of the proceeds into an IRA, subject to the following restrictions:

1 The distribution you received must represent your entire interest in your employer's plan.
2 Only the portion that includes your employer's contribution and earnings can be rolled over tax-free.
3 The rollover must be completed within 60 days after you receive the distribution.

You may roll the distribution over even if you did not establish an IRA account previously. For example, assume you are leaving one firm in which you were not eligible to set up an IRA (i.e. prior to 1982 your employer had a qualified plan). You still would be allowed to establish an IRA with your distribution from the first qualified plan. Since 60 days is such a short time, if you are getting a lump sum distribution it is important for you to plan adequately in advance to choose an IRA consistent with your investment objectives.

ROLLOVER OF PROCEEDS FROM SALE OF PROPERTY

If you receive a lump sum distribution after 1978 from a qualified plan that consists either wholly or partly of property other than cash, you may qualify to receive a tax-free rollover. You can contribute the proceeds of the sale of the property to an IRA other than an endowment contract within 60 days of the distribution date.

For example, assume you received a qualified lump sum cash distribution of $10,000 and corporate bonds valued at $40,000 on January 1, 1980. You sell the bonds on January 15, 1981 for $45,000. On February 1, 1981, you rollover $55,000 (10,000 + $45,000) into an IRA account. You would not have to pay a capital gains tax on the $5000 gain.

PARTIAL ROLLOVER FROM SALE OF PROPERTY

You may not wish to allocate the entire proceeds of the distribution you receive. If you allocate part of the proceeds of your distribution to an IRA, you will have tax obligations, either ordinary income or capital gains, for the part of the proceeds you exclude from the IRA. The portion of the proceeds rolled over will be tax-free until those funds are taken out of the IRA.

DETERMINING TAX LIABILITY

Your tax liability can be ordinary income, capital gains, or both. Ordinary income is computed by multiplying the fair market value of the property on the date of the distribution by the ratio of proceeds retained to the total proceeds of the sale.

The amount of capital gain or loss is computed by multiplying the difference between the fair market value of the property on the sale date and the fair market value on the distribution date by the same ratio (retained proceeds divided by total proceeds).

When you receive cash and property in a qualified distribution and don't roll over the entire proceeds into an IRA, the allocation of the cash rollover and the allocation of the property rollover must be determined. There are two options available to you. You can make your own selection by filing a written designation with the IRS. This selection must be made no later than the due date for filing the return in question.

If you do not make a selection, the rollover is prorated between the cash distribution received from the plan and the value of any property received as determined on the distribution date. It is to your advantage to make the selection that will minimize your immediate tax liability.

YOUR OWN CONTRIBUTION

If you have made contributions to your employer's plan, you are permitted to indicate which portion of the lump sum distribution was associated with your contributions and which portion of the money and property was associated with your employer's. You must make this designation by the due date for filing your tax return for the year. If you do not make this designation, each item, property, or money distributed will be prorated, based on the proportion of total employee-to-employer contributions.

You cannot rollover any portion of your contributions. The amount that can be rolled over is limited to all or any part of the employer's contribution.

KEOGH PLAN ROLLOVER

Under certain circumstances, you can rollover a lump-sum distribution from a Keogh plan into an IRA. You must either have reached age 59½ or be disabled at the time of the distribution to be eligible.

QUALIFIED PLANS AND IRA ROLLOVERS

If an employer's qualified plan ends, employees can rollover their balance tax-free within 1 tax year after plan termination. This rollover is permitted even if you continue to work for the same employer.

PARTIAL ROLLOVERS OF LUMP SUM DISTRIBUTIONS

Under the latest revisions of the law, you may rollover tax-free any part of the distribution placed into an IRA with 60 days of the distribution date. The amount eligible for IRA that you choose not to rollover is taxed as ordinary income. The amount is not eligible for income averaging nor does it qualify for capital gains treatment.

TAX SHELTERED ANNUITY

Recent changes in the law have benefited employees who are recipients of lump sum distributions under a tax sheltered annuity by an employee of a tax-exempt organization or a public school. If you are the recipient of such a distribution, you can rollover the taxable portion of a lump sum distribution or transfer made after 1978 to an IRA.

SURVIVING SPOUSE

A surviving spouse can rollover any portion of a lump sum distribution completed after 1978 from an employer's qualified plan to an IRA.

SALES OF SUBSIDIARY OR CORPORATE ASSETS

You may be eligible for a tax-free rollover if you are an employee of a corporation and receive a distribution from a qualified retirement plan in connection with a liquidation, sale, or other termination of the corporation's parent-subsidiary. The same situation could result if your corporation sells or transfers assets to another corporation and as a result you receive a distribution.

You are eligible for a tax-free rollover if the following conditions exist:

1 No employees of the employer corporation or the acquiring corporation are active participants in a distributing retirement plan at the time the distribution is made.
2 The distribution is made no later than the end of the second calendar year after the calendar year in which the termination of the parent-subsidiary or controlled group relationship, or the sale or transfer of assets occurs.
3 The distribution constitutes the balance to your credit under the plans and is paid to you in one tax year.

SUMMARY

Legislation effective in 1978 has made it easier for individuals to participate in IRA rollovers. The most significant change is related to partial rollovers. Before 1978, if you received a distribution from an employer's qualified plan or profit-sharing plan, you would have to place all of the distribution into an IRA.

Now you can allocate any portion of the employer's distribution into the IRA. Any portion of the employer's distribution you choose not to place in the IRA will be treated as ordinary income by the IRS.

You may be eligible to establish an IRA with funds contributed by your employer to a qualified plan. When you receive a distribution from your employer, you are eligible to open an IRA account. You must, however, open the account within a fixed time period after the distribution. Remember that your savings in opening the IRA are twofold:

1 You postpone paying ordinary income on the distribution you place in the IRA.
2 The funds placed in the IRA will earn tax-free income as long as you do not withdraw any funds from the IRA.

11 Self-Employed Plans (Keogh)

Keogh plans were authorized initially by Congress in 1962 by the Smothers-Keogh Act, or the Self-Employed Individual Retirement Act of 1962. The intent of the act was to enable self-employed individuals to establish tax sheltered retirement plans for themselves and their employees. Contributions to a qualififed Keogh plan, within established limits, may be deducted from income, and income earned on assets in the plan are tax-free. When funds are withdrawn from the plan at retirement, taxes must then be paid by the recipients of the income.

In 1974, the Tax Reform Act (ERISA), which modified the 1962 legislation, was passed by Congress. Under the Tax Reform Act, the maximum deductible contribution was increased from 10% of earned income not to exceed $2500 to 15% of earned income not to exceed $7500 per year. In addition, a provision in ERISA was introduced allowing self-employed individuals to set up a different type of Keogh plan, known as defined benefit Keogh plans. These plans allow contributions to exceed the $7500 maximum contribution for other Keogh plans, called defined contribution plans. In 1981 the tax laws were revised to allow up to $15,000 per year contributions, starting in 1982.

The most severe restriction associated with Keogh plans is the requirement that self-employed individuals *must* include their employees in any Keogh plan they establish for themselves. Self-employed people who do not want to establish Keogh plans for their employees can establish IRA plans for themselves as an alternative. Under the IRA plan you are allowed to contribute a maximum of $2000 per year of your earned income.

DEFINED CONTRIBUTION PLAN

A defined contribution plan provides an individual account for each participant. Benefits are based on the amount contributed to the participant's account and any

117

income, expenses, gains and losses, and forfeitures of accounts of other participants that may be allocated to a participant's account. A major limitation of the defined contribution plan is the maximum amount that can be contributed to the plan each year. That maximum, which is explained in detail in this Chapter, can be no higher than $15,000 per year.

DEFINED BENEFIT PLAN

According to the IRS, a defined benefit plan is any plan that is not a defined contribution plan. In practical terms, the contribution to the defined benefit plan is based on the desired retirement benefits. Contributions can be made, subject to specific limitations, to meet these desired retirement benefits. There is no yearly maximum contribution of $15,000 specified for the defined contribution plan.

You are allowed to have a retirement benefit equal to a percentage of each year's earnings. The percentage depends on your age when you enter the plan. The following table is applicable:

Age	Percentage
30 or Less	6.5%
35	5.4%
40	4.4%
45	3.6%
50	3.0%
55	2.5%
60 and over	2.0%

The percentage is applied to earned income up to $50,000 and does not change during one period of participation. The yearly benefit cannot exceed the lesser of $75,000 or 100% of the highest average 3-year compensation.

CONTRIBUTIONS—DEFINED BENEFIT PLAN

Defined benefit contributions are not subject to the 15% limitation associated with defined contribution plans. The contributions are based on the amount necessary to provide the specified retirement benefit. This calculation is determined and provided to the IRS by an enrolled actuary.

Your initial contribution to a defined benefit plan would initially be 70% higher than it would be with a defined contribution plan. Subsequent contributions would vary depending on the investment return and any changes in annuity rates.

This type of plan is more expensive to establish and maintain than the more common defined contribution plan. For example, banks that establish this type of plan—and not many do—normally charge more than $200 per year to establish and maintain it.

CONTRIBUTIONS—DEFINED CONTRIBUTION PLAN

The maximum contribution in any tax year that can be made to the plan is the lesser of (1) $15,000 or (2) 15% of earned income.

Example

In 1982, Lee Morgan, self-employed, earns $90,000.

Maximum Limitation	$15,000
15% × $90,000	$13,500
Limit	$13,500

The *minimum contribution* may be equal to the lesser of (1) $750 or (2) 100% of earned income if less than $750.

In other words, the IRS code allows minimum contributions above the 15% maximum if 15% of earnings are below $750.

Example

In 1978, Robert Smith, self-employed on a part-time basis, earns $700.

Maximum limitation	$750
100% of earned income	$700
Minimum	$700

QUALIFICATION

An individual who has earned income from personal services for any tax year is considered a self-employed individual and may be covered as an employee under a qualified plan.

The Self-Employed Individuals Tax Retirement Act of 1962 permits self-employed individuals to be treated like employees. Therefore, they may be included in qualified pension, annuity, profit-sharing, and bond purchase plans. *However, a plan that includes self-employed individuals must provide benefits for employees on a nondiscriminatory basis.* In other words, employers cannot set up self-employed plans for themselves and exclude other employees at their discretion.

Many self-employed individuals who are eligible to set up self-employed plans choose to set up IRA accounts for themselves. In that way they can get some tax benefits without the additional expenses of establishing retirement plans for all employees. An employer who establishes his or her own IRA account is under no obligation to set up retirement accounts for employees. Since the IRA upper contribution ($1500) is less than the upper limit for Keogh accounts ($7500), a smaller retirement fund would result.

When a plan includes self-employed individuals, none of whom are owner- −employees, the qualification requirements that apply to plans of corporate employers in general apply.

For example, a qualified plan must:

Be in writing.

Be in effect within the tax year for which qualification is sought.

Be the type of plan contemplated by the statute: (When a self-employed individual is covered, it must be a pension, profit-sharing annuity, or bond purchase plan as defined in the regulations.)

Be established by the employer for the benefit of employees or their beneficiaries.

Be a funded plan—that is, trust, custodial account, insured, or bond purchase plan.

Benefit a stipulated percentage of employees or, alternatively, the employer may establish a classification of employees not found by the Internal Revenue Service to discriminate in favor of highly paid employees.

Not discriminate in favor of the highly paid employees through contributions or benefits.

Owner—employees can establish plans that include themselves. If so, the plan must meet the qualifications outlined above, as well as additional ones that apply specifically to owner—employees. For example, a plan that includes owner—employees must limit the amount of contributions made on behalf of any owner—employee to the contributions made for other employees covered in the plan. In other words, the owner cannot allocate 15% of his or her earnings to the plan and allocate only 10% of the earnings of the other covered employees.

An employer can establish a plan that permits employees to make additional *voluntary* contributions. These contributions can be up to 10% of the employees' pay. The contributions are not tax deductible, but earnings on the contributions accumulate tax-free. Employees who allow their employees to make voluntary contributions can also make voluntary contributions. This contribution cannot exceed 10% of earned income or $2500, whichever is less. Voluntary contributions cannot be made if the plan is limited to self-employed persons.

The owner—employee may elect to set up a plan separate from the other employees. If so, contributions made to the *owner-employees* plan cannot exceed contributions made for other employees in the other plan.

If the owner-employee receives any premature distribution, no contribution may be made in behalf of that owner-employee for 5 tax years after the year the distribution is made.

ELIGIBILITY

The plan must be established for each full-time employee having 3 or more years of continuous service. The plan does not have to be established for employees included in a collective bargaining agreement or for nonresident alien employees who do not earn income in the United States.

INVESTMENT ALTERNATIVES

You have the same investment alternatives with Keogh plans that you have with IRA plans. Since the contributions you make with Keogh plans can be greater than those allowable under IRA accounts, you do have a little more flexibility with certain types of investments. For example, establishing an IRA account with a brokerage firm is discouraged because of the odd lost costs and the fixed administrative costs. For larger annual contributions than the $2000 IRA maximum, this alternative is more attractive if stock purchases can be made in full lots. Administrative costs, normally fixed, would be spread across a larger asset base and would represent a smaller percent of assets in the plan.

In general, investment alternatives that can be more attractive in Keogh plans than in IRA plans are those with the following characteristics:

Fixed administration costs.

Lower percentage costs with larger investments.

Higher expected percentage return on assets with larger investments.

As pointed out in Chapter 9, you should be wary of purchasing government retirement bonds for Keogh plans since you cannot roll them over into any other investment form. With any other investment, you can switch, without federal penalty, after 1 year.

ADVANTAGES

There are two primary advantages associated with self-employed retirement plans:

1   A tax deduction is allowed for funds that are contributed to these plans. These contributions would not be taxed until withdrawals from the plan are initiated.

2   The income earned on the funds invested in the plan is not taxable until the funds are withdrawn.

Example

John Roberts started a plan in 1978 at age 25 and does not expect to extract funds from the plan until age 65 in 2018. The funds Mr. Roberts puts in the plan starting in 1978 and any income earned on those funds in that year and in subsequent years will not be taxable until 2018, assuming Mr. Roberts does not make any withdrawals until that year. If Mr. Roberts' retirement income is less than his average income during his working years, Mr. Roberts would be paying lower taxes than he would have had he not initiated a Keogh plan.

DISADVANTAGES

Although there are significant tax advantages associated with the use of Keogh plans, there are significant disadvantages if the funds are withdrawn prematurely or if excess contributions are made.

Premature Distributions

Except in case of disability, an owner-employee cannot withdraw funds from the plan prior to age 59½ without incurring penalties. The penalty for a premature distribution is 10% of the amount received.

The 10% penalty is in addition to the normal income tax that must be paid. There may be an additional penalty depending on the method of investment selected. For example, if the alternative investment was in bank certificates of deposit (CDs), there would probably be additional penalties in terms of losing 90 or 180 days of interest.

Example

In 1980 John Jones needs money urgently to meet a personal emergency. He is not disabled. He is considering the withdrawal of $1000 from his Keogh plan, which is invested in a 9% $5000, 8-year certificate of deposit. He is in the 40% income bracket.

If he withdraws the $1000, he must pay a $100 penalty (10% of $1000) to the IRS. He would also have to pay on income tax of $400 (40% of $1000). Mr. Jones would probably lose some interest on his CD, depending on his agreement with the bank that is custodian of his plan. The penalty for early withdrawal of funds from uncompleted CDs is 180 days of interest if the maturity of the CD is 1 year or longer. Therefore, there would be an additional loss of $225 (180/360 × 5000 × 9%). In summary, the total penalty and tax of the early withdrawal of $1000 would be $725 ($100 + $400 + $225).

As the example illustrates, the penalties associated with early withdrawals can be severe. Individuals who qualify for Keogh or IRA plans must give serious consideration to having adequate emergency reserves exclusive of Keogh or IRA retirement plans, because the penalties of early withdrawal can be severe.

An individual is disqualified from making contributions to a Keogh plan for 5 years after a premature distribution. An owner-employee is permitted to withdraw voluntary contributions from a qualified plan without penalty.

A tax-free rollover may be made prior to age 59½ when a Keogh plan is terminated. In this way, the 10% is avoided and income taxes do not have to be paid. The plan owner will not be able to participate in any Keogh plan for 5 years after the rollover. There may be other penalties, however, based on the form of investment. As indicated in the previous example, there may be lost interest if a rollover results in terminating a CD contract before maturity.

Excess Contributions

If more funds are contributed to a plan than are allowed, there is a 6% excise tax imposed on the excess contribution.

Example

John Smith earns $50,000 in 1978.

Maximum contribution allowable (15% × 50,000)	$7500
Amount contributed in plan in 1978	$8000
Excess contribution	$ 500
Penalty	$ 30

The tax is cumulative. An excess contribution made in 1 year is subject to tax in subsequent years unless a correction is made.

SUMMARY

For self-employed individuals, Keogh plans provide a vehicle by which individuals can shelter up to $15,000 of their earned income and also shelter the earnings on their investments. There is a wide variety of investment options available to satisfy any investment objective.

One major disadvantage is that once the funds have been invested they are not accessible until age 59½ without significant penalties.

The second potential disadvantage is that employers who establish Keogh plans themselves must set up plans for all of their employees. If they prefer not to establish plans for all employees, they can establish IRA accounts for themselves, thus restricting their maximum contribution to $2000 per year.

12 Traditional Investments

Whether you decide to concentrate on traditional or nontraditional investments, there are two important investment evaluations that you must make. First you must determine what your primary investment goals are. Then you must determine how to achieve your investment objectives. Specifically, how active a role do you plan to take in achieving your investment objectives?

There are two extreme positions you can take. You can be active in every investment decision. You can do your own research regarding every stock, bond, or real estate venture and essentially use brokers simply as order takers to executive your decisions.

The other extreme position would be to turn over your income/assets to a trusted investment advisor, and allow him or her to invest for you, given your investment objectives.

Obviously you do not have to assume either extreme position. You can make some independent investment decisions and also use investment advice from professionals in selected fields. There is no right solution for everyone. The strategies you use should be based on factors such as the time you are willing to spend, your investment acumen, the amount of money you have to invest, and the track record of your investment advisor.

In this book no attempt is made to sway you one way or the other regarding the role you should play, since it should be your decision. However, some of the alternatives available regarding investment advisers and the associated advantages and disadvantages are pointed out.

COMMON STOCKS

Overview

You can consider investment in common stocks in two separate time periods associated with your retirement planning. The first period occurs before retirement when you are still working full-time and wish to build up your capital base. The second period is subsequent to your retirement, when you are probably more concerned with dividend income than with capital growth.

Pre-retirement

Prior to retirement your major concern should be selecting leading stocks in growth industries. Industries that should be of interest to you in this category are data processing, energy, leisure, and mining (precious metals). Your major concern in selecting companies should be those that have shown a higher growth rate than their competition in both sales and earnings. Your broker should be able to help you select companies that fall into this category. If you want to do your own research, Value Line, Standard & Poors, and Moody's are reliable sources of information.

You may prefer to have diversified holdings, and prefer professional investment advisors to make your selections for you. If so, you should consider purchasing a no-load mutual fund which has shown better than average growth. The No-Load directory, referenced in the discussion of mutual funds in this chapter should be valuable to you. The directory does not contain investment history of the various funds. You can obtain that information from Wiesenberger's Investment Companies Service, Standard & Poors, or from *Forbes'* annual survey published each August or September.

Even if you decide to select your own securities, you can obtain valuable information from the best performing mutual funds. At no cost the funds will send you their latest quarterly report containing their holdings at that time, as well as their latest purchases and sales.

Recent surveys have shown that smaller companies in the aggregate have outperformed larger companies in terms of stock market performance when performance is measured over a long time. Therefore, you should not restrict your selection to large companies. There are many sources available that identify small growing companies. Many of the larger brokerage firms conduct selected studies leading to the identification of growth companies. Many of these studies are available at no cost. You can also examine the latest report of the leading mutual funds specializing in small companies. *Barron's*, a weekly newspaper, is another source you should consider for information about small, growing companies as well as general financial conditions.

During the pre-retirement period your primary objective probably will be growth. If so, you should not be too concerned with high dividends. In fact, if the dividend payment for a specific stock represents too high a percentage of earnings, you should question purchasing that stock for your growth portfolio. If a stock is paying more than 50% of its earnings in dividends, it is unlikely that the company can be a true growth company since it is reinvesting a relatively small portion of its income.

Postretirement

After you have reached retirement age, your investment objectives probably will change considerably. You may no longer be as concerned with growth as with income and preservation of capital.

You should now be considering common stocks that have paid dividends each quarter for years and have a history of increasing dividends. You should also examine earnings growth patterns, since it is not likely that a company can continue to increase its dividend payout if earnings are not increasing as well. Just because a company has had a solid history of dividend payment and growth does not mean that this pattern will continue. Industries and companies can run into difficulties that will have an impact on dividend policy as well as the market price of the common stock.

It is a good idea to diversify your holdings so that if one company runs into problems the impact on you is minimal. If your asset base is too small to diversify among many companies, you should consider investing in no-load mutual funds that specialize in income securities and have a good performance history. More detailed information on mutual fund investment is contained later in this chapter.

Historically, the industry most consistent in paying high dividends and increasing dividend payout is the utility industry. Although the stocks of the auto industry and steel industry at times have provided good dividends, the current problems these industries face in the world suggest that they are too speculative for most retirees' holdings.

Ideally, you would like to receive high dividends and also see your investments increase in value. Although this can happen, you will find that as general interest rates rise the value of your securities that are primarily dividend-oriented will fall. Accordingly, you should not be too surprised to see the value of your investment go down as interest rates rise. This will be true even if you invested only in the most conservative, well-managed companies. However, if interest rates fall, the value of your securities should increase in value.

If you are dependent on dividends from your investment to provide you with necessities, you certainly do not want to invest in any company whose future is uncertain, and whose dividend is questionable. There are other investment alternatives to consider that can provide you with more guaranteed income. For example, annuities from insurance companies and long-term government bonds are two alternatives that will provide you with more secure income. These investment alternatives have some negative factors, however, such as the lack of growth potential.

From a tax viewpoint, corporate stocks have a limited advantage. Up to 1980, the first $100 ($200 for a joint return) you received in income was tax deductible. In 1981, this exemption was doubled to $200 ($400 for a joint return). In 1982, and thereafter the exemption will be $100 ($200) again.

There are some stocks, mostly utilities, that have a special tax advantage. One advantage is that some or all of the income you receive is not taxable as dividends. These distributions are categorized as return of capital. When you sell the securities, your buying price must be adjusted by any tax-free dividends you have received.

Example

You purchased 100 shares of ABC company at $100 per share. The company pays $5.00 per share in distributions for 5 years, which, according to the company, are not taxable but are a return of capital. For 5 years you did not have to pay any tax on the distribution. Assume you now sell the shares for $105 per share. According to the IRS, your adjusted cost is not $100 per share but $75.00 because you received $25 in total distributions over 5 years, thus reducing your effective cost. You must report a profit of $30 ($105 − $75) per share. You would pay taxes on your profit at the capital gains tax rate, since you have held the securities for more than 1 year.

Although this type of security seems attractive, there are two additional factors you should consider. First, the tax status of the stock can and does change. The company may have obtained this special tax status because of a specific sale of property. Once the distributions related to these proceeds have been exhausted, the tax status for future distributions will be taxed at normal rates.

Second, once you reach retirement age, your tax situation will probably change considerably. If most of your income is nontaxable, there may be limited advantages of this type of distribution. Standard & Poors and Moody's publish a list of companies whose distributions are wholly or partially tax exempt. Your broker should be able to obtain a list for you.

A second tax advantage originated in the 1981 tax legislation. Effective in 1982, stockholders in qualified public utilities can elect to receive dividends in common stock rather than cash. If you elect this option, the dividends will not be taxed as ordinary income, but at capital gains rates when the stock is sold. The stock must be held longer than 1 year. The limit is $750 ($1500 joint) per year.

Summary

Common stocks offer you the opportunity to achieve investment objectives such as income and growth. During the 1970s, the stock market in the United States did not perform well in the aggregate. Selected industries and companies, however, did very well, as will always be the case. Successful investing in the stock market in the years ahead will require ongoing research and continual reevaluation by either you or your investment advisor. Many industries in the United States are fighting for survival because of complex factors. U.S. industry is now facing difficult foreign competition in virtually every field. The combination of foreign competition and continual U.S. inflation will make it more difficult than ever for U.S. companies to show real growth in sales, earnings, and dividends. Therefore, you must be very selective in the stock market. If you don't have the time to do your own research or have an advisor who has demonstrated his/her skill in difficult times you should limit your stock market exposure and concentrate on the other investment alternatives discussed in this book.

BONDS

Overview

When you purchase a bond, you are essentially loaning money to some entity such as the federal government, another government agency, or a corporation. Bonds are long-term investments that normally do not mature for 10 years or more.

When you purchase a bond, the lender agrees to pay interest to you at a specific interest rate, known as the coupon rate, until maturity. For example, assume you buy an AT&T Bond with a 20-year maturity at a coupon rate of 10%. Each bond is sold for $1000 on January 1, 1981. AT&T effectively promises to pay you $100 per year (10% × $1000) for each bond for 20 years. Normally, interest is paid on a quarterly basis. At the end of 20 years, if you still hold the bond, AT&T will then repay you $1000, which is referred to as the face value of the bond.

You do not have to hold any bond until maturity. You can sell your bond on the open market. The price you receive for your bond will depend on two factors: interest rates and the stability of the borrower.

If interest rates have gone up since you purchased your bond, you will probably lose money if you sell your bond. Consider the previous example. If interest rates rose from 10% to 11%, no one would be willing to buy your bond paying 10% for $1000 if they could buy a new issue that paid 11%. Therefore, the market price of your bond would fall to reflect the higher interest rates prevailing in the market.

If interest rates had gone down since you purchased your bond, you would be able to sell your bond at a premium—that is, more than $1000—to reflect the fact that investors in new bonds would not be able to obtain rates as high as 10%.

The other factor that has an impact on bond prices is the ability of the buyer to pay interest and repay the principal at maturity. If you purchase a bond issued by the U.S. Treasury you will receive a lower interest (coupon) rate than you would if you purchased a bond issued by any corporation at that time. The reason is safety. You are virtually guaranteed that the U.S. government will honor its commitment and repay its interest and principal. When you purchase a bond from a corporation, you do not have the same guarantee. As soon as a corporation gets into the kind of financial difficulty that Itel or Chrysler have, the price of its bond drops because it can no longer be taken for granted that the company can repay its obligations.

As soon as a company misses an interest payment you can be assured that the price of its bond will drop dramatically. Thus, it is *crucial* that you understand the financial status of the issuing company. Standard & Poors and Moody's both rate and continually reevaluate the debt ratings of all major corporations. The best ratings are AAA, AA, and A, respectively. Any rating below A is considered somewhat risky. These ratings change, however. You may purchase a bond with a good rating, and over time that rating can drop as the financial conditions of the company deteriorate. If this happens, the value of your bond will fall.

There are several ways that you can protect yourself from losses in the bond market. One way would be only to buy bonds issued by the U.S. Treasury. Your interest rate would be somewhat lower, but you would at least be assured of your interest and principal payments. However, even if you buy U.S. treasury bonds you cannot be ensured against losses from changes in interest rates if you do not hold your bond to maturity. *Regardless of the quality* of the bond you purchase, the price of the bond will *always* change in the market because of changes in interest rates. The quality of bonds can only protect you from price changes that reflect the market's perception of the lender's ability to repay its debt.

Another way to protect yourself in the bond market is to buy a cross section of bonds—that is, many bonds in different industries. If you cannot afford to buy enough different bonds to diversify properly, you can purchase a no-load mutual bond fund with a good track record.

Although it is impossible to protect yourself completely from price changes because of fluctuations in interest rates, you can protect yourself somewhat by buying bonds at different time intervals. You can use this strategy whether you are buying individual bonds or purchasing bonds in mutual funds.

Call Provisions

You should be aware of one major difference between government bonds and corporate bonds. Corporations generally protect themselves from lower interest rates in the future by including a "call" provision in the agreement when they sell bonds. The purpose of this provision is to allow them to recall the bonds after a minimum number of years so they can issue new bonds at a lower interest rate. If the corporation recalls the bonds, it must pay a small premium to the bond holder for the recall.

Example

ABC company issued a 20-year bond in 1980 with a coupon rate of 13%. It included a call provision that allowed them to recall the bond at 103% of par at their option after 5 years. If interest rates fall any time after 1985, ABC can pay you $1030 for each bond you hold and retire that issue. The company could then issue a new bond with a coupon rate of 10%, for example, and save a great deal of money over the remaining 15 years.

There are a number of options you have to assure your self of long-term income. One option is to buy U.S. government bonds that have no call provision. You can buy new bonds directly from the Federal Reserve or you can purchase new bonds or existing bonds on the open market through a bank or broker. You will pay a small sales commission if you buy bonds on the open market. If you buy bonds directly from the Federal Reserve you pay no sales commission. One time to buy a bond already issued is when you do not expect to hold the bond for as long as 10 years.

Discount Bonds

Another option for obtaining a guaranteed income without concern about a recall is to purchase bonds issued many years ago at a low coupon rate. These bonds, known as discount bonds, would be selling in the market a prices well below par, that is, below $1000. It is extremely unlikely that these bonds would ever be called below maturity by the issuing corporation since interest rates have gone up since the bonds were issued. There would be no advantage to the company to recall them. From your viewpoint, the low coupon rate is not a disadvantage since you are buying the bonds at a discount. You must take into consideration the tax aspects of buying discount bonds. When the bonds mature, you will have to pay capital gains taxes since you will receive more back at maturity than the price you paid for the bond.

If you consider buying discount bonds to obtain income for a long period of time, make sure the bonds are discounted because interest rates have fallen and not because the company is in trouble. Make sure that the bond rating of the company is good before you purchase the discount bond. Although money can be made buying discounted bonds of corporations in trouble, it is a very speculative type of investment and not consistent with the objective of a long-term guaranteed rate of income.

Convertible Bond

A convertible bond is one that can be exchanged for a specific number of common shares of the issuing corporation under specified conditions. From an investor's viewpoint, convertible bonds would be a good investment if the price of the common stock increased substantially after the bond was issued.

Corporations issue convertibles for two basic reasons: They can sell a bond issue more easily if the issue is a convertible with favorable terms, and they can set the coupon rate lower on a convertible than on a straight bond issue, thus saving interest costs.

The conversion conditions for a convertible are established such that an increase in the price of the common stock would be required before the conversion of the bond to stock makes economic sense.

For example, assume a common stock was selling for $15/share. A corporation might issue a bond convertible into 50 shares of common stock. Unless the price of the stock rose above $20/share, no one would convert. As the price of the common approached $20, the price of the bond would go up—as long as there was a sufficient time for the conversion privilege left.

A convertible bond holder does not have to actually convert the bond to make a profit. He or she can simply sell the bond. For instance, in the example above, if the price of the stock rose to $25/share, the price of the bond would be approximately $1250 (50 shares × $25/share). Once the price of the stock goes above the break-even point ($20 for this example), the bond price increases (decreases) in value by the amount of the increase (decrease) multiplied by the number of shares that the bond can be converted to (50 shares in this example).

The primary disadvantage of the convertible to an investor is that if the common stock price does not increase so that it is close to the break-even point, the value of the convertible will be based solely on the value of the bond. If the coupon rate on the bond is low, relative to other bonds with the same rating and maturity, then the price of the bond will fall below the initial issue price, generally $1000, unless interest rates in general have gone down.

Another important factor for the investor to consider is the rating of the bond. In general, the ratings of convertible bonds are somewhat lower than other bonds. The reason is that smaller, less well-known corporations might be unable to sell straight bond issues. Accordingly, you should be wary investing in a convertible unless you are satisfied that the company is financially stable.

New Bond Vehicles

During 1980 and 1981 it became difficult for corporate treasurers to issue straight debt because the public wasn't buying and because the interest rates were so high. Accordingly, a number of new types of bond issues have been introduced in order to promote bond sales in general at more favorable rates for the issuing corporation.

One type of new issue is the bond that is sold at a discount when issued. The advantage of this instrument, from the investor's viewpoint, is that he or she knows the corporation will not call the bond before maturity.

Another new type of bond is the variable rate bond. The rate of return is not fixed but adjusted after a specified time, such as 3 months, based on changes in the rate of return of a bellwether issue such as Treasury bonds. This type of bond provides protection to the investor from capital losses even if interest rates increase. The disadvantage is that investors cannot "lock-in" high interest rates. If long-term rates fall, the rate of return on these bonds will also be reduced.

Many new issues, include features related to the common stock of the corporation. For example, some packages offer warrants, options to buy the common stock at a fixed price for a specified time. Alternative bonds and common stock are offered in one package. From an investor's viewpoint, these alternatives can be better investments than straight bond issues if the common stock prices increase in value. If you consider this type of investment, make sure you find out the rating of the bonds. If the common stock price does not increase, the success of your investment will depend on the yield of your bonds. Before you make a commitment, review the yields for comparably rated bonds with the same maturities. You should know if you are accepting a lower yield because of the common stock features offered. Lower bond yields will translate into lower bond prices if the equity features of your package become worthless or decrease in value.

Bonds During Retirement

Bonds do not normally have much of a place in your investment program while you are in your working years and are trying to develop a capital base for retirement. When you retire, you should consider bonds as one option that provides you with guaranteed income. Other options you could consider are annuities and high quality stocks that have a history of continuous dividends and periodic increases over time.

When you decide which investment vehicle is best at providing income for you, you should look at other factors such as the adequacy of income, the importance to you of leaving an estate, and your desire to increase your capital base.

Bonds are a fairly limited type of investment vehicle. Although they provide a steady income over time, they do not offer any capital appreciation potential unless interest rates fall. Within the last few years the rate of return obtainable from bonds has not been sufficient to provide a real return above the rate of inflation. That situation is not expected to change very much. Therefore, if you are interested in developing a capital base during your working years, it is not likely that long-term bonds will be an effective vehicle. About the best you can hope for is that your rate of return will keep pace with inflation.

After retirement you may want to consider investing in bonds, depending on your capital base and your required income. If your capital base is sufficient, you may want a guaranteed income, and there are alternatives discussed in this section that can provide it. The major problem after retirement, of course, is inflation. What appears to be a sufficient income now may not be in 5 or 10 years. Accordingly, you may want to invest only a portion of your capital base in a fixed income vehicle such as bonds, and invest the rest of your capital in alternatives that can increase in value.

MUTUAL FUNDS

Why Interest in Mutual Funds

Individuals traditionally have invested in mutual funds for one or more of the following reasons: professional management, diversified holdings, liquidity, ease of buying and selling, automatic reinvestment of distributions, and bookkeeping services. There is such a wide variety of mutual funds now available that a mutual fund can be found to meet almost anyone's primary investment objectives.

For many years the selection of funds was restricted to common stock funds, bond funds, and combination (balanced) bond—stock funds. Since the mid-1970s, many other funds have become available, such as municipal bond funds, money market funds, precious metal funds, commodity funds, and funds that specialize in foreign securities. These newer funds have been developed as a result of changes in federal regulations, higher interest rates, and new demand factors in the marketplace. Investors today are concerned with high taxes, protection from inflation, and investment flexibility.

Types of Mutual Funds

There are many categories of mutual funds from which to select depending on your investment objectives. The major types of funds are common stock, bond, balanced, money market, municipal bond, municipal bond money market, and special purpose funds such as energy funds or precious metal funds.

The type of fund you select should be based on your income and your investment objectives as well as on the amount of risk you are willing to take.

Sources of Information

Since there are so many mutual funds available, the task of selecting one is not simple. Before you select a fund you should determine your investment objectives. Then you can select the category of fund that meets those objectives, for instance, common stock fund, precious metals, or money market.

Once you have narrowed your search to a couple of categories of funds, you should do some research regarding the past performance and other characteristics of the individual funds. The following are major sources of information on mutual funds:

1 Wiesenberger Services, Inc. (1 New York Plaza, New York, NY 10005) Wiesenberger publishes *Investment Companies* each year, which contains detailed information on every major mutual fund. They also publish a monthly report that summarizes the best performance in the industry.

2 *Forbes* Magazine (60 Fifth Avenue, New York, NY 10011) In August or September *Forbes* publishes an in-depth summary of mutual fund performance for the previous 12 months and for prior periods of up to 10 or 12 years. The summary is well organized in that performance of individual funds are presented in logical groupings such as money market funds, no-load growth funds, and so forth. A narrative also accompanies the charts highlighting the best performers for the last year with a readable explanation of recent performances and current trends.

3 No-Load Mutual Fund Association, Inc. (Valley Forge, Pennsylvania 19481). The association will send you for $1.00 a no-load directory that summarizes the basic information for the larger no-load (no sales commission) funds. Past performance is not included in the directory. The directory includes information such as investment objectives, minimum initial deposits and subsequent deposits, Keogh/IRA participation, and addresses and toll-free numbers so you can obtain prospectuses.

4 Fundscope (Suite 700, 1900 Avenue of the Stars, Los Angeles, CA 90067). Fundscope publishes a monthly summary performance.

Final Selection

The major factors you should take into consideration before you select a fund are the following:

Your investment objectives.

Investment objectives of fund (as specified in prospectus).

Past performance of fund (especially the latest performance).

Sales commissions (if any) and fees.

Management of fund (you want to be sure that management hasn't changed recently if you are making your selection based on recent fund performance).

No-Load Funds

It may be possible to find a load fund that has performed better historically than the best no-load fund of the type you are interested in. Before you select any load fund, however, you should consider the probable length of time you expect to hold the fund.

One of the major disadvantages of buying any load fund is the immediate loss of sales commission to you if you decide to sell the fund shortly after your purchase. If you decide to switch out of a no-load fund you incur no penalty for changing your mind. Thus you have much more flexibility in switching either from one no-load fund to another or from a no-load fund to another form of investment.

In very volatile markets this type of flexibility is indeed valuable. Consider the situation in late 1979 and early 1980 when short-term interest rates were very high. You could have invested in the no-load money market funds and received a rate of return higher than 15%. When short term interest rates started to drop in the second quarter of 1980, you could have switched either to no-load bond/common stock funds or to other investment forms without paying sales commissions on the purchase or sale of your mutual fund shares.

There seems to be much more instability in the financial markets now than there was in prior periods. Because of that instability, it is advantageous to take investment positions that allow you to switch investments without incurring high sales commissions. Certainly there are other ways to obtain flexibility at low cost, but for both the small and large investor the use of no-load mutual funds has much to recommend it. No-load funds are available in virtually every category of mutual fund, and nearly all of the money market funds (next section) are no-load funds.

No-load funds are purchased directly from the fund itself. The no-load directory referred to earlier in this chapter contains the names, addresses and telephone numbers (toll-free) of all the major no-load funds.

Money Market Funds

One of the most successful types of mutual funds in recent years has been the money market fund. A money market fund is essentially one whose investments are limited to low-risk, short-term securities. Money market fund portfolios consist essentially of treasury bills, high rated, commercial paper, bank certificates of deposit, and bankers acceptances. Maturities are generally less than 1 year and many funds buy only securities that mature in 6 months or less.

The major reasons that these funds are so popular are safety of principal, flexibility in withdrawing funds, and a relatively high rate of return. Money funds are popular with corporate treasurers as well as individuals with either a great deal of assets or limited assets.

Since the investments are generally short-term, there is very little risk in losing principal even if you invest for only a few months. Even when interest rates fluctuate dramatically, there is relatively low risk with respect to your initial investment. The rate of return you receive may vary significantly from month to month because of changes in interest rates, but your initial capital will not be jeopardized as long as the length of your investment is in months or years as opposed to days.

Almost all money market funds are no-load. Some funds may charge a small redemption fee. The prospectus will indicate what charges, if any, you would incur. Most funds have no fees other than the investment advisory fee, which will normally be ½ of 1% per year. There is no way to avoid the payment of that fee, which to the investor is transparent since it is taken out of the assets automatically, normally at the end of each month.

Most money market funds allow investors the option of using checking privileges with their money market account. The majority of funds have a $500 minimum per check. This minimum is set to avoid high administrative costs that would occur if investors used their money fund as a typical checking account. The major advantage of using checks drawn on your money market account is that you will receive interest until the check clears. That is one of the primary reasons that many corporations use money market accounts. When short-term interest rates peaked in the first quarter of 1980, as well as much of 1981, money market funds were yielding in excess of 15%. There is a great deal of difference among the funds regarding minimum initial deposits, minimum subsequent deposits, and minimum net balances that you are required to leave in the fund. Most money market funds require a minimum of $1000 to open an account; some require more than $1000; some have no minimum at all. Some funds require subsequent deposits to be at least $1000; others have a higher minimum; most will have a lower minimum for subsequent deposits.

There is a very simple way to bypass a high minimum subsequent deposit. Assume you would like to deposit $100. The fund has a minimum subsequent deposit policy of $1000. You simply write a check drawn on the fund for $900 and deposit it in your bank checking account. You then write a check for $1000 drawn on your bank account and deposit it in your money market account. You have effectively deposited $100 very simply without any additional costs. Most money market funds do not charge for the check writing option. The major advantages of the money market funds are for the small investor are the relatively high rate of interest and flexibility. Money market funds normally pay a much higher rate of return than the typical passbook bank account.

Investors with more than $10,000 to invest have more options to obtain rates equivalent to those offered by the money market funds. Six-month bank certificates and treasury bills offer comparable rates of return. The money market funds, however, can be sold without commission or penalty. A commission would have to be paid if an investor had to sell a treasury bill prior to maturity. If an investor had to cash a 6-month certificate prior to maturity, she would lose 90 days interest on her investment. In fact, a bank does not have to allow an investor to withdraw funds prior to maturity on a time certificate. A number of banks have refused to do so.

The money market fund does have some disadvantages relative to other alternatives. Money market funds are not federally insured. Treasury securities are insured; bank certificates of deposit are federally insured up to $100,000 per account. There are no significant tax advantages associated with money market funds. Income from treasury securities are exempt from state and local taxes.

Many money market funds provide plans whereby investors can participate in IRA and Keogh plans. These options are discussed in detail in Chapter 9.

Municipal Bond Funds

One of the most significant problems you face today is higher taxes simply because the federal income tax tables are not yet indexed to inflation. The net result is that if you get a 10% raise in salary and inflation goes p 10%, you are in fact worse off than before because you have to pay more federal income taxes, and, in most states, more state income taxes.

One way to counteract this problem to some extent is to minimize the taxes you pay on income from your investments. If you invest in municipal bonds, your income from these bonds is exempt from federal income taxes and in some cases from state and local taxes. Investors who want the tax advantages of investing in municipal bonds but prefer a diversified portfolio to spread the investment risk can consider municipal bond mutual funds.

There are many municipal bond funds to choose from, and many are no-load funds with good track records. You can examine the track record of this type of fund the same way you would any other type of fund.

The major disadvantage of this type of fund is lack of protection from inflation. Investors who are concerned with capital growth should not invest heavily in this type of fund. Your major investment objective should be tax-free income. Otherwise you should be selecting another type of investment.

There is a relatively new class of mutual fund, the money market municipal bond fund, which is a specialized type of municipal fund. The fund management invests only in short-term municipal instruments. The advantage of this type of fund is that there is lower risk that your capital would go down in value because of the shorter maturity. One disadvantage of this investment is that if long-term rates fall you would have been better off in a regular municipal bond fund holding securities with longer maturities. However, if long-term rates rise, you would be better with the money market municipal funds than with regular municipal bonds.

Precious Metal Funds

In an inflationary environment commodities in general go up in value, and precious metals in particular generally go up more in value than most other forms of investment. Since there has been so much speculation recently in precious metals, there has been much more interest in mutual funds specializing in this segment of the market.

When the precious metal prices go up dramatically, the mutual funds specializing in this area historically have price increases that outperform the rest of the market. In 1979, the majority of the best performing mutual funds specialized in metals. Some of these were no-load funds. As metal prices go down as they did at the end of 1980 and the beginning of 1981, these funds do not perform well.

Precious metal funds sometimes charge a higher investment advisory fee than the typical mutual fund. It is not unusual for this type of fund to charge a 1% or higher advisory fee rather than the more standard ½ of 1% for typical funds. In a volatile market, however, a 1% fee is not that high if the fund management is making good decisions.

One of the problems an individual faces in the metal market is to make too large an investment at peak prices. By investing in equal increments, using dollar cost averaging, an investor can minimize the risks of buying at peak prices and have a profitable investment if metal prices go up in the long run. Although it is possible to use dollar cost averaging without using mutual funds, it can sometimes be very difficult, especially when metal prices are high. For example, if an investor is interested in buying gold and wants to invest $100 a month, he may not be able to make a purchase for 6 months or longer if an ounce of gold costs $600 or more.

Flexibility

There are many sound reasons to consider mutual funds in your investment program. The type of mutual fund you choose should be determined by your financial position, your retirement objectives, and the state of the financial markets. Your selection should be based on past performance, present management, fund objectives, and fee and commission structure. For example, when you have many working years ahead of you, are interested primarily in growth, and can afford some risk, you should consider growth common stock funds or perhaps commodity funds.

If you are concerned that the U.S. rate of inflation will be much higher than inflation in other countries, you could consider investment in mutual funds that specialize in investing in common stocks of foreign countries where the inflation rate has been historically less than in the United States. For example, in the 1970s Japan, West Germany, and Switzerland were able to control inflation better than the United States. If the Japanese yen, German mark, and Swiss franc becomes more valuable than the dollar, your investment through mutual funds in stocks of companies in those countries will also be more valuable. This investment option is discussed in more detail in the next chapter.

You may feel that stock prices are too high and you don't want to run the risk of losing your capital when stock prices drop. An alternative to consider would be a switch to no-load money market mutual funds until you think other types of investments have more potential.

You may feel that gold and/or silver has more growth potential than other forms of investment. There are several mutual funds, some of them no-load funds, that specialize in precious metals. To minimize your risk you should consider dollar cost averaging—that is, investing in equal increments over time. In that way you will be buying more shares when metal prices are low and less shares when prices are high.

You may reach a point during your life when you are concerned with the high level of income taxes you are paying. You should then consider the possibility of investing in a municipal bond fund. The income you receive from a municipal bond fund is exempt from federal taxes.

When you reach retirement age you may want a fixed rate of return. At that point you may want to consider investments in a bond mutual fund. Although the value of your assets will fluctuate based on changes in interest rates, you should be able to obtain a relatively fixed income without affecting your capital base very much unless there are dramatic changes in interest rates.

As your financial circumstances and objectives change over time you should be looking for different forms of investment. Although there will always be investments other than mutual funds that can meet your investment objectives, you will always be able to find a class of mutual funds consistent with your goals. As your investment objectives change or if you are dissatisfied with the performance of any fund you have selected, it is very easy to switch to another fund or to another form of investment.

BANK TRUST DEPARTMENTS

Banks provide investment advisory services for their customers who use the banks' trust services. You should consider the investment advisory services of a bank if you wish to set aside funds in trust for individuals and want these funds managed conservatively. If you are concerned about your health and want to ensure that your funds will be invested properly even if you become incapacitated, you can consider a bank trust department.

Bank trust departments normally do not manage individual accounts unless they are worth a minimum of $100,000. If the amount of your investment is less than the minimum for individual management, many banks will pool smaller investments into "comingled funds," which are similar to mutual funds. Banks normally have a yearly investment advisory fee of 1% of assets per year with a minimum of $100 a year.

The bank may have different funds with different investment objectives such as income or capital appreciation. Your assets would be apportioned in these funds dependent on your investment objectives.

Most people use banks as investment advisors only if they wish to use some type of trust account. Some banks will provide investment advisory services without the use of trust accounts.

The performance of bank trust departments in managing funds varies widely among banks. You should compare your bank's performance to that of other banks as well as to leading mutual funds. *The American Banker,* a daily newspaper devoted exclusively to banking news, periodically publishes comparative information regarding the investment performance of major trust departments. Although the performance of trust departments can change, the latest performance history is the best guideline you have to expected future performance.

When you meet with the officials of a trust department, ask them for the latest performance statistics for the bank's trust funds, and ask for a comparison with the other leading trust departments in your geographic area. Trust department officials will know how their portfolio performance compares to other banks. When you do this type of comparison you should look at performance not only for the last year but for a number of years. Comparison on a 5-year basis should be adequate. The Computer Directions Advisors in Silver Spring, Maryland has conducted a study encompassing the years 1970–1979 comparing the performance of bank trust departments. According to that survey, in the aggregate the performance of bank pools of common stock has not done as well as Standard & Poors index of 500 stocks. During the last 5 years, the bank pools' performance also trailed the market, but the gap is a smaller one in comparison to the Standard & Poors average. During the last 5 years the bank pool stocks rose 76% and the Standard & Poors average rose 79%.

Many of the banks in the survey outperformed the averages considerably. Thus your problem in selecting a bank to invest your funds for you is similar to selecting a mutual fund. There has been and will continue to be significant differences in investment performance among banks. Therefore, you must compare prior investment performance before you select a trust department to invest your funds.

There are several methods you can use to protect your beneficiaries in a trust agreement. You can instruct your lawyer to include the following provisions:

1 Give beneficiaries the right to replace trustees if the investment performance of the trustees does not meet certain criteria.
2 Appoint a respected co-trustee who would consult with the bank before investment decisions were made.
3 Delineate clearly the responsibility of the trust manager.

REAL ESTATE CONSIDERATIONS

As you approach retirement age you will be faced with a number of decisions related to housing. Do you plan to move? Will you rent or own your home? Do you want a one-family home or a condominium?

Where to Live?

Where you live is a personal decision. Some of the factors you should consider are climate, cost of living, recreational activities, age group, and your desire and ability to visit friends and relatives. Many people move a long distance from their friends and relatives and find that they do not see these people as often as they anticipated for many reasons. One of the most important factors is cost. In an era of double-digit inflation, a majority of retirees start pinching pennies in retirement much faster than they had anticipated.

If you are considering a move to an area that you are not familiar with, there are a few options you have that can save you some aggravation later. Take vacations in the area that you are considering for retirement. After your retirement, if you are still not sure where you want to live, rent for 6 months or a year rather than buying a home or condominium right away. That approach will give you more flexibility to change your mind about where to live.

Condominiums

As you approach retirement you should be considering whether you wish to own your home or condominium or rent an apartment. If you own your home, you should consider whether the property is too large for your needs and whether you want the burden of maintaining a large home. Even if you expect the property to continue to increase in value, is that an important objective for you in retirement? You may find that your cash flow will improve dramatically if you sell your home and move to a smaller apartment or purchase a one- or two-bedroom condominium.

You should consider the acquisition of a condominium for many reasons. Once you purchase one, a large part of your essential living costs will be fixed. Although your maintenance costs will go up, they should represent a relatively small percent of your total housing costs. You will only be responsible for the maintenance of the inside of your condominium. Your maintenance fee will cover the other costs such as maintaining the grounds, recreational areas, and the outsides of the buildings.

If you select a condominium carefully, making sure that the condominium is being maintained properly, the maintenance fees are reasonable, and the condominium is in a good neighborhood, you can expect the property value to increase. Condominiums have increased in value in most areas of the country to the same extent that other types of real estate have.

New Condominium

If you are considering purchasing a new condominium, be very careful before you make a commitment. You should retain an experienced attorney in the area. Obtain all the required documents for his or her review. Specifically, you want your attorney to review the sales contract, bylaws, charter, and deed.

You should determine whether your funds are comingled with the builder's money. It is to your advantage if the funds are maintained separately. In that way you have more protection if the condominium is not built for any reason. You should make sure that it is written into the contract that you will receive your funds back in case the condominium is not built.

Make sure that the proposed maintenance costs are reasonable. You should be able to do that by comparing the proposed costs with those of similar condominiums in the area. Determine if the company responsible for the maintenance of the property has other condominium maintenance contracts in the same geographic area. If so, you should be able to make a fair comparison.

You should determine if the builder has constructed other condominiums. If so, visit them and talk to owners to get their reactions. You also can determine to what extent property values have gone up on other condominiums the developer has built.

One of the things you and your lawyer should examine carefully is possible leasing arrangements retained by the builder. Although it is not as common a practice as it once was, a number of builders retain ownership of certain property such as land and lease it back to the condominium owners. The initial leasing fee may seem reasonable, but after the initial lease expires the builder can then increase the fee dramatically. In many states this practice is not legal. If at all possible, you should avoid any such arrangements whereby the builder or any other party retains ownership of any property that you use.

You should also be wary of any contract provision wherby the builder or any other party has a noncancellable contract to maintain the condominium. Obviously with that type of agreement you have no viable options, and your maintenance costs will certainly be higher than they would be in a more competitive environment.

Preretirement

Although condominiums have many advantages during retirement, there is no reason that you shouldn't consider them before retirement as well. Many people before retirement would like to retain the tax advantages of being a property owner without the responsibility of maintaining a large home and associated land.

Condominiums are growing in popularity and will continue to do so for many reasons. Inflation has made it difficult for many people to own large homes. Utility bills and other costs associated with maintaining a home have been increasing at a faster pace than most other expenses. Accordingly, many people are looking for alternatives that will somehow reduce the percent of their income spent on basic housing costs. That percent is at an all-time high, and it is not likely to be reduced with energy costs continually climbing. Condominiums probably will continue to increase in demand, and property values should increase for condominiums at a rate at least as high as those of other real estate alternatives.

Existing Condominium

It is certainly easier to evaluate an existing condominium than a new one. You have the advantage of being able to determine how well the property is being maintained. You should talk to as many owners as possible, hear their grievances and their positive impressions. You should be able to find out exactly what the maintenance costs are. Determine how fast they have gone up. Find out to what extent property values have gone up.

You should still use an attorney to review the deed, sales contract, charter, and bylaws. If your attorney is not familiar with condominium documents (and you should not assume that every attorney is), find one who understands such data. Ask before you hire an attorney what things you should be concerned about in purchasing a condominium. If he or she doesn't respond with some of the major considerations discussed in this chapter, consider another attorney.

Real Estate After Retirement

Real estate investment has many advantages in growth potential and as a tax shelter. After you retire, the advantages to you of investing in real estate will undoubtedly change as your tax status changes. For example, when you own your home, all of your interest payments and real estate taxes are tax deductible. Before retirement, the after-tax costs of these expenses are much smaller than they are after retirement. Therefore, it will be more expensive for you to maintain the same home in after-tax dollars. If your income during retirement is significantly less than it was prior to retirement, you should determine whether you wish to maintain the same residence. If you do, your housing costs as a percent of total income will probably be much greater than they were prior to retirement.

Real estate will probably continue to be a good inflation hedge even after your retirement. You may be concerned about your capital base eroding too fast because of inflation. You can expect that the value of your home will go up during your retirement. Therefore, an option you can consider is retaining your residence at the beginning of your retirement with the expectation of capital growth and with the plan of selling it later and moving to less spacious accomodations with a larger capital base.

Another option is renting your property during your retirement. One advantage to this is rental income, which could be increased periodically. Another advantage is that your capital base will increase to keep up with inflation. The potential disadvantages are the maintenance of the property and the possibility of not being able to rent the property continuously. The location and condition of the property are major factors in renting.

During retirement you will be faced with inflation; the only question is of degree. If you will be on a fixed income and are concerned that your capital base will erode and jeopardize your living standard, you must examine those real estate alternatives that will help you maintain a capital base keeping pace with inflation. Maintaining good real estate property certainly is one of those alternatives.

Sale of Residence

If you are at least 55 years old, you may be able to completely avoid the taxes on any profits up to $125,000 that you have made on the sale of a residence. To claim this exclusion, you must pass three tests:

1 You must elect the exclusion.
2 You must be over 55.
3 You must have owned and lived in the home for at least 3 of the 5 years preceding the sale date of the property. If you are 65 or older you do not have to meet this requirement if you owned and used the property for 5 of the 8 years preceding a sale occurring before July 26, 1981.

This exclusion can be used only once in your lifetime. Therefore, even if you are old enough to claim the exclusion, if you plan to continue to own your residences—whether they are single-family homes, condominiums, or cooperatives—you may want to postpone taking the exclusion. Under other IRS tax regulations, regardless of age, you can postpone paying taxes on the profits from the sale of residences as long as you purchase other residences with your profits within two years and the new residence is at least as expensive as the one you sold.

The implication of these two IRS regulations is that although you may take up to the $125,000 exclusion after age 55, you don't have any incentive to take the exclusion until you decide not to continue to live in a residence you own. In fact, if the total profit you have made on the residences you have lived in is less than $125,000, you have an incentive to continue to own residences until you have used up the $125,000 exclusion. The exclusion is not restricted to profits on the last home you purchased. You can use the exclusion for all the residences you have owned. As an example, assume you owned three homes and made a profit of $30,000, $40,000 and $65,000 when you sold them. Your total profit was $135,000. Utilizing your exclusion of $125,000, you only have to pay taxes on $10,000 of profit if you meet the three criteria outlined above. If you are younger than 55, the present tax laws give you an incentive to continue to own your home at least until you reach age 55.

Reverse Mortgages

If you reach retirement, have a need for more income, and have equity in your home, you can consider a reverse mortgage. A reverse mortgage is a vehicle whereby you borrow money from a financial institution each month based on the equity you have in your home.

There is a major disadvantage associated with this technique. The loan will have to be repaid at some point, and you may be forced to sell the property to pay off the loan. If the value of your real estate does not increase significantly, the bank may not be willing to extend the mortgage. Unless you expect to acquire other assets in the future that you can use to pay off the mortgage, you should avoid this vehicle.

The reverse mortgage is not very popular now and it is not likely to be in the future.

Multiple Properties

At retirement, you may have a lot of equity in your property. You may have decided that you want to live in a smaller home, apartment, or condominium. However, before you sell your existing residence to purchase a smaller one, consider your other options. You may be able to rent out your existing home, obtain a second mortgage, and use the proceeds to put a down payment on the residence in which you plan to live.

In this way you can use the rental from your original property to maintain the second property. Since you are moving from a larger residence to a smaller one, the rent you receive should exceed your payments for your new residence. Moreover, your capital base should be increasing since the value of both properties should be going up in value.

This approach allows you some protection against rising maintenance costs on your new residence as well as protecting your capital base. You should be able to increase your rental payments to help cover your increased expenses, and the value of both your properties should increase if they are basically good properties in good areas.

You should consider this strategy if you are confident of renting the initial property without problems, if the property can be maintained at a reasonable cost, and if the property is in an area where property values are likely to increase.

Adjustable Rate Mortgages

You should be aware of a new trend in mortgages toward adjustable rates. Banks and savings institutions have lost a considerable amount of money on long-term traditional mortgages because interest rates have been fixed, but the financial institution's cost of money has increased dramatically. To provide some protection for financial institutions, the regulatory authorities have allowed adjustable rate mortgages to be introduced. With these mortgages the lender can raise or lower the interest rate of the loan based on changes in general interest rate levels. These rates can be adjusted at the end of 1, 3, or 5 years based on the initial agreement. Lending institutions are phasing out fixed rate mortgages.

You may be able to choose the type of mortgage instrument you can obtain. For example, a savings and loan institution may offer you an adjustable rate initially at 17% or a fixed rate of 19%. The potential disadvantage of the adjustable mortgage is that if interest rates go up, the rate you pay on your mortgage will also go up. Some types of mortgage agreements restrict the rate increase (or decrease) to ½ of 1% per year; other agreements allow the rate to go up 1% each year. Some agreements limit the increase to 5% over the time of the mortgage; other agreements have no upper limit.

An increase of two or three percentage points on a mortgage makes a difference of thousands of dollars over the term of the mortgage. If you obtain a mortgage during a period in your life when your income is generally fixed and you are on a tight budget, you should avoid adjustable mortgages.

Shared-Appreciation Mortgages

With a shared-appreciation mortgage, the lender of funds lowers the interest rate as much as 40% in exchange for the same percentage of the appreciation of the residence when the property is sold. These types of mortgages are relatively rare but may gain in popularity as financial institutions become more interested in capital appreciation than in interest income. For example, assume the going mortgage rate of 16%. A financial institution could reduce the rate to 10%. Assume a home was purchased for $50,000 and was subsequently sold 5 years later for $100,000. The lender would receive 40% of the $50,000 gain, or $20,000.

This type of a mortgage would be advantageous to you in retirement when you purchase a new residence if you are more concerned with reducing your interest payments than with capital appreciation.

There are potential disadvantages with this type of mortgage. Some lenders specify in their agreement that if the home is not sold after a specified time, such as 10 years, the homeowner must pay the lender the agreed on percent of appreciation of the property. With this type of agreement, the homeowner would have to pay for an appraisal and pay the lender for up to 40% of the property's appreciation. If the property owner does not have the money, he or she would have to borrow funds at prevailing market rates to pay the lender. Moreover, the balance of the old mortgage might have to be refinanced at prevailing rates.

This type of mortgage should be avoided by families interested in improving the property with their own labor. The loan agreement normally allows only the cost of materials to be deducted from any property appreciation based on improvements. Only home improvements completed by contractors would be deductible from property appreciation.

Although shared-appreciation mortgages appear to have some short-term advantages, depending on the agreement, there can be long-term disadvantages that far outweigh the short-term advantages. You should not use this type of mortgage without a competent attorney familiar with the provisions of these types of mortgages.

13 Nontraditional Investments

The need for investors to look carefully at nontraditional investments becomes apparent when compound growth rates of different classes of investments are compared between 1968 and 1979. During that period the U.S. consumer price index went up 6.5%. Common stocks (3.1%) and high grade corporate bonds (5.8%) did not do as well.

Although single-family homes went up 9.6% in value, which is more than the inflation rate, the largest gains were made by nontraditional investments in diamonds (11.8%), silver (13.7%), and gold (19.4%).

Prices of gold and silver fell sharply at the end of 1980 and during the first half of 1981 due in large part to high short-term interest rates available in the United States. High interest rates can slow down increases in metal as well as diamond prices. However, as long as world wide inflation persists, it is likely that investors throughout the world will continue to look to metals and diamonds as inflation hedges. There are many reasons to suggest that the new growth patterns may not change very quickly.

Corporations in the United States are facing efficient foreign competition, rising energy costs, strong unions, and consumer resistance to higher prices. It is not likely in these circumstances that corporation earnings, and therefore stock prices, will show growth rates above the U.S. inflation rate. The rate of return on long-term bonds also is not likely to be higher than the inflation rate. Although real estate has done fairly well up to 1980, the combination of high energy costs, high interest rates, and lower real wages limits growth in real estate prices.

The dollar lost much of its value in the 1970's both with respect to other currencies and to gold because of high U.S. inflation. In 1980 and the first half of 1981, the dollar has made a dramatic comeback because of high interest rates in the United States. When investors fear paper money because of inflation, gold and other tangible assets become more popular. That is why gold, silver,

153

diamonds, and other commodities increased in value dramatically in the 1970's. If interest rates start falling, there will be renewed interest in these tangible assets.

There will undoubtedly continue to be wide fluctuations in metal prices as well as in other commodities. The underlying factors suggest that there will continue to be strong interest in investing in these hard assets. Therefore, it is likely that on a long-term basis the price of these assets will rise.

Investors concerned with planning their retirements in an inflationary environment must be aware of changing economic conditions and changing investment opportunities. If inflation remains in double digits, which is not unlikely, it will become very important for you to educate yourself concerning the new investment alternatives and to decide whether you can afford *not* to change your investment habits if your investment program has not kept up with inflation.

INTERNATIONAL INVESTING

The primary reasons for investing in foreign securities is to protect yourself against the weakness of the dollar with respect to other currencies. Assume there are two companies, similarly managed and of equal financial strength, and growth potential. One company is located in the United States, and the other is in a country that has a strong currency expected to increase in value with respect to the dollar on a long-term basis. In that scenario, you would be better off investing in the foreign security if you could purchase and sell the foreign security without a lot of red tape. Unfortunately, it is not always easy to get accurate information concerning foreign securities.

Other reasons to consider the purchase of foreign securities are that they provide diversification from the U.S. security market in general and represent investment opportunities not available in the U.S. securities market.

U.S. Environment

There are many factors operating in the United States that are not conducive to good stock performance. These are high inflation, low productivity growth, government regulation, low profitability, and dependence on foreign raw materials. If a foreign country provides a better economic environment for corporate profitability and has a strong currency, the securities of the strong companies in that country should prove to be good investments.

The Value of the Dollar in Comparison to Other Currencies

During 1980 and the first half of 1981, the dollar has increased dramatically in value relative to other major currencies. From 1970 to 1979, the currencies performing best were the Swiss franc, the German mark, and the Japanese yen. If economic conditions in these countries remain stable, their rates of interest will continue to be less than the inflation rate in the United States on a long-term basis. The inflation rate is the key to the strength of a currency.

Exhibit 13-1 indicates the value of world currencies compared to the U.S. dollar from a 1969 base. As the chart shows, of the seven currencies used in the comparison, only the currency of the United Kingdom decreased in value relative to the dollar. The Australian currency remained on a par with the dollar. The rest of the currencies increased in value relative to the dollar from 20% to over 260% from 1979 to 1980. The Swiss franc and the German mark were by far the best currency performers. It is no coincidence that both Switzerland and Germany have been able to control inflation better than other countries.

Rate of Return

U.S. industry has lost its competitive edge in major areas such as automobiles and steel. In 1980 Japan took the lead from the United States in the manufacture of automobiles. In mass production industries volumes are important. If large companies cannot maintain high sales volume, massive losses can result. Witness the situations of Chrysler, Ford, and General Motors in 1980. For the sake of the U.S. economy, it is hoped that this situation can be turned around. In the interim, however, investors should be considering those foreign companies that have demonstrated leadership in major industries both in terms of increased market share and high return on investment.

Stock Market Performance

During the last 10 years the stock markets in many countries have outperformed the U.S. stock market. From an investors standpoint you should be interested in your total return on investment. You should be aware, however, that when you

Exhibit 13-1   Currency Value Comparisons
1969 = 100

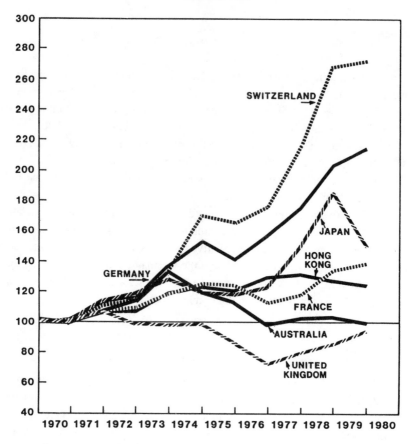

invest in foreign securities, there are two components associated with your total return: the return from appreciation in the stock price and the return caused by currency movements.

From 1970 to 1979 taking both stock price changes and currency changes into consideration, the following countries' stock markets showed performances superior to the U.S. stock market: Hong Kong; Japan; Switzerland; Germany; France; and the United Kingdom (see Exhibit 13-2). The stock market in the United Kingdom in the aggregate outperformed the U.S. stock market despite the loss in value of the pound to the dollar. That situation is the exception, however. Examination of Exhibit 13-2 shows that in general the countries that had more favorable foreign currency movements in comparison to the United States also had more favorable stock market performance.

Exhibit 13-2   Comparative Stock Market Performance: Average Annual Rates of Return, 1970−1979

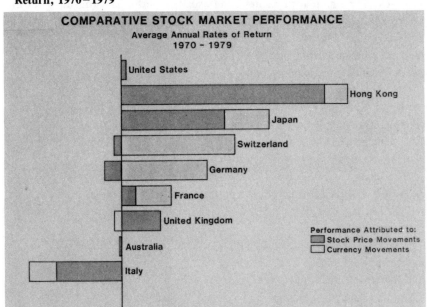

High rates of inflation will continue to make life difficult for corporate executives in the United States. Inflation makes it more difficult to replace capital assets. Moreover, inflationary pressures make it difficult for the Federal Reserve to keep interest rates down for any significant time. This in turn makes it difficult for U.S. corporations to maintain the status quo and very difficult to expand. It will not be easy for U.S. corporations in an inflationary environment to outperform foreign companies, which in many instances have more government support and less regulatory requirements.

From a U.S. investor viewpoint, you should consider placing some of your assets into alternatives that will provide you with more diversification. These alternative investments include foreign securities, Swiss annuities and insurance, and precious metals.

Mutual Funds

For most investors it is impossible to research either currency conditions in foreign countries or the major companies in these countries. One way to invest in foreign securities is to invest in one of the mutual funds that specialize in foreign securities. Some mutual funds have had excellent performance results over the last decade, especially in comparison to most mutual funds invested solely in U.S. securities. Mutual funds specializing in foreign securities that have had good to excellent performance results are the Templeton Fund, The Japan Fund, and the Scudder International Fund.

The Templeton Fund is a loan fund that has had excellent results. For a number of years, U.S. residents could not purchase shares in this fund, but they can now. The Templeton Fund does not preclude investments in U.S. securities. If the management of the fund feels that U.S. securities are the best investments available, U.S. securities will be emphacized in the portfolio.

The Japan Fund is a closed investment company whose shares are traded on the New York Stock Exchange. The performance of that fund has been excellent over the last 10 years. The managers of the fund invest in securities of companies in any country.

The Scudder International Fund is a no-load fund that contains only foreign investments. Its long-term performance has also been good. In 1980 the major investments of this fund were in high technology Japanese stocks and in Austrailian banks and engineering companies. Scudder, Stevens & Clark, who manage the fund, also manage other mutual funds that invest in U.S. securities.

Individual Foreign Securities

Many brokerage firms do not have specialists in foreign securities. If your broker does not and you are not satisfied with the overall performance of your investments, you should consider using a broker who does research foreign securities and makes timely recommendations accordingly. You may not want to place all your investments in foreign securites, but if your holdings are large enough, a broker who is not at least considering some foreign investments for you may not be acting in your best interests.

One way to evaluate the performance of your present broker is to compare the performance of your portfolio over several years to a mutual fund that concentrated in foreign securities during the same time. If the mutual fund performed much better than your portfolio, you should consider changing your investment strategy.

You should not be satisfied with the performance of the U.S. securities market if it does not keep pace with inflation. You are the one who will have to live on the assets you have at retirement. If these assets are not growing fast enough, you must consider other alternatives.

Comment

It is not easy to change investment habits. Unfortunately, we are faced with an economic environment that is destructive to future retirees. If you want to retire in comfort, you must choose your investment alternatives with extreme care.

Most U.S. citizens want to invest in American things. That is fine if you can afford it. You should monitor the international environment, and be prepared to invest some of your assets in foreign investment alternatives, if U.S. inflation gets out of control.

GOLD

Anyone who is concerned about inflation should become knowledgable about gold. Since 1977 gold prices have soared. In general gold prices go up whenever investors are concerned about the stability of currencies and whenever international flareups occur.

Although many investors have profited from gold, the fluctuations in prices have been dramatic. Therefore, even if the long-term prospects for gold prices are good, an investor has to be very careful about timing. For example, in the beginning of 1980 gold was selling as high as $850 an ounce. Investors who waited until then to make their purchases had severe losses thereafter if they were forced to liquidate their investment.

Supply

One of the major reasons that gold has remained in such high demand is its scarcity. All the gold in the world would not fill a good-sized room. Moreover, gold is durable; it has industrial use; it is popular in jewelry. For all of these reasons, it is likely that gold will continue to be valuable.

Investment Alternatives

There are many alternatives in gold investments: coins; ingots; jewelry; bonds; delivery orders; gold certificates; bank accounts; commodity futures; commodity options; mutual funds; stock options; and stocks.

These alternatives vary considerably in their degrees of risk as well as in the amount of investment required. They all have on thing in common however; the performance of the investment will depend on what happens to the price of gold.

GOLD COINS

One of the easiest methods of investing in gold is through gold coins. Gold coins are produced by South Africa, Mexico, Austria, and Canada. The most popular coin is the South African Kruggerand. The Kruggerand is available now in 1-ounce, ½-ounce, ¼-ounce, and 1/10-ounce denominations. There is a higher percent commission for the smaller denominations of Kruggerands than for the one ounce coin. Normally the sales commissions are from 3–10% for the purchase of coins. Coins from other countries are generally available in 1-ounce and ½-ounce denominations.

The advantages of gold coins are liquidity, availability in small quantities, and easy storage. One of the disadvantages is that if you buy in small quantities you will pay a relatively high commission in comparison to other forms of gold investment such as bars.

When you invest in gold coins, you can spread your investment out over an extended time. This technique is advantageous during periods of wide fluctuations in gold prices. In this way you can avoid making a large investment at a time when you are concerned that the gold price has peaked.

One of the potential disadvantages of gold coin investment is security. You have the responsibility and associated cost of finding a secure place to store the coins.

You can purchase gold coins at one of the nationwide branches of Deak-Perera. Many banks now offer gold coins for sale at their major branches.

Gold Mining Stocks

There are some advantages in investing in gold mining stocks. Some of the important ones are capital growth, diversification, and dividends. The primary disadvantages are possible political problems, labor problems, certain tax disadvantages; and volatility in metal prices.

South Africa is the world's largest gold producer and has more than 30 publicly held mining companies. American investors can purchase shares in these companies through the purchase of American depositary receipts (ADRs).

ADRs are traded over the counter in the United States and are sold in the same way that other stock certificates are.

One of the disadvantages of purchasing South African stocks is that American and other foreign investors must pay a 15% South African tax on dividends. This tax is deductible on your U.S. tax return.

The most important factor that affects the price of shares of these stocks as well as the stocks of other gold mining shares is the per ounce price of gold. As long as the price of gold continues to increase, investment in these stocks should be a good inflation hedge for you unless the political environment changes. Many of these mines have extensive ore deposits of gold and other metal deposits as well.

Seven finance companies in South Africa control the major South African Mining Companies. They are:

Anglo American Corporation of South Africa, Ltd.

Anglo-Transvaal Consolidated Investment Co. Ltd.

Barlow Rand Group.

Consolidated Gold Fields, Ltd.

General Mining & Finance Corp. Ltd.

Johannesburg Consolidated Investment Co. Ltd.

Union Corporate Ltd.

Each of these finance companies has mining affiliates associated with it, and each mining affiliate has its independent securities. You can get detailed information about individual securities from your broker. Other sources you can consider are *Dollar Devaluation* and *Gold Share Investments* by Walter Lynch (120 Broadway, New York, NY 10005) and the book *Double Your Dollars in 600 Days*, by Ira Cobleigh, published by Harmony Books, New York.

Jewelry

Gold jewelry normally sells at a very high premium over the par value of gold. You can expect to pay a minimum of three times the value of gold if you purchase jewelry. You will not be able to resell jewelry to a wholesaler for anywhere near the price you paid on a short-term basis. Therefore, you should not buy gold jewelry for pure investment reasons. If you want to buy jewelry because you like it, fine. If you want to make an investment, consider other forms of gold.

Gold Certificates

Gold certificates are an attractive investment alternative for investors who can invest a minimum of $1000. When you purchase a certificate you are effectively purchasing a specific number of ounces of gold which is stored for you, at minimal cost, in places such as Switzerland and Delaware.

Certificates are sold by Deak-Perera, Dreyfus, Republic National Bank, and Citibank. The minimum purchase requirements vary among the selling organizations. Citibank sells $1000 certificates. The minimum purchase requirement of the other sellers is somewhat higher.

The sales commission is nominal, generally 3%. Therefore, you can make a profit on your investment in a relatively short period of time if the price of gold goes up. There is no minimum holding period. The certificate you hold can be sold with no problem; it is very liquid.

Stock Options

If you are willing to risk losing all of your investment with the potential of large gains, you can consider the option market. You can purchase "calls" on gold mining stocks if you think the price of gold and accordingly the price of the stock will go up in the short run. A call is an option to buy 100 shares of stock at a fixed price for a specific time, 30 days to 1 year. The longer the time of the option, the more expensive the price of the option.

If you think the price of gold will go down, you can purchase "put" options. A put option is an option to sell 100 shares of stock at a specific price. The time periods for puts are the same as for calls.

Purchasing puts and calls is very speculative because if the underlying stock price does not move in the direction you expect it to, you will lose *all* of your investment. However, if the stock price does move in the right direction (up for calls, down for puts) you can make a substantial profit. The reason to consider purchasing options is that you can make a higher percentage of profit on your investment with options than you can if you buy the underlying stocks. This situation holds true only if the price change is sufficient to outweight the costs you incur in buying the options.

You can get more information on options from your broker. The American

Stock Exchange has a number of free readable booklets available through your stock broker. These booklets discuss all the major option alternatives. Examples are provided to illustrate the conditions under which different options would be profitable investments.

The option market is not restricted to gold stocks. You can use options for virtually all major listed stocks. Your broker can tell you which stocks are traded on the option market. If you decide to become very active in the option field, you may want to consider a brokerage firm and/or broker that specializes in options.

Commodity Futures

Commodity futures should be considered only by investors who are willing to take substantial risks with their capital and have a large capital base to start with. Many brokerage firms will not consider customers for commodity accounts unless they have $50,000 in risk capital. Each firm sets its own minimum requirements.

When you purchase a futures contract, you obtain the right to buy a specific amount of gold at a fixed price on a specified date. Gold futures are sold in minimum contracts for 10 ounces. The value of your contract can change each day depending on market conditions. The reason futures are so speculative is that you are only putting up a small percent of the total purchase price. For example, if the margin requirement for gold is 5%, with a $5000 investment you control $100,000 worth of gold. If the per ounce price of gold goes up 10% on paper, you would have a gain of $10,000 on a $5000 investment. Unfortunately, the opposite scenario holds true also. If the price of gold drops, your broker will ask you to put up additional capital; otherwise you will have to sell your contract and incur a loss. There are fixed limits for each commodity regarding the maximum price change that can occur in 1 day. Accordingly, you know in advance the maximum you can lose in 1 day.

Unless you are willing to take a *great deal of risk* and can afford substantial capital losses, stay away from commodities.

You can purchase futures from selected brokers and from commodity brokers. An excellent source for information on commodities is COMEX, 4 World Trade Center, New York, NY 10048. They have an excellent brochure explaining the ''nuts and bolts'' of commodity training. The brochure contains information about investing in all commodities, not just gold. You can purchase futures in other metals such as silver, grains, and livestock.

Before you purchase gold futures or any other futures, make sure you understand the potential losses you can incur with your investment. It is critical to understand that your losses are not restricted to your initial investment. There is a significant difference between the risks associated with purchasing options and purchasing futures. With options your potential loss is limited to the price you pay for your option. With futures your loss is unlimited. To limit your losses you must sell your futures contract. Very few investors have the stomach to absorb losses as quickly as is possible in the futures market.

Most brokers will tell you to cut short your losses and hold on to your winners. It's sound advice, but if you start out with losses, it can be a painful experience—one that very few investors can handle easily.

Ingots

You can purchase gold ingots in various sizes. The weight can range from 16/100 of a troy ounce to 400 ounces. You can purchase ingots from Swiss banks (U.S. branches), coin dealers, precious metal dealers, and selected U.S. banks. The markup will vary depending on the size of your purchase. For small purchases the markup will be approximately 5%. Sales commissions are generally 1%. There are additional fees for insurance and storage of at least 1%.

You have the option of holding the gold yourself. If you do, however, you will probably have to have the ingot assayed. That cost can be from $50 to $100. If you purchase ingots in sealed plastic you may be able to avoid the assaying fee. There should be no additional cost of buying the ingot sealed in plastic.

Mutual Funds

There are a number of mutual funds specializing in gold, either bullion or mining stocks. Some of these funds are diversified by investing in other precious metal holdings such as silver as well. As you would expect, these mutual funds did very well in 1979 and early 1980 when gold prices went up dramatically. However, on a long-term basis they did not do as well as other funds that were more diversified.

One of the advantages of investing in gold mutual funds is dollar cost averaging. This is especially important with a commodity such as gold whose price goes up and down dramatically. With dollar cost averaging you invest a fixed sum at regular intervals. In this way, you are buying more shares when the gold price goes down and less when the price goes up. The advantage of the technique is that you avoid making too large an investment when the gold price is at its peak. As long as the long-term gold price trend is upward, dollar cost averaging is a useful technique. With many of the funds, however, a minimum investment of $1000 is required. High minimums make it difficult for you to use dollar cost averaging effectively unless you can afford to make consistently large investments.

Many of the gold funds charge a higher yearly investment advisary fee than other types of mutual funds.

Summary

As long as we continue to have a high rate of inflation, gold will remain an attractive investment alternative. The basic problem for most investors will be to avoid purchasing at peak prices. Since no one can predict with certainty the peaks and valleys of gold prices, a conservative strategy would be to make purchases over an extended time rather than investing one lump sum.

Conservative gold investors should consider gold mutual funds, coins, ingots, certificates, and a cross section of the major gold mining stocks. Speculative investors can consider options. Very speculative investors can investigate gold futures.

You must remember that there are disadvantages with gold investment. You will not receive dividends with most forms of investment, and there can be dramatic price fluctuations. It is unlikely that gold will increase very much, if at all, when short-term interest rates for investments such as Treasury bills, 6-month certificates of deposit, and money market funds are high in relation to the inflation rate. You must weigh these disadvantages against the expectation that the value of gold will increase on the average more than traditional investments as long as inflation persists in the United States and the rest of the world.

SILVER

Since 1971, the price of silver has gone up dramatically. Moreover, since 1976 there has been another surge in the price of the metal. Prices went down in late 1980 and 1981.

There are a great many factors indicating that silver will be a good inflation hedge. Some of these factors include:

Continued expected use in electronic and photographic industries.

Hoarding of silver in many cultures.

High price of gold influencing more peeople to turn to silver.

Demand for medallions and commemerative coins.

More investors turning to hard metals to avoid holding currencies.

Silver not easily substituted for in industrial use.

Many large silver mines have been worked out.

World production of silver much less than world consumption in the last few years.

Since there are many factors pointing to higher silver prices it seems reasonable for investors to consider some investment in silver as a good inflation hedge.

Forms of Investment

There are four basic forms of silver investment: bullion, futures, coins, and stock. Your selection should be based on factors such as the size of your investment and the degree of speculation you are willing to take.

Bullion

You can buy bars of silver in various sizes. The most common sizes are 10, 100, and 1000 troy ounces. You should purchase bars only if they are certified by a reputable refiner. The largest U.S. refiners are Handy and Harman and Englehardt Metals.

You do not have to take possession of the bars. You can elect to have them stored for you at a nominal cost in a bank or a warehouse facility specializing in metals. Make sure that any facility holding your metals is adequately insured.

The value of your bars will fluctuate based on the silver troy ounce price quoted in the paper each day. To make sure you are getting the best price, buy only from dealers who have a long history of buying and selling metals.

Futures Market

If you can afford to speculate, you can consider the futures market. Contracts are sold from 1 month to 15 months for 5000 ounces or multiples thereof.

The margin requirements for silver trading was 10% in 1980. Accordingly, if silver is selling for $20 an ounce, you can control a 5000 ounce contract worth $100,000 with an initial investment of $10,000. If the price of silver falls, you will have to put up additional capital or lose part or all of your investment. The current maximum fluctuation is 20 cents per ounce each day. This means you can lose or gain up to $1000 per day for each contract, not taking commissions and other fees into account. You can expect to pay approximately $100 in fees and commissions for each contract.

You can obtain a detailed explanation of the details of the silver futures market from the New York Commodity Exchange (COMEX) at 4 World Trade Center, New York, NY 10048. They have an excellent brochure that includes information about silver and all other commodities traded on COMEX. Future options are traded on both COMEX and the Chicago Board of Trade.

Margin

There are some silver dealers who will allow you to purchase bars of silver on margin. In this type of transaction you put up a percent of the total purchase price and borrow the difference. You pay interest charges as well as commissions and storage charges in most situations.

This type of transaction is different from the futures market in the sense that you are borrowing money and accordingly paying interest. In the futures market, although you are only putting up a portion of the total value of your transaction, you are not borrowing money.

The advantage of buying on margin rather than playing the futures market is that your capital will not be wiped out quickly in short-term downward moves. If the futures market moves down quickly, you will lose all of your investment quickly unless you can put up additional margin. With a margin account you can withstand short-term movements more easily, although you will have to put up additional capital if the silver price goes down very much. You should not buy on margin if you do not have sufficient capital to withstand short-term fluctuations.

Silver Coins

Silver coins have become more popular as an investment vehicle because of the increases in the price of silver. One of the advantages in selecting coins as an investment alternative is that a large investment is not required. You can buy a few coins or bags containing $1000 worth of silver at face value.

The value of silver coins goes up as the per ounce price of silver rises. The value of silver coins can also go up because of the relative scarcity of a particular coin. Because of this twofold value of silver coins, they generally sell at a premium above the price of bullion.

You can obtain more information about investing in silver coins from the two most respected periodicals in the field, *Coin World* and *The Numismatist*.

Common Stocks

The major advantage of investing in silver common stocks is that you obtain a current return on your investment. None of the other forms of silver investment pays a dividend or return of any type.

There are some potential disadvantages of common stocks you should consider: the political environment where the mine is located; price sensitivity of the mine when the ore is of relatively poor grade; the labor situation at the mine; and possible disasters such as cave-ins.

You can get up-to-date information about the current financial status and future prospects of any major silver mine from your broker and other reliable sources such as Value Line, Standard & Poors, and Moody's.

Some of the major stocks that you should examine are: ASARCO (NYSE; Rosario (NYSE); Sunshine Mining (NYSE); Texas Gulf (NYSE); Day Mines (AMEX); Callahan (NYSE); Hecla (NYSE); United Keno Hill Mines Ltd. (Toronto Exchange); Agnico-Eagle (Toronto Exchange).

If you cannot afford to diversify you should consider a no-load mutual fund with a good history that specializes in metals.

Bonds Convertible into Metal

Sunshine Mining initiated a unique bond instrument that may become popular. Sunshine issued a bond convertible at a future date into a specified number of ounces of silver. Until conversion or maturity (in 1995) the bond pays 8½%. The price of this bond has fluctuated a great deal as the price of silver has changed dramatically. Investors were very anxious to buy this bond when it was issued since they felt that silver prices would increase and the value of the bond would go up accordingly.

In the future, other companies may follow Sunshine's lead since the issue was quickly oversubscribed. This type of issue combines income and price appreciation potential because its price is linked to the price of silver. The risk associated with this type of issue depends on several factors: the price of the metal the financial status of the company; and the capability of the company to pay off its bondholders in the required quantity of metal.

It is important to examine the bond rating of the issuing company. Standard & Poors and Moody's rates the bonds issued by major corporations. Convertible issues are commonly issued by companies whose ratings are below average. The convertible feature makes it feasible for many companies to issue bonds that they could not otherwise. In addition, the convertible feature allows the issuer to pay less (lower coupon rate) than it would for a straight bond issue.

DIAMONDS

Within the last 10 years there has been much more interest in the United States in purchasing diamonds as investments. In other cultures, especially in Europe, there has been a longer history of diamond investments.

There are many reasons for the rising popularity of diamonds in the United States. The major one is that Americans have been "buried" with statistics indicating which investments have been outperforming inflation and the traditional investments. Diamonds fall in this category. The supply and production of South African diamonds is controlled by the DeBeers Group. For many years they have restricted the supply of uncut diamonds to their customers to ensure a steady increase in worldwide diamond prices.

Another reason that diamonds are more in demand as investments is the "Prudent Man Rule," part of The Employment Retirement Security Act of 1974 (ERISA). The prudent man rule under ERISA governs investment activity and applies to all fiduciaries. The fiduciary must invest solely in the interest of the participants and beneficiaries, and for the exclusive purpose of 1) providing benefits to participants and their beneficiaries and 2) defraying reasonable expenses of administering the plan. The fiduciary should act in the same manner as a prudent man familiar with such matters acting in a similar capacity. The fiduciary will also be required to diversify the investments of the plan so as to minimize large losses, unless under the circumstances it would be prudent to diversify. Based on this rule, trustees have increased exposure to liability in their investment decisions. Trustees are no longer restricting themselves to traditional bond and stock investments. They are including in their portfolios investments that they believe will provide an above average rate of return, preserve capital, and minimize taxes. One of the advantages of investments in diamonds is that taxes are deferred as long as the diamonds are held. From a tax viewpoint this is superior to bond or stock investments whose interest and dividends are taxable.

Moreover, from a trustee's viewpoint it is easier to invest in a diamond on a long-term basis than it is to hold a common stock. Diamonds have shown a much more stable growth pattern than individual common stocks (or bonds) have.

Industry Structure

DeBeers Consolidated Mines controls the production and distribution of approximately 90% of all rough diamonds mined in the world. DeBeers makes these diamonds available several times each year in London to a select group of diamond brokers. The diamonds are offered at prices determined by DeBeers. No bargaining takes place. If the broker wants to stay in the diamond business, he or she must buy at the DeBeers price. The DeBeers group has been very shrewd in controlling diamond supply and increasing the diamond price systematically. At the retail level, diamonds have increased in value at a rate of approximately 12.5% compounded annually since the beginning of the twentieth century. This rate of increase is far superior to any of the popular stock market averages. The rate of increase is also superior to the increase in gold prices since the beginning of the twentieth century.

There can be a significant difference between the wholesale and retail price of diamonds. A 50–100% mark-up is not unusual. Unless you know someone in the business or you are a large customer you would probably pay at least a 50% mark-up. Therefore, investing in diamonds on a short-term basis is simply not profitable. You must be prepared to invest in diamonds for a minimum of 2 years if you are a small buyer.

If you are interested in quick turnover of your assets for profits, you should consider a different investment vehicle. Gold, silver, and stocks and bonds are examples of investments in which spreads between wholesale and retail prices are relatively narrow, normally less than 10%. Accordingly, you can make a profit quickly if prices move favorably. With diamonds you must be much more patient.

Diamonds will not provide any income to you. If income is an important investment criterion, you must include other investments in your portfolio such as bonds, certificates of deposit, stocks, or annuities.

Diamond middlemen operate on a relatively high mark-up—50% or more. Therefore, you will not be able to sell your diamond at a profit very quickly if you are reselling to your supplier. For example, assume you purchase diamonds at a retail price of $10,000; the cost to your supplier was $6666. Your diamond must increase in value by 50% before your supplier would be willing to pay you $10,000 for the diamonds your purchased. If diamonds increase in value at a rate of 13% per year it would take you 3 years to break even. If you could sell the diamond at its retail value, you would not have to wait as long before breaking even. Unless you are in the diamond business, however, you will be selling your diamonds back to middlemen who will offer you less than wholesale prices.

Checklist

If you are interested in investing in diamonds, consider the following guidelines to further your knowledge and protect your investment.

1 Contact the Gemological Institute of America, 580 Fifth Avenue, New York, NY. Determine what courses they have available that suit you. The institute offers both correspondence courses and residence courses. Ask them to recommend periodicals and other sources of reliable information. They should be able to provide you with reliable dealers and investment advisary firms specializing in diamonds.

2 Store your diamonds in a safe place such as a safety deposit box.

3 Insure any diamonds you own.

4 Review carefully any money-back agreements. You should specifically review any disclaimers that would void the agreement. If you are offered a guarantee of this type, it will undoubtedly affect the price you pay for the diamonds.

5 Obtain written statements regarding the quality of the diamonds you purchase as well as warranties and any other services that are offered you.

6 When you decide to buy diamonds, determine the size, quality, and other characteristics you are looking for based on the amount you have to invest. Then you will be in a position to compare prices among several diamond dealers.

7 When you decide to sell, use multiple diamond dealers to ensure that you receive the most favorable prices. After you have surveyed the professional market, you may want to consider selling your diamonds to a private party. Since the mark-up is so high in this business, if you can find a person who is interested, you should be able to negotiate a price favorable to both of you.

Characteristics of Diamonds

The major characteristics of diamonds are the Four Cs: Carat; Color; Clarity; and Cut.

The carat is the weight of the diamond. In general heavier diamonds are worth more proprotionately than small diamonds. For example, a 1-carat diamond would be worth more than two ½ carat diamonds of the same quality. Investment quality diamonds are generally between ½ and 5 carats.

Diamonds are specified in terms of "points." One carat is equal to 100 points. It is important when ordering diamonds to specify minimum carat size since values can vary significantly if the size of a diamond is slightly below a specific size. For example, a diamond of 99 points may be valued on a different scale than a diamond of a full carat.

Color refers to the shade of white in the diamond. Colorless diamonds are the most valuable. The exact color can be determined through the use of a spectrophotometer that measures color precisely. The Gemological Institute of America (GIA) has established a scale used to compare colors. On that scale the rarest color is graded D. Other grades that are considered to be of investment quality are E, F, G, and H.

Clarity refers to the passage of light through the stone. All diamonds contain some flaws that restrict the passage of light. Experts check clarity with a magnifying hand lens.

The best rating on the GIA scale is flawless (FL). Other good ratings in descending order of clarity are IF, VVS_1, VVS, VS_1 and VS_2. The initials stand for internally flawless, very very slight inclusions, and very slight inclusions.

The cut is the geometric figure of the diamond after it has been shaped from a rough stone. A round cut shows a diamond's best qualities and is generally more valuable than other shapes. The pear shape and the oval may be used to increase the wieght of a cut diamond.

Advantages and Disadvantages of Diamonds

Advantages

1   Diamonds have been and probably will continue to be a good inflation hedge. Diamonds will very likely continue to increase in value because of the DeBeers Group control of the market.

2   You can verify the quality of any diamond you purchase because of the standards established by the Gemological Institute of America.

3   Diamonds can be used as collateral for other financial transactions.

4   Investments in diamonds provide you with a tax advantage if you retain them for a long time. Until you sell the diamonds at a profit you do not have any tax liability. In contrast to other types of investment, once you select a quality diamond there is really no advantage in selling it to purchase another diamond that you feel will appreciate at a faster rate.

Disadvantages

The major disadvantages of diamond investments are related to liquidity, income, and the length of time you probably must hold a diamond before it becomes profitable. One way to ensure liquidity is to purchase a diamond from a merchant who will guarantee to buy it back. You should understand, however, that the merchant does not have to repurchase the diamond at a profit to you.

PLATINUM

Platinum is another metal that you should give some attention to. It will probably be a good inflation hedge because of its scarcity. Platinum is used both for jewelry and for industrial use.

Approximately one third of the world's platinum is made into jewelry. In most cultures other precious metals are preferred for this use. Japan is the exception. In Japan more than half of the metal is used for jewelry and has been even more popular than gold.

Industrial use

Platinum is widely used in a number of industrial applications. It is used extensively in automobile; chemical; petroleum; and electrical industries and will probably continue to be used since there is no comparable substitute. The qualities that make platinum unique are its high melting point; its high resistance to corrosion; and its unique catalytic properties.

The most extensive use of platinum in industry is in the automotive industry. It is used specifically for automotive exhaust pollution control. In the face of recession the federal government may relax its pollution control standards, but on a long-term basis, it can be expected that the government will insist on strict pollution standards that will ensure a steady demand for platinum in the automotive industry.

Wartime Usage

Platinum is a vital element in war. As long as the threat of war exists, the federal government will stockpile the metal. Russia is one of the world's major producers of platinum. This is another reason that the United States will probably add to its inventory of the metal to eliminate any dependence on Russia as a supplier.

Supply Factors

The leading producers of platinum are South Africa, Russia, and Canada. The foremost of these has been South Africa, which has the advantage of owning extensive properties with relatively high platinum content. Platinum is mined with other metals, predominately copper and nickel.

The demand for copper and nickel will affect the availability of platinum since platinum is produced as a by-product of these metals. Any reduction in the demand for these metals will have a positive impact on platinum prices.

In the future it is expected that platinum prices will increase because of the following factors: Russia will probably restrict its supply; higher mining costs; uncertain political climate in South Africa; increased industrial demand; and an expected increase in demand by individuals searching for tangible investments that will keep pace with inflation.

Price Trends

The price of platinum rose dramatically in the 1970s. Although there have been temporary drops in the price of the metal, the price for a troy ounce of platinum has consistently gone up. The following table indicates the price trend per troy ounce based on average prices.

1970	$132
1973	$152
1976	$168
1978	$206
1979	$352
1980	$437

Alternate Investments

There are three basic ways you can invest in platinum: stocks; bars; and the futures market.

You can obtain a detailed explanation of the futures marekt from the New York Commodity Exchanges (COMEX) at 4 World Trade Center, New York, NY 10048. They will provide you with an excellent brochure which includes information about commoditis traded on COMEX. Futures options are traded on both COMEX and the Chicago Board of Trade.

The stock whose companies control the most extensive mines is Rustenburg Platinum Holdings Ltd. The stock can be purchased in the United States through the purchase of American depository receipts (ADRs). The mines are in South Africa.

Other stocks that will appreciate in value if platinum prices rise are: Union Corporation (ADR); Bishopgate (London Stock Exchange); International Nickel (NYSE); and Lydenburg Platinum (London Stock Exchange). Since the price movements of these stocks can be volatile, you should not purchase them indiscriminitely. Use the research capability of your brokerage firm before you invest so that you have a good understanding of earnings projections, recent price movements, and the political climate.

You should also consider the purchase of mutual funds that specialize in metals. Using that option you should benefit from overall price increases in metals without being overly dependent on the fortunes of one or two selected companies.

Investment in platinum bars in another alternative you can consider. They are generally available in sizes from 1 ounce to 100 ounces. You will find, however, that it is much more difficult to buy and sell platinum than gold or silver. There are far fewer dealers.

14 Tax Savings Hints

Some of these topics have been discussed in other sections of this book. However, since minimizing taxes is so important an objective, a summary is presented here.

MAJOR FEATURES OF THE ECONOMIC RECOVERY ACT OF 1981

Tax Reduction   Congress authorized three rounds of reductions in individual tax rates: 5% on October 1, 1981, 10% on July 1, 1982, and 10% on July 1, 1983.

Indexing   There will be annual adjustments to income brackets, personal exemptions, and the zero bracket amount, based on the inflation rate, starting in 1985.

Retirement Planning   The eligibility requirements were relaxed so that employees covered by company pension plans can also contribute to IRA plans. The maximum contribution to IRA plans was increased from $1500 to $2000. The IRA contribution is no longer restricted to 15% of earned income. For Keogh plans, for self-employed workers, the limit on deductible contributions was increased from $15,000 to $30,000. One new restriction was introduced. Individuals with self-directed plans, starting in 1982, can no longer purchase gold, silver, diamonds, or fine arts for IRA/Keogh investments.

Estate and Gift Tax   The federal estate tax exemption, which was $175,000 in 1981, will be increased in steps to $600,000 by 1987. Spouses will be able to leave all of their estate to a surviving spouse without paying an estate and gift tax. The maximum tax rate will be reduced, on taxable transfers above $5 million, from 70% to 50% on transfers above 2.5 million. The rate will be reduced 5% a year from 1982 to 1985.

Gift Allowance   The annual tax-free limit of $3000/individual was increased to $10,000; for a joint spousal gift a $20,000 gift is allowable.

176

Utility Dividend In 1982, common stockholders of qualified public utilities can exclude up to $1500 ($3000 if jointly held) in dividends if they elect to reinvest the proceeds to purchase additional common stock. The dividends will be taxable at capital gains rates when the stock is sold if the stock is held for more than one year.

Savings Certificates After October 1, 1981, banks and savings institutions can offer 1-year certificates that yield up to 70% of the yield on 52-week treasury bills. The interest is tax-free up to $1000 for individuals and $2000 for joint returns.

Dividend Exclusion The dividend and interest exclusion, which was $200 ($400 for joint returns), reverts to $100 ($200) in 1982 and will hold for subsequent years.

Marriage Tax Relief Starting in 1982, there will be a 5% exclusion of the income of the lower-earning spouse, up to a $1500 maximum exclusion. The exclusion percentage will be increased in steps until 1983 when the percentage exclusion will be fixed at 10% with a $3000 maximum.

Stock Options The 1976 law that imposed ordinary income taxes on executive stock options if there was a gain when the option was exercised was repealed. Under the revised law, profits on stock options are taxed only when the stock is sold.

Americans Working Abroad Americans working and living abroad, starting in 1982, can exclude up to $75,000 of wages and salary. This exclusion increases $5000 a year to $95,000 in 1986. An American would have to spend 11 of 12 months outside the United States to qualify.

Contributions Taxpayers who use the standard deduction can deduct 25% of their contributions up to $100 a year in 1982 and 1983. The allowable deduction is 25% up to $300 in 1984; 50% with no upper limit in 1985; and 100% with no upper limit in 1986. This deduction will no longer be in effect after 1986 unless Congress modifies the legislation.

FILING REQUIREMENTS

The IRS establishes higher income limits for filing for individuals older than 65. For example, for 1980 tax returns an individual older than 65 would not have to file an income tax return if his or her gross income was below $4300. For joint returns the limit is $6400, and if your spouse is also older than 65, the limit goes to $7400. These limits are modified periodically by the IRS, and you can get the latest information by contacting your local IRS office.

Even though you may not owe any taxes, if your gross income is below these limits you certainly should file if any taxes have been withheld so you can receive a refund.

If you are self-employed, you must file a return if your net earnings are more than $400. You must pay self-employment tax on your net earnings even if you are receiving Social Security benefits.

TAX-FREE INCOME

The following sources of income are tax-free. Do not report them on your tax return as reportable income.

Social Security retirement payments.

Railroad Retirement annuity.

Portion of annuity payment that is a repayment of your cost.

Interest on tax-exempt securities.

The first $100 ($200 for jointly owned securities) of dividends paid out of earnings by a taxable U.S. corporation. For your 1981 return $200 ($400 joint) of dividends and interest income are tax-free.

The IRS, in its free publication, *You and Your Income Tax*, provides a complete list of items that can be excluded from gross income on your tax return.

EXTRA EXEMPTIONS

When you reach age 65 you will receive an extra tax exemption. When your spouse reaches 65 he or she will also receive an extra deduction. Thus when both you and your spouse are 65 or over, you are entitled to four exemptions on your tax return.

TAX CREDIT FOR THE ELDERLY

A tax credit for the elderly is available to people over 65 who do not receive Social Security or Railroad Retirement benefits. The credit is also available to individuals under 65 who receive income from a public retirement system.

The maximum credit for a single person in 1980 was $375; the maximum credit for a married couple was $562.50. The IRS can modify these amounts in any tax year.

The amount of your credit is computed by taking 15% of a base amount from which some tax-free retirement benefits are subtracted. The base amount for single persons or when only one spouse is eligible is $2500; the base amount for a couple when both spouses are eligible for the credit is $3750; the base amount is $1875 if you are married and file a separate return. You may claim the credit on a separate return only if you and your spouse have not lived together during the tax year.

The base must be reduced by Social Security payments, Railroad Retirement payments, some tax-free pension/annuity income, and half of adjusted gross income above stipulated amounts based on marital status. If you are single, that amount is $7500; married and filing a joint return, $10,000; married and filing separately, $5000.

Example

You are married and both you and your wife are over 65. You received $1000 in Social Security payments and earned $12,000 during the tax year. Therefore, if you file a joint return, $2000 ($12,000−$10,000) must be deducted from your base ($3750).

Initial base		$3750
Adjustments:		
Social Security	$1000	
Income adjustment, 50% × (12,000−10,000)	$1000	$2000
Adjusted base		$1750
Credit (15% × adjusted base)		$ 262.50

TAX DEFERRED EMPLOYER SAVINGS/INVESTMENT PLANS

Many employers now offer deferred savings/investment plans providing attractive tax shelters. Since the details of these plans vary, you should find out if your employer has such a plan and, if so, examine all of the details.

As a result of the 1981 tax law changes, you may be able to participate in an IRA program through an employer-sponsored pension program. If you are eligible, and do participate, your contributions, up to $2000/year, would be nontaxable until you withdraw the funds. You should recognize, however, that if you do participate in an IRA program there are limitations on your flexibility in withdrawing funds without penalty prior to age 59½ (see Chapter 8). After age 59½ you may withdraw funds without penalty.

Even if your employer develops an IRA program, you may elect not to participate. You may still be able to make contributions to an employer pension plan in which your contributions are not tax deductible. Yet there still would be tax advantages for you since any increase in value, whether from interest, dividends, or capital gains, would not be taxable until you withdrew funds from the plan. Although you would not have the immediate tax advantage of an IRA program you would probably have more flexibility in being able to withdraw funds without penalty. Moreover, any capital gains would be taxed at a lower rate than in an IRA plan. All withdrawals from IRAs are taxed at ordinary income rates.

If you leave your current employer, you will probably not be able to leave your funds in the plan. That will depend on the specific plan of your employer. However, even in that situation you will have a few options available to you that should minimize your taxes. You will be able to rollover any of your *employers'* contributions to an IRA plan. IRA rollovers are discussed in Chapter 10. By utilizing an IRA with your lump sum distribution you postpone paying any taxes until you withdraw funds from your IRA.

Another option you have with an employer's lump sum distribution is 10-year averaging. If you select 10-year averaging, you spread your tax liability out over a 10-year period. You pay taxes as the single head of household rate regardless of your marital status. The most important factor, however, is that the distribution is taxed as if it were your only income. Your other income is not a consideration in computing the tax liability for the distribution. This is very important for individuals or family units whose other income is considerable.

As an example, assume you just received a $100,000 distribution from your employer because you changed jobs. Of the $100,000, you contributed $50,000, and $50,000 represents your employer's contribution plus dividends, income, and capital gains. You do not have to pay any tax on your $50,000 since you have already been taxed on it. Your only options are related to the $50,000 that is or will be taxable. If you place the $50,000 or any part of it into an IRA, you will postpone taxes until you withdraw funds from the IRA account. At that time, all of your withdrawals will be taxable at *ordinary income* tax rates.

If you select 10-year averaging, you pay taxes at the single head of household rate for the next 10 years. However, you will be paying taxes on the basis of $5000 per year ($50,000÷10 years). You will be paying the same income tax on the $5000 whether you earn $100,000 or nothing in other income. With 10-year averaging the tax is computed separately from your other income. Accordingly, you tax bite is relatively small.

If you select the IRA option, you can, when you reach age 59½, make withdrawals so that you also spread your distribution out over a 10-year period. If you have no other taxable income at that time, you would also be minimizing your tax payments.

The primary advantage of 10-year averaging in comparison to IRAs is that you have access to your money right away, and you have no restrictions on the manner of investing your distribution. The disadvantage is that although you minimize your tax payment, you can no longer defer taxes on your employers' distributions or any earnings you have made in the plan. A complete explanation of 10-year averaging including eligibility requirements is described in the next section of this chapter.

The primary advantage of the IRA rollover is that you can continue to postpone your tax liability. The principal disadvantages are that once you commit yourself to an IRA plan, you cannot obtain funds before age 59½ without incurring prohibitive penalties. Another disadvantage is that you are somewhat constrained in switching your investments. You can only transfer from one type of IRA investment to another once each year.

You have the option of paying taxes on your distribution in the next tax year rather than using either 10-year averaging or IRAs. From a tax viewpoint, there is no advantage in that option.

TEN-YEAR AVERAGING

The use of 10-year averaging is a very attractive option for anyone receiving a relatively large taxable distribution from a qualified profit-sharing or retirement plan. You are eligible to use 10-year averaging if you meet the following requirements:

1 Payment must be from a qualified pension or profit-sharing plan.

2 You must receive *all* that is due you under the plan.

3 The payments must be made within 1 year of your taxable years. (In other words, you cannot retire and wait 2 years before receiving distributions and then claim 10-year averaging).

With 10-year averaging you spread your tax payments over a 10-year period in equal payments rather than pay all your taxes in 1 year. In addition, the tax rate is much lower than it would be if you simply reported your distribution as ordinary income.

If you elect 10-year averaging, your taxes are based on the unmarried individual's tax rate schedule regardless of your marital status. The tax is based *only* on the amount of your distribution. The tax is *independent* of any other income you report in any of the 10 years you use income averaging.

For example, assume you receive a taxable distribution of $20,000. With income averaging, you would pay taxes at a rate of 7%. Other effective rates are as follows:

If your distribution is	Your effective tax rate (1980 Tables) is
$ 30,000	11.1%
40,000	13.7%
50,000	15.4%
75,000	17.9%
100,000	19.2%

This tax rate in almost every case will be lower than the tax rate you pay on your regular income. You can compute your tax savings using 10-year averaging by multiplying the amount of your taxable distribution by the difference in rates between the 10-year averaging rate and the rate you pay for your ordinary income.

You can learn more details about 10-year averaging from the IRA publication *Your Federal Income Tax* and publication 575, *Pension and Annuity Income*.

REAL ESTATE—$125,000 EXCLUSION

The tax laws are beneficial to owners of real estate in many ways. This is true for investors in income property, land, and private residences. The recent changes in the tax laws provide an excellent *one-time* tax shelter for owners of private residences after they reach age 55. After that age you are allowed up to a $125,000 income tax exclusion for any profits you have made on real estate you have sold. This exclusion is accumulative in the sense that it applies to all residences that you have bought and sold during your life as long as you continue to purchase new residences within the allowable time (24 months) after you sell your previous residence.

For example, assume that you buy a home for $45,000 in January 1960. You sell the home in December 1970 for $60,000. In June 1971, you purchase a co-op for $75,000. In December 1975, you sell the co-op for $100,000. In January 1976, you buy a condominium for $120,000. You are now 56 and you still own the condominium. You have a total of $40,000 in profits—$15,000 from the first home and $25,000 from the co-op. You could sell your existing condominium for up to $205,000 without incurring any income tax liability. If you sold your condominium for $205,000 you would have a total profit of $125,000 for all three residences ($15,000 + $25,000 + $85,000).

If you sell your condominium for more than $205,000 and *do not* buy another residence, you will have to pay a capital gains tax based on the amount you received over $205,000. Assume you sell your condominium for $225,000. You would owe capital gains tax on $20,000 ($145,000 − $125,000 exclusion). You are only allowed to take the exclusion once in your life, after age 55.

As long as you continue to purchase residences more expensive than the last one you sold, you can effectively postpone any tax liability on any profits you have made on the sale of your residences. If you decide you no longer wish to be a homeowner after you reach age 55, it is to your advantage to use your option of the $125,000 one-time exclusion.

The exclusion gives individuals an incentive to continue owning personal real estate, at least until they have a $125,000 gain.

It should be remembered, however, that you can postpone income tax liabilities indefinitely during your lifetime by continuing to own your home. For example, a man has over a $200,000 gain on personal property he has bought and sold. If he remains living in a residence he owns, he will not incur any income tax liability. If he sells the residence and does not purchase another within 24 months he will have an income tax liability.

In summary, there are two major tax shelters available to you in your personal residence:

The $125,000 lifetime exclusion after age 55.

The continuous postponement of income taxes by continuing to own your home.

DISCOUNT BONDS

Whenever interest rates go up, bond prices go down. If interest rates go up significantly, many quality bonds will be selling at a discount from par—that is, the value of the bond at maturity. This situation provides you with an opportunity to purchase bonds at a discount, hold them to maturity, and receive a capital gain, which is taxable at lower rates than ordinary income.

For example, assume that a top quality bond maturing in 1990 is selling for $900. Assume also that the coupon rate is 8%. If you purchase 10 bonds for $9000, you will receive $80 per year in interest income, and you will receive $10,000 in 1990 at maturity. The difference between the $10,000 you received and the $9000 you paid, or $1000, would be treated as a capital gain for federal income tax purposes.

This type of investment is attractive for high income tax bracket investors who are not as concerned with present income as they are with assured capital gains that are taxed at favorable rates.

Individuals who have long-term losses on securities may want to consider the purchase of discount bonds to counteract the losses. The IRS only allows you to deduct 50% of any long-term losses. If you have gains to offset the losses, however, you effectively are allowed credit for all your losses. For example, assume you have a loss of $1000 on some stock. The IRS would allow you only a $500 credit against your taxes. If you had a $1000 gain to offset against the loss, you would be able to get credit for the complete $1000 loss and save the tax on $500.

MUNICIPAL BONDS

If your income is high enough, you may find that you can obtain a higher after-tax return with municipal bonds than you would with taxable investments.

CUSTODIAN ACCOUNTS   185

All income on municipal bonds is exempt from federal taxes. If you reside in the state where the bonds are issued, you are exempt from state taxes as well.

Municipal bonds are rated by Standard & Poors and Moody's as to quality of issue. Although in the aggregate municipal bonds have been safe investments, you should not purchase municipal bonds indiscriminately. You should only buy issues that are top rated unless you are willing to take risks with your capital in exchange for a 1−2% higher rate of return.

The one disadvantage associated with municipal bonds is the lack of capital appreciation potential. Unless you buy bonds at a discount from par, at maturity you will receive exactly the amount that you initially paid for the bond. You will have no protection from inflation as far as your capital base is concerned. You should invest in municipals if your primary concern is tax-free income, not capital appreciation.

In 1981 congress passed legislation that reduced income taxes 25% over three years, 1981−1983. You may find, as this legislation goes into effect, that you can obtain a higher after-tax return from other investments such as government or corporate bonds.

GIFT TAXES

Under the current law there is one unified tax schedule that applies to gifts and estates. The basic intent of the law was to apply the same tax rate whether gifts are made during your lifetime or after your death. However, you can reduce your overall estate/gift tax by making gifts during your lifetime. For example, you can give up to $10,000 tax-free to each of as many individuals as you like without incurring a gift tax. If your spouse agrees, the tax-free gift can be $20,000 per married couple to each individual. There is no limit to the number of individuals to whom you can give gifts.

CUSTODIAN ACCOUNTS

A convenient and inexpensive method of minimizing taxes is the use of custodian accounts. Gifts of money or securities can be made to minors using this device. A custodian can be a parent, guardian, grandparent, brother, sister, uncle, or aunt. In some states the custodian can also be an adult or a financial institution.

Once the account is established, the assets in the custodian account can be used only for the benefit of a child. The money may not be used by a parent to provide basic necessities for the child. When the minor reaches majority age (which varies from state to state), the property in the custodian account is turned over to him or her.

The income that the account earns is taxable to the child, not to the custodian. Therefore, as long as the taxable income of the child is lower than the taxable income of the custodian, there is an overall tax advantage.

If you die while you are the custodian of an account, the value of the account is included in your estate for tax purposes. If you are concerned about minimizing your estate taxes, you should consider whether you would prefer your spouse or another eligible individual to be custodian of the account. You will be subject to a gift tax if you provided more than $10,000 ($20,000 if jointly with your spouse) in assets within 1 year to a custodian account.

INSURANCE OWNED BY A BENEFICIARY

Until the 1981 tax changes were made, there was some advantage in having your spouse own your life insurance policy, assuming he or she was the beneficiary. The proceeds of life insurance are included in your estate if you are the owner of the policy. Based on the 1981 tax law changes, your spouse will not have to pay any estate taxes on property he or she receives from you starting in 1981. Therefore, there is no longer any tax advantage in having your spouse own your life insurance policy.

There still may be an advantage in having a beneficiary other than your spouse own your policy. For example, assume you have no spouse, or the beneficiary of your policy is not your spouse. If the size of your estate, including the insurance proceeds, exceeds the allowable estate tax exemption ($600,000 in 1981), there could be some tax savings if your beneficiary owns the policy. If you decide to use this option, the beneficiary must pay the premium. If he or she does not have sufficient income to pay the premium, you can give him or her up to $10,000/year tax-free under the amended gift tax laws passed in 1981.

IRAS/KEOGHS

Starting in 1982 all workers can contribute to IRA plans up to $2000 of their earned income. Self-employed individuals can now contribute to Keogh plans up to 15% of their employment earnings up to a maximum of $15,000 per year. All earnings contributed to IRA and Keogh plans are deductible from your taxable income. Any earnings on your investment would accumulate tax-free until you withdraw the funds. As early as age 59½ you can make withdrawals without penalty. You would pay taxes on all the money you withdraw but probably at a reduced rate since your taxable income should be lower at retirement than it was during your working years. See Chapters 8–11 for a fuller discussion of IRA and Keogh plans.

REAL ESTATE SYNDICATES

A syndicator is a person or group that organizes real estate partnership ventures for investors—essentially a middleman between the investors and the developer. He or she is responsible for selecting the property, arranging for its purchase, and working with the developer on construction. In some situations, the syndicator is also the developer.

Normally syndicators do not incur any risk. They make money by taking commissions and/or retaining a percentage of ownership of the partnership. Syndicators will generate some revenues for themselves even if the rest of the partners do not obtain an adequate return on their investments. Therefore, you must investigate the background of syndicators and analyze their performance with respect to other syndications they have been associated with.

The major advantage of real estate syndications is an initial tax advantage. In the first few years of your ownership you will probably be able to deduct losses on your investment even if your are receiving a positive cash flow. Another advantage is that you will not be playing an active role. You put up the capital, and the syndicator manages the investment.

There are many potential disadvantages. Syndicators take their share out of the capital immediately. Start-up expenses can be high. In many syndications the property is not selected until after the capital has been put up. In that situation you would be investing without knowing what property you are purchasing. Although there may be initial tax advantages, eventually you will have tax liabilities. It is important to examine the eventual tax impact of your investment with your tax preparer.

Real estate syndications can be successful when syndicators know what they are doing. Do not go into any syndication unless the syndicator has an established track record, and it has been demonstrated that the syndication will have a tax advantage *for you*. The optimum situation for you would be if you have a high income during the first few years of the syndication when you anticipate taxable losses and expect to have little or no income when you would have to report gains.

A tax shelter is of no value to you if the investment itself is not good. If you think that the only advantage in the investment is the shelter, don't invest your money. Look first at the investment. Then look at the tax aspects. You should use this philosophy for any tax shelter investment, not only for real estate syndications.

Real estate tax shelters established under a limited partnership structure have a more favorable tax advantage than other tax shelters. Federal laws were changed in 1976 and 1978 to restrict the advantages of investing in other tax shelters. Before the laws were changed, large writeoffs were allowable with limited risk, since an investor was allowed to deduct expenses in excess of the investment. The new laws limit deductions for nonreal estate investments to the investors' risk capital. Accordingly, investors are allowed to take deductions in excess of their initial investment only if they are willing to risk losing more than their initial investment.

CAPITAL GAINS

If you buy and sell common stocks and bonds, it is very important that you understand the tax code with respect to the difference between short-term and long-term capital gains and losses. If you hold a security for 1 year or longer, the tax status is long-term; otherwise it is short-term.

If you sell a security at a profit, your tax liability is much greater if you hold a security for less than 1 year—your profits will be taxed at ordinary income tax rates. If you hold a security for longer than 1 year, the tax is 40% of your ordinary income tax rate. Therefore, it is to your advantage to hold securities that you have made a profit on for at least 1 year before you sell them. An exception would be a situation in which the price of the security is volatile, and there is a high probability you could lose your gain if you held the security for a year.

If you are holding securities that are selling for less than you paid for them, you should consider selling them before you have held them 1 year to get the maximum tax advantage. If you sell securities at a loss before you have held them for 1 taxable year, you may deduct 100% of your loss up to $3000. If your short-term losses exceed $3000, you can carry forward your loss to subsequent years.

For example, assume you lost $7000 on a short-term basis in 1981. You could deduct $3000 from your taxable income on your 1981 tax return. You would still be able to take a $3000 deduction on your 1982 return and $1000 on your 1983 return.

If you sell securities at a loss after you have held them for longer than 1 year, you may only deduct 50% of your loss up to a maximum of $3000 per year. For example, assume you lost $10,000 on securities that you held for more than 1 year in 1981. You are allowed a total deduction of $5000. You can claim a $3000 deduction on your 1980 return and a $2000 deduction on your 1981 return.

No one likes to take a loss on an investment. Therefore, people hesitate to sell securities just to be able to take a short-term capital loss. But you don't have to stop there. If you feel that the stock will recover, you can rebuy the same stock 31 days or later after your sale. Another alternative is to buy a similar security in the same industry simultaneous with your security sale. In that way, if industry stocks make a comeback you can recover some or all of your loss. Meanwhile you have established a short-term loss for tax purposes.

If you purchased the same security within 30 days before or after your sale, the IRS considers the transaction to be a "wash sale." You would not be allowed a tax deduction in that situation since your position essentially would not have changed.

You can net long- and short-term capital gains and losses on your tax return. If you have both long-term gains and long-term losses, the net result of all your transactions would be reported. If the result is a gain, 40% of the gain is reportable. If the result is a loss, 50% of the loss up to $3000 is deductible.

You can match short-term gains with short-term losses. If the net result is a gain, you would report the net gain and pay tax at your ordinary income rate. If the net result is a loss, you would be able to deduct the net loss up to $3000 for 1 tax year and carry forward any excess.

If you have a net long-term gain and a net short-term loss, you would deduct the short-term loss from the long-term gain. If the loss is greater than the gain, you can deduct the gain up to $3000 in 1 year. The loss can be carried forward as a short-term loss in subsequent years. If the long-term gain exceeds the short-term loss, you would report 40% of the excess.

If you have a net short-term gain and net long-term loss, you would deduct the long-term loss from the short-term gain. If the gain is greater than the loss, you would report the gain as ordinary income. If the loss is greater than the gain, you could deduct 50% of your loss up to $3000 per year, with a carryover to subsequent years if 50% of your loss exceeds $3000.

If you have net short-term gains and net long-term gains, or net short-term losses and net long-term losses, they are treated separately in the same manner described earlier.

Once you have established a long-term loss, it is to your advantage to offset the loss with either a short- or long-term capital gain. If you report a long-term loss without an offsetting gain, you are allowed to deduct only 50% of your loss. Naturally you should not be selling securities that you feel have growth potential only to offset long-term capital losses. However, you should recognize the tax advantages associated with matching gains against long-term losses.

If you have substantial long-term losses in your portfolio, you may want to consider purchasing high quality bonds that are selling at a discount because of a low coupon rate relative to current prevailing rates. As the bonds approach maturity the discount will be reduced until maturity when there will be no discount. At maturity, you will receive the face value of the bond. If you have held the bond longer than 1 year, you will have a long-term capital gain that can be offset against the long-term losses you have for your other securities. Thus you would be able to offset 100% of your long-term losses rather than 50%, up to the value of your gains on the bonds. You should not use this strategy, however, if you feel that the securities you have already lost money on will continue to go down in value. You must weigh the tax advantage against the possible gains you could obtain if you simply sold your securities at a loss and reinvested the proceeds elsewhere.

INCORPORATION

Under the regulations of ERISA, professionals who incorporate can establish profit-sharing plans and set aside up to 15% of the annual compensation for each participant. The amount of money that is put aside is not taxable when the funds are put into the plan.

The major advantage of using this type of profit-sharing plan within a corporate structure is that the maximum contribution is higher than it would be with an IRA or Keogh plan. For example, in 1979 the maximum contribution was $32,000 in contrast to the $1500 and $7500 maximums for IRAs and Keoghs respectively. The maximum contribution will be adjusted in subsequent years based on a cost-of-living factor.

Exhibit 14-1 Tax Shelters

Type of Shelter	Deductions to Shelter Income	Income Deferral	Leverage	Non Taxable Income — Federal	Non Taxable Income — State	Non Taxable Income — Local	Capital Risk Factor	Liquidity	Growth Potential	Income	Eligibility Requirements	Limit on Investments
IRA		x					Variable	Low	Variable	Variable	Yes	Yes
Keogh		x					Variable	Low	Variable	Variable	Yes	Yes
Real Estate	x	x	x				High	Low	High	Variable	No	No
Oil and Gas (Limited Partnership)	x	x					High	Low	High	Variable	No	No
Annuity		x					Variable	Variable	Variable	Variable	No	No
Municipal Bond				x	Variable	Variable	Variable	High	Low	Medium	No	No
Treasury Instruments				Partial	x	x	Low	High	Low	High	No	No
Common Stocks			x	Partial			Variable	High	Variable	Variable	No	No
Savings Certificates				Partial			Low	Variable	Low	Medium /high	No	No

Criteria

Note: A "Variable" rating indicates that there is a wide selection of investment opportunities available. The rating for a particular selection could be from low to high.

TAX SHELTER INVESTMENT COMPARISON

The following chart (Exhibit 14-1) summarizes the major features of the tax sheltered investments we have reviewed. It is worth repeating that you should not select an investment simply because of its tax shelter aspects.

It is important to understand the value of tax shelters at different points in your life. When your income peaks, the value of tax shelters will be more significant. When you retire or decide to work part-time, you should reexamine the role that tax shelters should play in your investment planning process. Regardless of when you do your planning, however, do not lose sight of the fact that tax shelters are but one aspect of the investment planning process and that other important investment objectives such as growth potential, liquidity, risk of capital loss, and income are equally significant.

15 Estate Planning

ESTIMATING THE VALUE OF YOUR ESTATE

You cannot do an effective job of estate planning without first developing a personal balance sheet (see Exhibit 15-1). Your assets should be separated into present assets, deferred assets, and assets in your estate. Your present assets should be broken down into liquid assets as well as nonliquid assets.

The most important figure for planning purposes will be the total net assets. This is the amount that is left after all your liabilities are subtracted from the sum of your present assets, your deferred assets, and the assets that will exist after your death.

During this process it is necessary to separate your assets by ownership—for instance, assets owned by you alone, your spouse alone, or joint ownership with your spouse.

IDENTIFY WHO WILL RECEIVE ASSETS

How you distribute your assets upon your death will depend on a number of factors, including providing for your dependents, state law, your personal wishes, and tax factors. In a well-designed estate plan each significant asset is examined and determinations are made about how it will be treated. You may decide to dispose of certain assets during your life and others at death.

Lifetime Transfers

You have many options available to dispose of your property during your lifetime. You can transfer property to your spouse, children, any other person, or

Exhibit 15-1 Statement of Assets and Liabilities

	Husband	Wife	Joint
Present Assets			
Liquid			$1,000
Checking Accounts			
Savings Accounts	$ 2,000	$ 3,000	
Stocks	100,000	10,000	
Bonds	55,000		
	$157,000	$13,000	$1,000
Nonliquid			
Residence	150,000		
Other real estate	100,000		50,000
Tangible personal property	20,000		
Life insurance—cash value	5,000	2,000	
	$275,000	$ 2,000	$50,000
Gross present assets	$432,000	$15,000	$51,000
Less liabilities			
Mortgages	100,000		30,000
Net Present assets	$332,000	$15,000	$21,000
Deferred Assets			
Retirement income plan:			
Vested	80,000		
Nonvested	20,000		
	$100,000		
Assets at death			
Personal Life Insurance			
(less Cash Value)	$ 50,000		
Group Life Insurance			
(as of 12/01/80)	150,000		
	$200,000		
Total net assets	$632,000	$15,000	$21.000

194

to charitable organizations. You can place certain property in a "living" trust. You can register property jointly with members of your family or with anyone else. The conditions under which you would consider any or all of these alternatives are discussed later in this chapter.

Transfers at Death

You can elect to transfer property at your death by will. Certain property can be passed by will and other property by contract or law. Assets that are passed by contract or law are considered nonprobate property.

NONPROBATE PROPERTY

Property that passes by contract is distributed because of beneficiary designation. Life insurance is the most common asset that is handled this way. Insurance proceeds are not allocated by will unless the policy is payable to the estate or to a trust created in the will. If the life insurance is not specifically passed by will, the assets resulting from the policy are not available for taxes and other estate settlement purposes. This does not mean, however, that the value of the life insurance is not included in the estate for federal estate tax computations as long as the deceased party owned the policy.

Corporate benefits such as profit-sharing plans and pension plans, in addition to life insurance, pass by contract according to the assigned beneficiary.

Assets can be distributed by contract in other ways than by beneficiary designation. Trust agreements are regulated by the terms of the trust instrument and do not become probate assets. The advantages and disadvantages of trust agreements are discussed in detail later in this chapter.

Another example of property that can pass by contract rather than by will is U.S. savings bonds. These bonds can be registered with a "payable on death" provision. This designation takes precedence over any contradictory provision specified in a will.

In a partnership agreement, a successor beneficiary can be designated if death occurs during the life of the agreement. This agreement is another example of a contractual agreement that would result in property being passed independent of a will.

Property That Passes By Law

If property is jointly owned, the property is passed by law. There are two common types of joint ownership: joint tenancy and tenancy in common.

In joint tenancy two or more individuals own an interest in property with the agreement that if one dies the survivor gets the entire property. In a tenancy in common each co-owner maintains control over his or her individual share of the property. The property can be transferred or sold during the lifetime of each co-owner or be passed by will. There is no right of survivorship. A tenancy in common is not a substitute for a will. Thus it is important to determine whether joint property is held in common or in joint tenancy. Normally tenancy in common ownership is used in business relationships.

PROBATE PROPERTY

Probate is the process by which property is transferred at death either by will or by intestacy. Probate property includes all property that is not transferred by a testamentary substitute such as contract or law. The provisions of a will relate only to probate property.

The executor of an estate is entitled to a commission on probate property only. Any property that is passed through a substitute for a will is not subject to commission. Other estate settlements costs, however, are generally fixed.

Many people have taken steps to avoid probate to ensure that assets pass immediately. Unfortunately, there can be just as many delays for some assets even if probate is avoided. For example, banks, insurance companies, brokerage firms, and transfer agents cannot legally release substantial amounts of money or property when property is held in joint name or is payable to beneficiary designation. Documentation must be provided and clearance must be obtained from the applicable tax authorities.

The paperwork will be the same whether the assets are probate assets or not. Therefore, you should not choose a testamentary substitute only to avoid probate.

Your selection of a substitute should be based on other factors such as tax considerations, and you should have the advice of proper legal counsel.

WILLS

Function of Will

The major function of a will is to control the disposition of your assets. You should use an attorney to prepare your will, and it should reflect the assets you now have as well as additional assets that will go into your estate at your death. The will should take into consideration your present family situation and be broad enough to accomodate contingency planning. If you use a fiduciary, you should give instructions and powers to the fiduciary so that problems can be dealt with. Your will should be signed under the supervision of an attorney.

Before you see your attorney, you should prepare a balance sheet. You should also make sure you understand the present form of ownership of all your assets. A competent attorney should discuss the advantages and disadvantages of changing the form of ownership of your assets with you and your spouse.

You should also decide which of the following are your primary objectives:

Financial support of spouse for life.

Financial support of children up to a certain age.

Management and preservation of certain assets.

Charitable contributions.

Establishment of guardians for children.

Minimizing taxes.

Spouse's Will

Your spouse should have a will drawn up that is consistent with yours. It is easier and probably less expensive to have wills of both spouses drawn up at the same time. Even if your spouse does not have substantial assets now, in the event that you die before your spouse, her or his estate will grow.

Intestacy

Dying without a will is called dying intestate. State law then determines how assets are distributed. Laws vary among states. In some states a surviving spouse would receive one third to one half of the property, and the children would receive the balance. If there are surviving children who are minors, it becomes a very expensive, tedious process. A court-appointed guardian would be required.

A simple will is not an expensive document. If you are concerned about the cost of drawing up a will, discuss fees with your attorney first. If you don't have an attorney, you can ask your bank to refer one to you, or you can ask your friends or business associates to recommend one. As your situation changes you can have your will modified inexpensively with a codicil. There is really no logical reason for you not to have a will.

TRUSTS

Function

A trust is an agreement in which the person who establishes the trust gives property to a trustee to invest and manage for the advantage of the beneficiary. A trust allows you to have some control over assets after your death, as well as during your lifetime. There are four parties to a trust: the donor, or trustor; the trustee; the beneficiary; and the remainderman. The maker of the trust is the trustor. The receiver and manager of the assets is the trustee. The individual who receives income is the beneficiary. The remainderman is the party who receives the residue of the estate on termination of the trust. One individual can function in more than one of these functions.

Objectives

One major objective of trusts is to provide proper management of assets. The trustee is selected to manage the assets because he or she has more management expertise than the beneficiaries. The trustee is given the responsibility to manage the assets and distribute income in accordance with the objectives expressed by the trustor.

One of the major advantages of the trust agreement is flexibility. The trustee can be given broad responsibilities allowing him or her to be selective in terms of determining whether principal should be invaded, to whom funds are to be allocated (in the case of multiple beneficiaries), and how much is to be allocated.

Revocable and Irrevocable Trusts

Trusts can be established during one's lifetime, in which case they are called "living" trusts, or inter vivos trusts. If the trust is created by will, it is called a testamentary trust.

A trust that can be changed by the donor is called a revocable trust. A trust that cannot be changed by the donor once created is called an irrevocable trust. Testamentary trusts are irrecovable. Revocable trusts become irrevocable after the death of the donor.

Tax Considerations

A revocable trust has no tax advantages to you. Since you can modify or eliminate the trust you will be subject to income and capital gains tax. At your death the value of the assets in the revocable trust will be included in your estate for estate tax purposes. With a sizable estate you have more of an opportunity to save taxes passing your property by will than you have by creating a revocable trust. Before you establish a revocable trust, you should examine other alternatives that would have the same effect but would have more favorable tax implications.

An irrevocable trust has definite tax implications. There may be a gift tax depending on the amount of assets involved. There may be an income tax if income is paid to an individual who is in a lower tax bracket than the donor. The advantage of the tax savings should be compared with the flexibility lost to the grantor who has essentially given up any claim to the property associated with the trust.

A common use of irrevocable trusts is to place assets in trust for children with the remainder to pass to the grandchildren after the death of the children. Although a gift tax must be paid, no estate tax is due either in your estate or your children's estate as long as the distribution is no more than $250,000 per child.

Power of Attorney

One way to maintain flexibility in a trust agreement is to use the power of attorney. This power enables the holder to review the trust years after the trust was created to determine if the disposition of the trust assets should be changed. This feature would be worthwhile if the economic situations of the beneficiaries have changed.

A general power of attorney allows the holder, upon his or her death, to direct that trust assets be distributed to anyone. General powers are taxable in the estate of the person to whom they are given. A limited power is almost as flexible as a general power but it is nontaxable for estate purposes to the person who holds it. A limited power can be as broad or narrow as you like. The only restriction is that the power cannot be exercised for the benefit of the person holding the power.

You can give a limited power to anyone, exercisable during her or his lifetime and after death, within the constraints you specify. You can specify that the trusts be continued for your children and assign power of attorney to them so they can plan for their families.

TYPES OF TRUSTS

Marital Deduction Trust/Residuary Trust

One of the major changes in the 1981 tax law pertained to allowable marital deductions. Prior to this law, based on the Tax Reform Act of 1976, you could give up to 50% of your estate or $250,000, whichever was greater, tax-free to your spouse. Based on the 1981 tax law, which is effective in 1982, you can leave any or all of your assets to your spouse without incurring a gift/estate tax. You do not have to put these assets into a marital trust to get this tax exemption. You may choose to use a trust, however, if you want someone other than your spouse to manage the assets.

On the surface it appears that because of this change in the law you should leave all of your assets to your spouse. This is not necessarily so because you should look ahead and examine the tax situation when your surviving spouse dies. When he or she dies, the whole estate will be subject to taxes.

The Tax Reform Act of 1976 combined the gift tax and estate tax into one unified tax. The tax changes passed into law in 1981 did not change the unified tax concept. Under this concept an individual was allowed a lifetime tax allowance, which could be applied against his tax liabilities. In 1981 this allowance as $175,625. If an individual did not make any gifts to one individual greater than $3000 ($6000 for joint gift) in 1 year, then the entire $175,625 would be available as an exemption to be deducted from the net estate before estate tax liability was computed. If gifts greater than $3000 to one individual were made, then the amount of the gift greater than $3000 would be deducted from the lifetime exemption allowance. For example, if one $8000 gift was made, the lifetime allowance remaining would be reduced to $170,625 ($175,625−$5000).

The 1981 tax change, effective in 1982, liberalized both the size of the exemption and the yearly allowable tax-free individual gift. (See Exhibits 15-2 and 15-3.) In 1982 the lifetime exemption was increased to $225,000. The exemption will be increased each year until 1987, when it will remain fixed at $600,000. The individual tax-free gift allowance was increased from $3000 to $10,000 ($20,000 if joint) per year.

If you believe that the size of your surviving spouse's estate will exceed the new lifetime exemption limits, you should consider establishing two trusts, a marital trust and a residuary trust. The assets that go into the marital trust will be available to your spouse only. The remaining assets, which will be available to anyone you select, could also be available to your spouse, based on the way you arrange the trust.

Essentially, you will be dividing your assets into two separate trusts. Any amount that you place in the marital trust will pass to your spouse tax-free. The amount that you place in the residuary trust may or may not pass tax-free based on the amount of assets that you place into it.

For example, assume you have $600,000 to bequest. You consider leaving $300,000 to your spouse in a marital trust and the remaining $300,000 in a residual trust to be accessible to your children and your spouse if required. Whatever amount you leave in the marital trust will not be taxable. If you leave $300,000 in a residual trust, it may be taxable depending on when you die. For example, if you die in 1982, an estate tax will have to be paid on $75,000 ($300,000−$225,000) since in 1982 the allowable exclusion will be $225,000. If you leave $375,000 to your spouse, and only $225,000 in the residuary trust, none of your estate will be taxable.

This approach can save considerable tax savings when your spouse dies.

Exhibit 15-2 United Gift and Estate Tax Rates (as of 12/31/81)

| If Taxable Amount Is | | The Tax Is | | |
Over	But Not Over	This	Plus %	Over
$ 0	$ 10,000	$ 0	18	$ 0
$ 10,000	20,000	1,800	20	10,000
20,000	40,000	3,800	22	20,000
40,000	60,000	8,200	24	40,000
60,000	80,000	13,000	28	60,000
80,000	100,000	18,200	28	80,000
100,000	150,000	23,800	30	100,000
150,000	250,000	38,800	32	150,000
250,000	500,000	70,800	34	250,000
500,000	750,000	155,800	37	500,000
750,000	1,000,000	248,300	39	750,000
1,000,000	1,250,000	345,800	41	1,000,000
1,250,000	1,500,000	448,300	43	1,250,000
1,500,000	2,000,000	555,800	45	1,500,000
2,000,000	2,500,000	780,800	49	2,000,000
2,500,000	3,000,000	1,025,800	53	2,500,000
3,000,000	3,500,000	1,290,800	57	3,000,000
3,500,000	4,000,000	1,575,800	61	3,500,000
4,000,000	4,500,000	1,880,800	65	4,000,000
4,500,000	5,000,000	2,205,880	69	4,500,000
5,000,000		2,550,800	70	5,000,000

Exhibit 15-3   Impact of 1981 Tax Law

Year	Allowable Unified Tax Exemption
1982	$225,000
1983	$275,000
1984	$325,000
1985	$400,000
1986	$500,000
1987 and after	$600,000

Year	Maximum Tax Rate
1982	65%
1983	60%
1984	55%
1985 and after	50%

Assume that your surviving spouse dies in 1987, and the size of the estate is $600,000. Assume also that the value of the residuary estate is then $200,000. There will be no tax on the $600,000 estate since in 1987 the allowable tax-free exemption will be $600,000. There will also be no tax on the $200,000 residuary trust, since that trust was already taxed in your estate. If you have not established a residuary trust, and left all your assets to your spouse, your spouse's estate will be $800,000, and $200,000 will be taxable. At the lowest marginal tax rate in 1987 of 37%, the estate tax on $200,000 will be $74,000. By having had the foresight to establish a residual trust you will have saved a minimum of $74,000.

The most effective long-term tax strategy is to leave as much as possible in the residual trust up to the limit of the exemption. By 1987, the exemption will be $600,000. Thus the optimum strategy for 1987, and thereafter, will be to divide the assets of the two trusts so that the residuary trust will have as close to, but not over, $600,000 left in it.

Example

Assume that Mr. Jones' estate was $940,000. He made no gifts during his life, and he died in 1987.

	Gross estate	$940,000
Less:	Expenses and liabilities	40,000
		$900,000
	Marital trust	300,000
	Tax on marital trust	0
	Residuary trust	$600,000
	Tax on residuary trust	0

In this example, Mr. Jones left the maximum amount possible in the residuary trust without incurring any estate tax. He left $300,000 to his spouse in a marital trust. None of that amount was taxable. Mr. Jones could have left all of his estate to his wife tax-free, but it would then have been more difficult for her to pass her estate on without incurring estate taxes.

Example

Mrs. Jones died in 1990. (The residuary trust was not taxable in Mrs. Jones' estate.)

	Gross estate	$840,000
Less:	Expenses and liabilities	40,000
		$800,000
	Allowable exemption	600,000
	Taxable estate	$200,000
	Approximate tax	$ 74,000

Example

Mrs. Jones died in 1990. (In this example assume Mr. Jones, who died in 1987, left his $900,000 estate tax-free to his wife and did not use a residuary trust.)

	Gross estate	$1,440,000
Less:	Expenses and liabilities	40,000
		$1,400,000
	Allowable exemption	600,000
	Taxable estate	$ 800,000
	Approximate tax	$ 320,000

By establishing a residuary trust, Mr. Jones saved approximately $250,000 on his wife's estate. Note that his wife could have access to the residuary trust if the trust agreement was drawn up properly.

Sprinkling Trust

A sprinkling trust is one in which the trustee can use his or her discretion in allocating income among two or more beneficiaries. This trust has three basic advantages:

1   It provides flexibility in that trust income can be allocated to beneficiaries who need the income the most.
2   It provides an effective barrier against creditors.
3   It can be used to reduce aggregate family income tax.

For example, assume the major beneficiary of the trust is your wife. She will have to pay income tax on any income she receives. Assume she is in a high income tax bracket. It would be advantageous to have as much income go to your children as possible. Your wife has a legal obligation to support your children. However, whenever expenditures are to be made for the children for luxury items such as vacation trips or an automobile, there should be no problem having funds allocated to the children to minimize the income tax.

Short-Term Trusts

Short-term trusts are used to divert income from a high income tax payer to a low income tax payer for the duration of the trust. After a specified term the trust ends and the assets in the trust revert to the donor.

An example of a short-term trust is a Clifford trust. The donation of the trust must be for the life of the beneficiary, or for at least 10 years and 1 day. Its purpose must be other than fulfilling a legal obligation of the trustor. The trustor must give up his or her right to the property for the period of the trust. If these requirements are met, the income from the trust assets are taxed to the beneficiary of the trust, not to the trustor.

Trust for Minors

The gift tax law as revised in 1981 allows you to give $10,000 per year to any party without incurring a gift tax. You and your spouse can jointly give $20,000 per year to anyone. You can establish trusts for your children and give up to $20,000 per year (jointly) to minimize the size of your estate for tax purposes. This will probably also reduce the income tax liability for the family since the trust or children should be paying income taxes at a lower rate than you.

The Uniform Gift to Minors Act is a convenient vehicle to give assets to children and take advantage of the annual allowable exclusion without setting up an expensive trust mechanism.

The 1981 tax law also stipulated that you can contribute an unlimited amount to your children without incurring a gift tax, if the funds are used for educational purposes.

Charitable Trusts

There is a wide range of charitable trusts available with various features. They can be created during your lifetime or by will. One popular form of trust is a charitable remainder trust. Under its provisions, benefits are payable to an individual either for life or for a period of years, and the remainder paid to charity. Lifetime charitable remainder trusts can have the advantage of reducing income taxes.

PARTIES INVOLVED IN ESTATE PLANNING

If your estate is of sufficient size, you may want to consider the advice of other parties in addition to your attorney. In the most complicated estate plan, you might use an accountant, a life insurance specialist, and a trust officer or financial institution.

If your estate is complicated, you should analyze the experience of your lawyer. Many attorneys handle only simple wills and are not competent at handling complicated estates. A large law firm would certainly be able to provide estate planning specialists.

A corporate fiduciary should be considered for relatively large estates. Most banks have minimum fees that preclude handling small estates. If you have a need for fiduciary services, you should see an officer in the trust department of a bank with a good reputation. Be prepared to discuss your requirements, and expect to learn about the bank's services, investment objectives, and fees. If you are considering using the bank's investment services, feel free to discuss the trust department's investment performance in comparison to the performance of competing trust departments.

KEY TERMINOLOGY

Executor (Executrix)

An executor is a man or institution appointed in the will to carry out the terms of that will. A woman so appointed is called an executrix. The executor or executrix serves until the estate has been distributed to the beneficiaries or trustees. His or her functions include probating the will; collecting assets; paying bills and taxes; filing or hiring someone to file state and federal estate tax returns; paying out the assets of the estate according to the terms of the will; getting receipts from the beneficiaries; and submitting a final accounting to the court of all receipts and payments.

In most states the executor's commission is fixed by state law and is based on the amount of the estate. If more than one executor is used, the commission can double.

There is no simple formula to determine who should serve as executor. If your estate is large, you should consider naming an executor experienced in handling the type of assets in your estate. You can name your spouse if you feel he or she is capable of handling the job. You can name co-executors, one a family member and the other a lawyer, bank, or trust company. In that way both your personal interests and business interests would be properly protected.

Trustee

A trustee is the manager and legal owner of the trust property. The trustee's function continues for as long as the trust agreement indicates. The trust is no better than the ability of the trustee. Although you may name a business associate or friend to serve as trustee, you should seriously consider a specialist in the field, a trust company, or the trust department of a bank. Some states specify fixed fees. Most states simply allow fees to be set based on competition.

Guardians

A guardian is responsible for the physical care and custody of minor children. A surviving spouse automatically has the right to be guardian of the children. The will should specify a guardian if both parents die.

Administrative Costs

Settlement costs can include executor's commission, attorney fees, special guardian fees, court costs, expenses of last illness and funeral, and incidental administrative expenses. The settlement of a sizable estate generally will require 2 or 3 years. Tax proceedings are largely responsible for this lengthy period.

JOINT OWNERSHIP

Many people use joint ownership in the belief that there are many advantages and no disadvantages. This is certainly not the case. In fact there are few advantages and many disadvantages.

Some apparent advantages of joint ownership are convenience; preventing claims to assets by creditors; reducing estate administration costs; expediting estate administration; and tax advantages in special circumstances. Some of the conveniences of joint ownership are the use of checking accounts, savings accounts, and savings bonds. In these situations assets can be easily liquidated by either co-owner.

State law determines whether joint property will be available for payment of claims by creditors of a deceased co-owner. In some states joint property cannot be claimed by creditors if the property is owned by a husband and wife. This potential advantage is a factor only when it is not expected that the estate will have sufficient assets to pay creditors.

There is normally a substantial delay in the transfer and use of separately owned property. This delay is avoided when the property is jointly owned in a form in which the survivor acquires all of the property.

There are tax advantages only in specific situations. There can be an income tax advantage when the co-owners file separate tax returns, and there would be a lower tax than there would be in filing one tax return. This advantage is only applicable when each co-owner contributed funds for the asset.

If common stock is owned jointly, $200 of dividends may be excluded by a married couple. If the stock is owned by one party, only $100 in dividends can be excluded.

When income property is owned jointly, one half of the income can be transfered without paying a gift tax. This would be an advantage only if half of the income exceeds $10,000, because even if the property were owned by one spouse, $10,000 per year can be transferred free of gift tax.

There are many potential disadvantages associated with joint ownership. These disadvantages are less income, less control, potential management problems, legal problems, and tax disadvantages.

One co-owner can lose income to the other's right to a proportionate share of the income. Control is lost because the co-owner does not have the sole right to determine how the property is to be used, managed, or sold. Moreover, an individual who places property in joint ownership can no longer dispose of the entire property by will, and, in the case of right of survivor ownership, the surviving spouse acquires all the property. Management problems may arise if the surviving owner does not have the necessary expertise to manage the property properly.

Placing property in joint ownership can result in legal problems associated with ownership and tax obligations that do not exist in individual ownership. A competent attorney should be able to assess the possibility of these problems.

There can be tax disadvantages from an income, gift, or estate tax viewpoint. Income tax liabilities can result if an individual sells or exchanges property in his or her own name to acquire property in joint ownership. In many situations a gift tax is applicable when joint ownership is created but the funds are provided by only one of the parties. There are exceptions such as joint tenancy by husband and wife in real estate, U.S. savings bonds, joint bank accounts, and joint brokerage accounts. A gift tax is generally applicable when a joint ownership is established using funds provided by another party.

Joint ownership can result in higher federal estate taxes in some situations. It is necessary for records to be maintained to demonstrate the contribution of each party to the acquisition of the property. For example, if records are not kept, the *entire* property can be taxed in the estate of the deceased even if both parties contributed funds toward the initial purchase. The burden of proof is on the surviving co-owner, not on the Internal Revenue Service.

The 1981 tax legislation has a definite impact on the advantages and disadvantages of joint ownership. There is now more of an advantage in owning property in one name, since property can be left to the surviving spouse on a tax-free basis. An asset willed to a spouse would be valued at the time of death rather than at the initial purchase price. If the property is sold, the taxes due would be less if the initial purchase price was less than the value of the property at the time of death.

Joint ownership is a complicated issue. You should always consult an attorney before you select on ownership option. If you currently have some property in joint ownership, you should review with your attorney the advisability of changing ownership from a joint basis to individual ownership.

Summary

Effective retirement planning is not easy. It would be a complicated process even without persistent inflation and changing economic and political factors. The planning process must be integrated with a continual monitoring process.

Tax laws continue to change. Some tax shelters will be eliminated, but it is hoped that others will take their place. You must review these changes annually and determine whether you should make any changes in your investment plans and programs.

Interest rates will probably continue to fluctuate a great deal. Different forms of investment will become more or less attractive based on these changes. You must be aware of these interest rate changes and modify your investment strategy accordingly.

International economics and politics will continue to play a significant role in our economy. You should monitor the international environment, specifically examining the inflation and general health of foreign economies. You should consider diversification by making some conservative foreign investments if it is apparent that other nations have lower inflation rates and healthier economies than our own.

Periodically you must review your total planning process. Has a change in the inflation rate afected your retirement goals? Are your initial objectives still valid? Have your financial obligations changed? Is your estate plan still valid? Is your will up-to-date? Are there new investment tools available that will make it easier to reach your financial goals?

A sound retirement plan is a moving target. The plan that you develop in 1981 may be obsolete in 1985 if you do not review and update your plan, taking into consideration changes in your personal life, revised income and estate tax laws, and more favorable investment opportunities.

Your future is at stake, and no one has more motivation or is better equipped to plan for it than you. Good luck.

Common Stock Glossary

Ask	The lowest price at which the owner is willing to sell a security.
At the market	An order to buy or sell securities at the best price your broker can get.
Bear	An investor who feels that market prices will fall.
Bid	The highest price a prospect is willing to pay for a security.
Big board	New York Stock Exchange.
Blue chips	Stocks with a long history of above average growth and increase in earnings.
Book value	Company's total assets minus liabilities and preferred stock value, divided by number of common stocks outstanding.
Broker	Agent who executes orders to buy and sell securities for a commission.
Bull	An investor who feels that market prices will rise.
Capital gain	Profit on the sale of a capital asset.
Commission	The broker's fee for buying or selling securities.
Convertible	Bond or preferred stock that can be exchanged into a fixed number of common stock shares for a stipulated time.
Current yield	The dividends or interest paid on a security divided by the market price of the security. The yield of a stock selling for $20 and paying $1 dividend per year would be 5%.
Dividend	Payment to shareholders of cash or stock in direct proportion to stock ownership. The company's board of directors approves each dividend.

Dollar cost averaging	Process of investing a fixed sum of money regularly in the same security. The advantage of the system is that more shares are bought at low prices and few shares at high prices, thus lowering the average cost per share.
Listed stock	Stock traded on a national securities exchange.
Margin	To purchase a stock on margin is to borrow a percent of the purchase price from your broker. The percent you can borrow is regulated by the Federal Reserve Board.
Margin call	A call from a broker requesting an investor who has purchased stock on margin to supply more capital to the broker. Margin calls are made when the stock price has gone down since the initial purchase. If the investor cannot put up additional capital, the stock will be sold.
Market price	The latest transaction price of a security.
Odd lot	Amount of stock less than a round lot. For most stocks 100 shares constitute a round lot.
Option	Right to buy or sell securities at a specified price within a specific time.
Over the counter	Market in which securities not listed on securities exchanges are traded. U.S. government securities are traded over the counter. The National Association of Securities Dealers (NASD) monitors this market.
Preferred stock	Category of stock with more characteristics of bonds than common stock. Preferred stockholders receive fixed dividends. Preferred stock remains outstanding indefinitely unless called for redemption by company at predetermined price. In case of liquidation, preferred stockholders' claims on assets are subordinate to bond holders but come before common stock holders.
Price earnings ratio	The ratio of current stock price to company earnings per share.
Prospectus	Document filed with the Securities and Exchange Commission by a company when a new issue of

securities is offered to the general public. The document contains highlights from the registration statement. The information is used by brokers and investors to evaluate the securities before purchase.

SEC	The Securities and Exchange Commission, a federal agency established by congress to protect investors.
Selling short	Process by which investor sells stock he or she does not own, borrowing stock initially, and subsequently buying the stock later to complete the transaction. Investors sell stock short when they expect the price to fall.
Spread	Difference between the bid and ask prices for a security.
Stock dividend	Dividend paid to stockholders in the form of additional common stock. The company normally uses this form of dividend to preserve cash for expansion.
Street name	Securities left by owner in the custody of the broker.
Warrant	Right to buy a security at a specified price, normally within a specified time. Warrants usually are offered as incentives to investors to buy other securities.

Mutual Funds Glossary

Asset value per share

The market value of the fund's portfolio divided by the number of shares outstanding. Each day the asset value per share is published in the mutual fund listings for the major funds. For no-load funds the asset value and the price of a share of stock are the same.

Capital gains distribution

Distribution made to shareholders when the fund has net long-term capital gains in a particular year. The shareholder normally has the option to accept this distribution in additional shares.

Closed end fund

Mutual fund with a fixed number of shares outstanding. The market price of a share of a closed end fund is based on supply and demand. That price can be more or less than the asset value per share.

Distributions

Payments to shareholders, either as capital gains distributions or income distributions. Shareholders normally have the option to accept distributions in cash or in additional shares.

Load fund

Fund in which the investor pays a sales commission to purchase shares in the mutual fund. An investor who invests $100 in a fund with an 8% sales commission would be receiving only $92 in assets.

Management fee

The amount that the management of a fund charges for its services. The fee is normally ½ of 1% per year, but it does vary among funds. The fee arrangement is disclosed in the prospectus. Management fees are associated with both load and no-load funds.

No-load fund

Fund in which there is no sales commission. No-load funds are normally purchased directly from the company since brokers have no incentive to sell them.

Open end fund

Mutual fund that offer to buy and sell shares continually to the public at net asset value. Number of shares outstanding fluctuates depending on supply and demand.

Reinvestment option

Option by which an investor can reinvest his or her distributions in additional shares of the fund. This option has no tax advantage. There may or may not be a sales commission depending on the policy of the fund, as indicated in the prospectus.

Bond Glossary

Accrued interest	Interest accumulated from the last interest payment to the present.
Amortize	Reduction of issuer debt by fixed payments on a regular basis.
Basis	Yield.
Basis point	1/100 of 1%.
Bearer bond	Bond not registered with the issuer; a cash equivalent.
Bond	Promissory instrument issued by corporations and governments; principal is usually paid off not earlier than 10 years, and interest is paid periodically. Interest rate is fixed at time of issuance.
Callable bond	Bonds containing a call provision allowing the borrower to recall the bond at a price higher than the issue price within a set period of time. Corporations normally use the recall provision when interest rates have fallen and they are able to issue bonds with a lower coupon rate.
Convertible bond	Bond backed by the general credit of the issuing corporation that can be redeemed for a specific number of shares of securities, generally common stock, under certain conditions.
Coupon	The attachment to a bearer bond required to receive interest payments. The coupon is submitted to the bank/brokerage firm to receive credit.
Current yield	Coupon rate divided by current market price. A 10% coupon rate on a $900 bond equals an 11% current yield.

Debenture	Corporate bond backed by the general credit of the issuing corporation.
Discount bonds	Bond selling below its par value. If a bond was issued at $1000, any time it is selling below $1000 it is selling at a discount.
Federal agency issue	Securities issued by federal agencies. These bonds are second in safety only to U.S. government issues. Some are federally insured. They are generally exempt from state and local taxes.
First mortgage bond	Corporate bond secured by a mortgage on some or all of the property of the issuing corporation.
General obligation bond	Municipal bond backed by the general credit of the municipality issuing the bond.
Maturity	Date on which the principal amount of a bond is payable by the issuer to the bond owner.
Municipal bonds	Bonds issued by municipalities—cities, towns, states—and are exempt from federal income taxation. If you reside in the area in which the bond is issued you generally are exempt from state and local taxes as well.
Point	For bonds one point is $10.
Premium.	The price above par that a bond is selling for. If a bond sold initially at $1000 par value is selling for $1100, it is selling for a $100 premium.
Ratings	The evaluations assigned by the rating services regarding the quality of an obligation. The most respected rating services are Standard & Poors and Moody's. Their letter evaluations are similar but not identical. For both services, AAA(Aaa) are the best ratings, B ratings are lower in quality and C and D ratings are the worst.
Registered bond	Bond registered with the issuer in the owner's name. The issuer is mailed a check directly by the issuer's paying agent when interest payments are due.

Serial bonds	Bonds redeemed on an installment basis in sequential order. Municipalities generally issue serial bonds.
Sinking fund	A fund of money produced through regular payments by the bond issuer that will be used to retire a certain amount of outstanding bonds on a predetermined schedule.
Term	Length of time that a bond is expected to be outstanding.
Treasury bills	Short-term marketable U.S. treasury obligations. They are offered on a discount basis in maturities of 90 days to 1 year. They are guaranteed by the U.S. government and are exempt from state and local taxes. (Treasury notes are available at maturities of greater than 1 year and less than 10 years. They are sold at par value. Treasury bonds have terms greater than 10 years and are also sold at par. All Treasury issues are exempt from state and local taxes.
Yield to maturity	True rate of return taking into consideration the current market price, interest to be received, and the value of the bond at maturity. This yield is important since it enables investors to compare the returns offered by bonds having different coupon rates and maturity dates.

Real Estate Glossary

Abstract	A short legal history of a piece of property, tracing its ownership (title) through the years. An attorney or title insurance company reviews the abstract to make sure the title comes to a buyer free from any defects.
Acceleration clause	A provision in a mortgage that may require the unpaid balance of the mortgage loan to become due immediately if the regular mortgage payments are not made or if other terms are not met.
Amortization	A payment plan by which the borrower reduces his or her debt gradually through monthly payments of principal.
Appreciation	An increase in the value of property.
Appraisal	An evaluation of a piece of property to determine its value—that is, what it would sell for in the marketplace.
Assessment	The value placed on property for purposes of taxation; may also refer to a special tax due for a special purpose, such as a sewer assessment.
Assumption of mortgage	The promise by the buyer of property to be legally responsible for the payment of an existing mortgage. The purchaser's name is substituted for the original mortgagor's (borrower's) name on the mortgage note and the original mortgagor is released from the responsibility of making the mortgage pay-

ments. Usually the lender must agree to an assumption.

Binder

A simple contract between a buyer and a seller stating the basic terms of an offer to purchase property. It is usually good only for a limited period of time, until a more formal purchase agreement is prepared and signed by both parties. A small deposit of earnest money is made to bind the offer.

Certificate of title

A document prepared by a title company or an attorney stating that the seller has a clear, marketable, and insurable title to the property he or she is offering for sale.

Closing

The final step in the sale and purchase of a property, when the title is transferred from the seller to the buyer; the buyer signs the mortgage, pays settlement costs, and any money due the seller or buyer is paid.

Closing costs

Sometimes called settlement costs—costs in addition to the price of a house, usually including mortgage origination fee, title insurance, attorney's fee, and prepayable items such as taxes and insurance payments collected in advance and held in an escrow account.

Commission

Money paid to a real estate agent or broker by the seller in payment for finding a buyer and completing a sale. Usually it is a percentage of the sales price and is spelled out in the purchase agreement.

Community property

In some states, a form of ownership under which property acquired during a marriage is presumed to be owned jointly unless acquired as separate property of either spouse.

Conditional commitment	A promise to ensure (generally with FHA loans) payment of a definite loan amount on a particular piece of property for a buyer with satisfactory credit.
Condominium	Individual ownership of an apartment in a multiunit project or development and a proportionate interest in the common areas outside the apartment.
Contractor	A person or company who agrees to furnish materials and labor to do work for a certain price.
Conventional loan	A mortgage loan not insured by FHA or guaranteed by VA.
Cooperative	An apartment building or group of housing units owned by all the residents (generally a corporation) and run by an elected board of directors for the benefit of the residents. The resident lives in a unit but does not own it—he or she owns a share of stock in the corporation.
Credit rating	A rating or evaluation made by a person or company (such as a credit bureau) based on one's present financial condition and past credit history.
Credit report	A report usually ordered by a lender from a credit bureau to help determine a borrower's credit rating.
Deed	A written document by which the ownership of property is transferred from the seller (the grantor) to the buyer (the grantee).
Deed of trust	In some states a document used instead of a mortgage. It transfers title of the property to a third party (the trustee) who holds the title until the debt or mortgage loan is paid off, at which time the title (ownership) passes to

the borrower. If the borrower defaults (fails to make payments), the trustee may sell the property at a public sale to pay off the loan.

Deed (quitclaim deed)

A deed that transfers only that title or right to a property that the holder of the title has at the time of the transfer. A quitclaim deed does not warrant (or guarantee) a clear title.

Deed (warranty deed)

A deed guaranteeing that the title to a piece of property is free from any title defects.

Default

Failure to make mortgage payments on time, as agreed to in the mortgage note or deed of trust. If a payment is 30 days late, the mortgage is in default, and it may give the lender the right to start foreclosure proceedings.

Delinquency

When a mortgage payment is past due.

Deposit

A sum of money given to bind a sale of real estate—also called earnest money.

Depreciation

A loss or decrease in the value of a piece of property because of age, wear and tear, or unfavorable changes in the neighborhood; opposite of appreciation.

Documentary stamps

In some states a tax in the form of stamps, required on deeds and mortgages when real estate title passes from one owner to another. The amount required differs from one state to another.

Easement

The right to use land owned by another. For instance, the electric company has easement rights that allow their power lines to cross another's property.

ECOA

Equal Credit Opportunity Act—a federal law that requires lenders to loan without discrimination based on race, color, religion, national origin, sex, marital status, or income from public assistance programs.

Encumbrance	Anything that limits the interest in a title to property such as a mortgage, a lien, an easement, a deed restriction, or unpaid taxes.
Equity	A buyer's initial ownership interest in a house that increases as the mortgage loan is paid off. When the mortgage is fully paid, the owner has 100% equity in the house.
Escrow	Money or documents held by a third party until all the conditions of a contracts are met.
Escrow agent	The third party responsible to the buyer and seller or to the lender and borrower for holding the money or documents until the terms of a purchase agreement are met.
Escrow payment	That part of a borrower's monthly payment held by the lender to pay for taxes, hazard insurance, mortgage insurance, and other items until they become due. Also known as impounds or reserves in some states.
FHA	Federal Housing Administration—a division of the U.S. Department of Housing and Urban Development (HUD). Its main activity is to insure home mortgage loans made by private lenders.
FmHA	Farmers Home Administration—a government gency (part of the Department of Agriculture) that provides financing to farmers or other qualified buyers (usually in rural areas) who are unable to obtain loans elsewhere.
Finance charge	The total of all charges one must pay to get a loan.
Firm commitment	An agreement from a lender to make a loan to a particular borrower on a particular property. Also an FHA or private mortgage

insurance company agreement to insure a loan on a particular property for a particular borrower.

Forbearance
The act of delaying legal action to foreclose on a mortgage that is overdue. Usually it is granted only when a satisfactory arrangement has been made with the lender to make up the late payments at a future date.

Foreclosure
The legal process by which a lender forces payment of a loan (under a mortgage or deed of trust) by taking the property from the owner (mortgagor) and selling it to pay off the debt.

Grantee
That party in the deed who is the buyer.

Grantor
That party in the deed who is the seller.

Guaranty
A promise by one party to pay the debt of another if that other fails to do so.

Hazard insurance
Insurance that protects against damage caused to property by fire, windstorm, or other common hazard. Required by many lenders to be carried in an amount at least equal to the mortgage.

Homeowners insurance policy
Insurance that covers the house and its contents in the case of fire, wind damage and theft, and covers the homeowner in case someone is injured on the property and brings a suit.

HUD
The U.S. Department of Housing and Urban Development.

Installment
The regular payment that a borrower agrees to make to a lender.

Insurance binder
A document stating that an individual or property is insured, even though the insurance policy has not yet been issued.

Insured loan
A loan insured by FHA or a private mortgage insurance company.

Interest	A charge paid for borrowing money. Also a right, share, or title in property.
Joint tenancy	An equal, undivided ownership of property by two or more persons. Should one of the parties die, his or her share of the ownership would pass to the surviving owners (right of survivorship).
Late charge	An additional fee a lender charges a borrower if the mortgage payments are not made on time.
Lien	A hold or claim that someone has on the property of another as security for a debt or charge; if a lien is not removed (if the debt is not paid), the property may be sold to pay off the lien.
Listing	Registering of properties for sale with one or more real estate brokers or agents allowing the broker who actually sells the property to get the commission.
Loan disclosure note	Document spelling out all the terms involved in obtaining and paying off a loan.
Mortgage	A special loan for buying property.
Mortgagee	The lender who makes a mortgage loan.
Mortgage interest subsidy	A monthly payment by the federal government to a mortgagee (lender) that reduces the amount of interest the mortgagor (homeowner) has to pay the lender to as low as 4% if the homeowner falls within certain income limits.
Mortgage origination fee	A charge by the lender for the work involved in the preparation and servicing of a mortgage request. Usually 1% of the loan amount.
Mortgagor	The person borrowing money for a mortgage loan.
Option (to buy)	An agreement granting a potential buyer the

	right to buy a piece of property at a stated price within a stated period of time.
PITI	Principal, interest, taxes, and insurance (in FHA and VA loans paid to the bank each month).
Plat (or plot)	A map of a piece of land showing its boundaries, length, width, and any easements.
Point(s)	One point is an amount equal to 1% of the principal amount of a loan. Points are a one-time charge collected by the lender at closing to increase the return on the loan. In FHA or VA loans, the borrower is not allowed to pay any points.
Prepaid items	An advance payment at the time of closing for taxes, hazard insurance, and mortgage insurance, which is held in an escrow account by the lender.
Prepayment penalty	A charge made by the lender if a mortgage loan is paid off before the due date. FHA does not permit such a penalty on its FHA-insured loans.
Principal	The amount of money borrowed that must be paid back along with interest and other finance charges.
Purchase agreement	A written document in which a seller agrees to sell and a buyer agrees to buy a piece of property with certain conditions and terms of the sale spelled out such as sales price, date of closing, and condition of property. The agreement is secured by a deposit or down payment of earnest money.
Real estate	Land and the structures thereon. Also anything of a permanent nature such as trees, minerals, and the interest and rights in these items.

Real estate agent	An individual who can show property for sale on behalf of a seller but who may not have a license to transact the sale and collect the sales commission.
Real estate broker	An individual who can show property for sale on behalf of a seller and who has a valid license to sell real estate. The real estate broker represents the seller and is paid a commission when the property is sold.
Realtor	A real estate broker or an associate holding active membership in a local real estate board affiliated with the National Association of Realtors.
Recording fees	The charge by an attorney to put on public record the details of legal documents such as a deed or mortgage.
Refinancing	The process of paying off one loan with the money (proceeds) from another loan.
RESPA	Real Estate Settlement Procedures Act—A federal law that requires lenders to send to the home mortgage borrower (within 3 business days) an estimate of the closing (settlement) costs. RESPA also limits the amount lenders may hold in an escrow account for real estate taxes and insurance and requires the disclosure of settlement costs to both buyers and sellers 24 hours before the closing.
Restrictions	Legal limitations in the deed on the use of property.
Right of rescission	That section of the Truth in Lending Law that allows a consumer the right to change his or her mind and cancel a contract within 3 days after signing it. This right to cancel is in force if the contract would involve obtaining a loan and the loan would place a lien on the property.

Right of way	An easement on property in which the property owner gives another person the right to pass over his or her land.
Sole owner	Ownership of a property by a single individual.
Survey	A map or plat made by a licensed surveyor showing the measurements of a piece of land; its location, dimensions, and the location and dimensions of any improvements on the land.
Tenancy-by-the-entirety	The joint ownership of property by a husband and wife. If either one dies, his or her share of ownership goes to the survivor.
Tenancy-in-common	Property owned by two or more persons with the terms creating a joint tenancy. In the event one of the owners dies, his or her share of the property would not go to the other owner automatically, but rather to his or her heirs.
Title	The rights of ownership of a particular property and the documents that prove ownership (commonly a deed).
Title defects	An outstanding claim or encumbrance on property that affects its marketability (whether it can be freely sold).
Title insurance	Special insurance that usually protects lenders against loss of their interest in property because of legal defects in the title. An owner can protect his or her interest by purchasing separate coverage.
Title search	An examination of public records to uncover any past or current facts regarding the ownership of a piece of property. A title search is intended to make sure the title is marketable and free from defects.
Truth in Lending Law	A federal law providing that the terms of a loan (including all the finance charges) must

be disclosed to the borrower before the loan is signed. It also contains a provision for the right of rescission.

VA

Veterans Administration—The VA guarantees a certain proportion of a mortgage loan made to a veteran by a private lender. Sometimes called GI loans, these usually require very low down payments and permit long repayment terms.

Zoning

The power of a local municipal government (city or town) to regulate the use of property within the municipality.

Estate Planning Glossary

Administrator	Individual or institution appointed by the court to administer the estate of a person who died without a will (intestate).
Attestation	Act of witnessing the signing of an instrument and subscribing to it as a witness.
Beneficiary	Person named to receive funds or property from a trust, insurance policy, or will.
Bequest	Gift of personal property by will.
Charitable trust	Trust in which part of a grantor's estate is used for charitable purposes.
Codicil	A supplement to a will, adding, changing, or deleting its provisions.
Community property	In selected states, property acquired by husband and wife is considered to be owned in equal percentages. Applicable in Arizona, California, Idaho, Louisiana, New Mexico, Texas, and Washington.
Custodian	One who has custody; a guardian or a trustee.
Decedent	A person who has died.
Devise	Give real estate by will.
Domicile	Place where a person has his or her permanent home.
Donee	A person who receives a gift.
Donor	One who makes a gift.
Estate	The assets and liabilities left by a person at death.
Executor/Executrix	Person or institution appointed by testator to carry out the terms of his or her will.

Fiduciary	Person invested with rights and powers to be used for the benefit of another.
Guardian	A person appointed with legal care and control over a person or property.
Holographic will	Handwritten will.
Inter vivos trust	Gift made during one's lifetime.
Intestate	Dying without leaving a will.
Irrevocable trust	Trust that cannot be revoked.
Issue	Descendants.
Joint tenancy with right of survivorship	Ownership of real estate by two or more persons with agreement that when one dies, the survivor gets the entire property.
Legacy	Gift of personal property made by will.
Marital deduction	Provision in the federal tax law that allows a person to give half of his or her estate to his or her spouse tax-free.
Marital trust	A trust that permits either spouse to give half of his or her property to the other without having to pay estate tax. Property would be taxable upon the death of the surviving spouse.
Power of attorney (appointment)	Giving an individual the authority to indicate the recipients of the assets of a trust.
Probate	The process by which the validity of a will is determined.
Residuary clause	Clause in the will referring to the remainder of the estate after other individual bequests of money and property have been taken into consideration.
Revocable trust	Trust that can be changed or revoked at any time during the grantor's life.
Sprinkling	Power given to a trustee to use discretion in making distributions to two or more beneficiaries.

Tenancy in common	Title of a piece of property held jointly by two people. Each individual has control over his or her share and can dispose of the property independent of the other owner.
Tenancy by the entirety	Title in which the names of husband and wife appear on the deed to their real estate.
Testementary	Pertaining to a will.
Testementary trust	Trust established by will.
Testator	Person making a will.
Totten trust	Trust in which the donor deposits funds in a bank in his or her own name as trustee for another. The donor retains control over the account and can withdraw any part of the account at any time. Upon the death of the donor, any balance goes to the beneficiary.
Trust	The holding of property set aside for the benefit of those for whom the trust was created. The property is managed by the trustee for the advantage of the beneficiaries.
Trustee	Person or institution designated by the trustor or assigned by the court to administer a trust.
Trustor	Creator of a trust.

Index